Thatcher

Thatcher provides an accessible and scholarly introduction to the personality and career of Britain's first female political leader and the twentieth century's longest serving Prime Minister. Providing a balanced narrative and assessment of one of the most significant figures of the post-war era, this new biography examines the reasons why Margaret Thatcher has been admired by many as the architect of national revival, yet loathed by others as the author of widening social and geographical division.

The book begins by examining the making of Margaret Thatcher, her education, the beginning of her political career and her rise through the Conservative Party to her unexpected election as leader. Moving on to her tenure as Prime Minister, Graham Goodlad then examines her impact at home and abroad, covering her controversial economic policies and hard line with the trade unions, leadership through the Falklands conflict and during the last decade of the Cold War, and influence on Britain's relationship with a more closely integrated Europe. Finally, the biography closes with a review of Thatcher's legacy before and after her death in April 2013, and considers how far she shaped the politics and society of the 1980s and those of our own time.

Thatcher is essential reading for all students of twentieth-century history and politics.

Graham Goodlad is Head of Politics at St John's College, Southsea. His most recent publication (with Robert Pearce) is *British Prime Ministers from Balfour to Brown* (Routledge, 2013).

ROUTLEDGE HISTORICAL BIOGRAPHIES

Series Editor: Robert Pearce

Routledge Historical Biographies provide engaging, readable and academically credible biographies written from an explicitly historical perspective. These concise and accessible accounts will bring important historical figures to life for students and general readers alike.

In the same series:

Thatcher

Graham Goodlad

Routledge
Taylor & Francis Group

LONDON AND NEW YORK

First published 2016
by Routledge
2 Park Square, Milton Park, Abingdon, Oxon OX14 4RN

and by Routledge
711 Third Avenue, New York, NY 10017

*Routledge is an imprint of the Taylor & Francis Group,
an informa business*

Durham County Council Libraries, Learning and Culture	
C0 1 73 64422 FF	
Askews & Holts	
B THATCHERMARGA	

British Library Cataloguing in Publication Data
A catalogue record for this book is available from the
British Library

Library of Congress Cataloging-in-Publication Data
Goodlad, Graham D. (Graham David), 1964- author.
   Thatcher / Graham Goodlad.
      pages cm. — (Routledge historical biographies)
   Includes bibliographical references and index.
   1. Thatcher, Margaret.   2. Prime ministers—Great Britain—
Biography.   3. Women prime ministers—Great Britain—
Biography.   4. Great Britain—Politics and government—
1979–1997.   I. Title.
   DA591.T47G66 2016
   941.085′8092—dc23
   [B]
   2015028242

ISBN: 978-1-138-01565-4 (hbk)
ISBN: 978-1-138-01568-5 (pbk)
ISBN: 978-1-315-64718-0 (ebk)

Typeset in Sabon
by Apex CoVantage, LLC
Printed in Great Britain by
Ashford Colour Press Ltd, Gosport, Hants

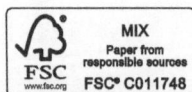

Contents

Acknowledgements

Thatcher copyright is reproduced with permission from the estate of Lady Thatcher. The publishers are grateful to the estate of Lady Thatcher for granting permission to reproduce copyright material.

Extract from 'My Style of Government': The Thatcher Years by Nicholas Ridley reprinted by permission of Peters Fraser + Dunlop (www.petersfraserdunlop.com) on behalf of the Estate of Nicholas Ridley.

Extract from Not For Turning by Robin Harris, published by Bantam Press. Reproduced by permission of The Random House Group Ltd and Thomas Dunne Books. All rights reserved.

Extract from My Style of Government by Nicholas Ridley, published by Hutchinson. Reproduced by permission of The Random House Group Ltd.

Extract from Splendid! Splendid! by Ian Aitken and Mark Garnett, published by Jonathan Cape. Reproduced by permission of The Random House Group Ltd.

Chronology

Date	Personal	Political	General
1925	MT born		
1943	Wins place at Oxford University		
1950	Contests Dartford constituency		
1951	Second attempt to win Dartford Marries Denis Thatcher		
1953	Mark and Carol Thatcher born		
1954	Qualifies as a lawyer		
1959	Elected MP for Finchley	Conservatives under Harold Macmillan win general election	
1961–4	Junior minister at Ministry of Pensions and National Insurance		
1967	Joins Edward Heath's Shadow Cabinet		
1970–4	Education Secretary	Conservatives under Edward Heath win general election	
1974	Shadow Environment and Treasury roles	Heath loses two general elections (February and October)	
1975	Wins Conservative Party leadership election		
1976		James Callaghan becomes Prime Minister	

(continued)

Date	Personal	Political	General
1978–9		Winter of Discontent	
1979		Assassination of Airey Neave (March)	
	Becomes Prime Minister (May)	Conservatives win general election with 43-seat majority (May)	Lancaster House agreement on Rhodesia; Soviet invasion of Afghanistan (December)
1980	'The lady's not for turning' speech (October)	Interim deal on UK's EC budget contribution (May); 1980 Employment Act; right to buy for council tenants (August); Michael Foot elected Labour leader (November)	
1981		Howe introduces controversial budget (March) SDP formed (March) Riots in Brixton (April), Liverpool (July) IRA hunger strikes; 'wets' purged in Cabinet reshuffle (September)	Ronald Reagan inaugurated US President (January)
1982		Falklands conflict (April–June); 1982 Employment Act (October)	

(continued)

Date	Personal	Political	General
1983	Re-elected with 144-seat majority (June)	Neil Kinnock elected Labour Party leader (October)	Reagan announces SDI project (March) US invasion of Grenada (October)
1984	MT survives Brighton hotel bombing (October)	Miners' strike begins (March) Fontainebleau council deal on budget rebate (June) Sale of British Telecom (November)	UK–China agreement on future of Hong Kong (December)
1985		Miners' strike ends (March) Abolition of GLC and metropolitan councils (July) Anglo-Irish agreement signed (November)	Mikhail Gorbachev becomes Soviet leader (March)
1986		Westland affair; Heseltine resigns from Cabinet (January) Single European Act signed (February) US warplanes attack Libya from British bases (April)	

(continued)

Date	Personal	Political	General
1987	Third general election victory, with 102-seat majority (June)	Unemployment falls below 3 million (June) Black Monday on Stock Market (October)	
1988	Bruges speech on Europe (September)	Retirement of Willie Whitelaw (January) Lawson's budget reduces top rate of income tax to 40%, standard rate to 25% (March) Education Reform Act passed (July)	
1989		Conservative losses in European Parliament elections (June) Howe demoted in Cabinet reshuffle (July) Lawson resigns as Chancellor (October) Sir Anthony Meyer's leadership challenge (November)	George Bush inaugurated US President (January) Collapse of communist rule in Eastern Europe (October–December)
1990		Poll tax riots in London (March) Iraq invades Kuwait (August) Britain joins Exchange Rate Mechanism (October)	German reunification (October)

(continued)

Date	Personal	Political	General
	MT resigns as PM (November)	Howe resigns; Heseltine challenges MT for Conservative leadership	
1991		Gulf War (January–February) Major negotiates Maastricht Treaty (December)	
1992	MT moves to House of Lords (April)	Major wins 21-seat majority at general election (April) Sterling forced to leave the ERM; MT campaigns against Maastricht Treaty (September)	
1993	Publishes *The Downing Street Years* (October)		
1995	Publishes *The Path to Power* (May)		
1997		Tony Blair wins general election for New Labour (May)	
2002	Publishes *Statecraft* (March) Announces retirement from public life (March)		
2003	Denis Thatcher dies (June)		
2010		David Cameron elected Prime Minister; end of New Labour era (May)	
2013	MT dies (April)		

Introduction

So transient are both power and fame that the deaths of most retired Prime Ministers arouse relatively little popular interest. By the time of their passing, the achievements and reverses of their time in office are only hazily recalled, outside the select circles of professional political commentators and contemporary historians. The passage of time draws a natural line under the controversies which, a few decades earlier, filled pages of newsprint and dominated the nightly TV bulletins. This was most definitely *not* the case when Margaret Thatcher passed into history on 8 April 2013, almost twenty-three years after her departure from Downing Street. Her place in the record books as Britain's first female political leader, and as Britain's longest serving twentieth-century premier, would always set her apart from others who attained the highest office. It was particularly remarkable that a woman of her modest social origins, as the daughter of a small shopkeeper in the East Midlands, could rise to the leadership of an intensely hierarchical and male-dominated Conservative Party. Yet there was far more to it than that.

Thatcher's obituaries invariably drew attention to her capacity to cause controversy. Andreas Whittam-Smith, for example, wrote in *The Independent* that 'while a heroine for many people, she was equally a hate figure for others. Indifference wasn't an option.'[1] His words echoed those of another noted political commentator, Peter Riddell of *The Times*: 'She never failed to make an impression; no one was neutral about her. That made her one of the most divisive politicians of her age – loved and loathed in equal measure.'[2] Admired by many as the architect of Britain's recovery from years of post-war decline and self-doubt, Thatcher was detested by others as a leader whose policies exalted material greed and entrenched social division. Even in death she continued to spark passionate argument. Thatcher was the first retired Prime Minister since Winston Churchill in January 1965 to receive a ceremonial funeral with full military honours, at which the monarch led the official mourning. The stately procession of the flag-draped coffin to St Paul's Cathedral brought central London to a standstill, with the cortège greeted by admiring applause. Elsewhere, particularly in deprived areas of northern England and Scotland, where many blamed her for the destruction of old industrial communities, others openly celebrated her demise in pubs and on the streets.

A controversial premier

Gender was undoubtedly critical to Thatcher's hold on the public imagination, in an age of uniformly grey-suited male politicians. Many of the nicknames given during her years of ascendancy – the Iron Lady, Attila the Hen, the Great She Elephant – reflected the supposed paradox of having a dominant, assertive *female* at the helm of the state. The term 'hand-bagging' became a widely used short-hand term for her frequently undiplomatic relations with other world leaders. Certainly, in staged photo-opportunities she was careful to be pictured playing stereotypically masculine roles, such as riding in a tank at military exercises. At the same time, she frequently presented herself as a thrifty housewife, shopping for bargains in the high street, in a way which would not have occurred to a male leader of the period, and she took immense trouble with her hair and clothes. Although never identified with the feminist movement, she sometimes laid claim to a greater determination, as a woman, to work hard at what mattered: 'If you want a speech ask a man. If you want something done, ask a woman.'[3] To her admirers she projected a feminine allure which formed a potent part of her political armoury. Conservative MP and diarist Alan Clark was sufficiently impressed, after encountering Thatcher early in her premiership, to compare her to the most glamorous figure in post-war Latin American politics: 'But goodness, she is *so* beautiful; made up to the nines, of course, for the television programme, but still quite bewitching, as Eva Peron must have been.'[4] Thatcher's critics, on the other hand, recoiled from her alleged lack of the qualities of empathy and compassion that were popularly associated with the female sex. Thus Channel 4's long-running satirical puppet show, *Spitting Image*, invariably portrayed her wearing a man's pinstriped business suit, snarling grotesquely and treating opponents and Cabinet colleagues alike with brutal disdain. The importance of image, and the way in which it sometimes contrasted with the underlying reality, is an important theme for students of Thatcher's political career.

In her years of power Thatcher stood out among post-war premiers, not only as a woman but also for the sheer assertiveness and drive which she brought to the role. Historian Peter Hennessy described her as 'a formidable shifter of business, a ruler of the state rather than its servant', a leader whose pronouncements showed no sign of 'the tolerance which is traditionally part of the British way of governance, of open discussion before decision, the very bone-marrow of collective government at the top'.[5] These character traits have been remarked upon by a range of commentators, both hostile and supportive. Journalist John Cole, who suppressed his personal antipathy towards Thatcher and her policies as the BBC's political editor for the greater part of her premiership, later wrote that her ministers were unanimous in 'treating her as a force of nature, almost a volcano, who had to be propitiated by those living on the slopes below'.[6] Her critics regarded her as harsh, aggressive and unwilling to listen to alternatives. To others, however, these were positive characteristics, which enabled her to overcome opposition and to achieve objectives which were in Britain's long-term interests. Nicholas Ridley, one of her most loyal Cabinet allies, recalled that her opponents said that 'she was bossy, she rode roughshod over people, she wouldn't listen, she was determined to get her own way. Such criticisms were in fact only an acknowledgement of the strength of her character and her determination'.[7]

Thatcher's premiership was also unusual for its length, which enabled her to make a real impact on the direction of policy making. She occupied Number 10 for eleven and a half years, clocking up three consecutive general election victories in 1979, 1983 and 1987. Thatcher herself was understandably proud of her long tenure, which was a record for the twentieth century. Yet her reputation was built mainly on the way in which she used her power. She took office at a time when the economy was experiencing poor growth, with inflation rising and competitiveness declining, and when Britain's international standing – with a perhaps excusable lack of longer-term historical perspective – was widely regarded as being at an all-time low. In power, Thatcher projected herself as spearheading a mission of national revival, breaking with the centrist political and economic settlement around which both main political parties had rallied since the Second World War. She challenged the assumptions upon which post-1945 governments had framed their domestic policies – the mixed economy, in which the state owned key industries and services and sought to maintain a high and stable level of employment; tolerance of growing trade union influence over national economic management; and the financing of a generous welfare state. She also sought to instil respect for traditional values of order and morality at home, and to re-establish Britain as a respected player on the global stage. In her memoirs she recalled her desire to limit the role of the state and to give greater scope to enterprising individuals to make their own choices. The task of government, she wrote, was 'to establish a framework of stability – whether constitutional stability, the rule of law, or the economic stability provided by sound money – within which individual families and businesses were free to pursue their own dreams and ambitions'.[8] Together with an emphasis on traditional 'family values' and law and order, and a robust nationalism, these ideas formed the core of the ideas widely known, from quite early in her term of office, as 'Thatcherism'. In this way she became the first Prime Minister since W.E. Gladstone, a century earlier, to give her name to an ideology.

Thatcher's embrace of these priorities entailed a self-conscious rejection of the notion of consensus between Britain's main political parties. Her notes for a speech to Conservative European Parliament candidates in February 1979, for example, contain the following key points: 'Need for Conviction – Not consensus. Can make changes happen around us – not wait for things to happen.'[9] Two years later she defined consensus as 'the process of abandoning all beliefs, principles, values and policies in search of something in which no one believes, but to which no one objects . . . What great cause would have been fought and won under the banner "I stand for consensus"?'[10] In remarkably similar terms, shortly before her departure from Number 10, she insisted that 'there would have been no great religions, no great philosophies, no great disciples of freedom in the world if they had gone out and said, "Brothers! I stand for compromise! I stand for consensus!"'[11] In place of the vaguely benevolent, middle of the road attitudes which typified post-war British politics, Thatcher projected a clear sense of direction, scornfully dismissing arguments which conflicted with her own beliefs: 'The facts, the facts,' she told a group of policy advisers on one occasion, 'I have been elected to *change* the facts!'[12] Her certainty about herself and her policies sometimes bordered on self-parody. One of her entourage recalled Thatcher ordering the deletion of the word 'perhaps' from the draft of a speech: 'I'm a conviction politician. I'm not in the "perhaps" business.'[13]

Thatcher's dominance of the political scene helped to make the 1980s a time of profound change. The extension of free market principles stood at the core of her government's economic policies. The privatisation of state-owned utilities, such as British Telecom, British Gas, water and electricity, caused the number of shareholders in the UK to increase from 3 million to almost 11.5 million. The sale of more than a million council houses created a new class of owner-occupiers. Business leaders welcomed a new toughness in government attitudes towards the trade unions, whose power was restricted by a series of laws restricting the right to picket and insisting on the balloting of members before a strike. Successful entrepreneurs also benefited from a long-term shift from direct to indirect taxation, with income tax rates, especially those levied on the better off, falling steadily across the decade. Thatcher's economic revolution stimulated a rise in living standards for its beneficiaries, especially in the more prosperous South, typified by the rise of the 'yuppie' – the young, upwardly mobile city trader, clutching, as a visible symbol of personal prosperity, one of the mobile phones which made their first appearance in the 1980s. Her admirers acclaimed her frequently stated desire to encourage self-reliance and to extend opportunity to those with the ambition to better themselves. As

Lord Lexden, the party's official historian, put it in 'Our Maggie', the commemorative film shown at the Conservative conference a few months after her death, she stood for 'enterprise, freedom, choice, competition, liberty'.[14]

Opponents took a much less benign view of the Thatcher decade. Not only the official Labour opposition but also old-style Tory paternalist critics within her own party attacked Thatcher's tolerance of high levels of unemployment. They highlighted the widening gap between rich and poor, and accused the government of wilful neglect of the old industrial areas of northern England, South Wales and Scotland. Former Conservative minister Ian Gilmour was among Thatcher's most articulate critics, condemning what he saw as an inflexible attachment to economic ideology, which engendered a spirit of selfishness and threatened the cohesion of the social fabric. 'Where others might see social conflict, poverty and misery', he wrote, 'she saw merely the benevolent working of an invisible economic providence.'[15] Her downfall was partly caused by the perceived unfairness of the community charge or 'poll tax', a means of funding local government which took little account of residents' ability to pay. The reappearance of beggars on the streets of major cities during the 1980s, a phenomenon little noticed for the previous two generations, was another visible symbol of social division.

Only slightly less controversial were Thatcher's foreign policies. Her period of office coincided with a series of momentous world events. Initially Thatcher faced a new and more dangerous phase of the Cold War, with the Soviet invasion of Afghanistan at Christmas 1979 reversing a decade of progress towards the reduction of tension between the Western and Eastern power blocs. By 1989–90, however, in partnership with US President Ronald Reagan and a new and more flexible leader of the Soviet Union, Mikhail Gorbachev, she had played a part in bringing the forty-five year conflict to an end. As her premiership came to an end Germany – divided since the end of the Second World War – was in the process of reunification.

Thatcher faced other challenges across the globe as Prime Minister. She negotiated a conclusion to two remaining issues left over from the era of the British Empire – the transition to black rule in Zimbabwe and a deal on the eventual hand-over of Hong Kong to communist China. In 1982, in an event which was to be of critical importance for her public image, and for the whole of her premiership, she despatched a naval task force to recover the Falkland Islands, following their occupation by Argentina. To many, Thatcher's role in these developments provided clear proof of her leadership qualities. Perhaps more than any other episode, the victory in the South Atlantic established her as a dominant figure, with most commentators in agreement that none of her recent predecessors as Prime Minister would have dared to launch so bold an operation. Malcolm Rifkind, who served as a junior Foreign Office minister in the 1980s before joining her Cabinet, recalled that, together with her skilful handling of East–West relations, the conflict 'restored the United Kingdom's reputation throughout the world as a significant power'.[16] Her critics, however, regarded her as unduly subservient to the wishes of the United States, masking Britain's relative decline by maintaining its status as a nuclear-armed power, and claiming a degree of independence and influence in world affairs which Britain no longer possessed.

Thatcher's growing hostility towards the process of European integration was viewed by many of her natural supporters as the greatest missed opportunity of her government. Although she played an important role in creating the European single market, which enabled the free movement of people, capital, goods and services across the Community, her period of office is better remembered for a series of conflicts with Britain's continental partners. Thatcher engaged in a long-running dispute over the size of Britain's contribution to the Community budget, before campaigning against the pace of economic and political union. The rifts which this issue caused with key figures in her Cabinet played a significant role in her fall from power in November 1990, and in producing the divisions which beset the Conservative Party for the subsequent decade. By the end of her term of office, Thatcher was widely seen as a negative force in European affairs, incapable of transcending her narrowly nationalistic prejudices. Typical of this viewpoint was the criticism offered by Peter Jenkins, a prominent liberal journalist of the period, who lamented Thatcher's failure 'to rise above her small-town shopkeeper prejudices' to offer the leadership which might have reconciled the British people to the European Community.[17]

Thatcher and the historians

It is unsurprising that so much has been written about Thatcher and her era. Historians have a formidable and still growing volume of sources on which to draw. Thatcher herself and nearly all her senior ministers wrote memoirs, as did a large number of her advisers, backbenchers and political opponents. These of course need to be treated with due caution as historical documents. Most appeared within a few years of Thatcher's departure from office in 1990, and so lacked the detachment which often comes with the passage of time. The main protagonists, not least Thatcher herself, were keen to set down their own version of the events in which they had taken part. A fuller appraisal is now possible, thanks to the work of the Thatcher Foundation in making available through its website (www.margaretthatcher.org) a body of primary material which is unrivalled in its scope. This is augmented by the work of Oxford University Press in collecting, on one CD-ROM, all of Thatcher's surviving recorded public statements from 1945 to 1990. These include transcripts of radio broadcasts and TV interviews, many of which would otherwise be virtually impossible to locate. Among twentieth-century British Prime Ministers, only Winston Churchill exerts the same degree of fascination for writers.

Scholarly study of Thatcher's governments began long before she left office. The most prominent line of interpretation in the early years, common both to sympathetic and hostile writers, was that Thatcher had decisively broken with the post-war consensus. Thus in *Thatcherism and British Politics*, which appeared in 1987, historian Dennis Kavanagh identified Thatcher and Clement Attlee as the two most important post-war British political leaders. Attlee had created the consensus as head of the 1945–51 Labour governments; Thatcher had dismantled it. This interpretation was broadly endorsed, though from a different perspective, by Shirley Letwin, an academic who also worked for the Centre for Policy Studies, a free market think tank founded by Thatcher and other leading Conservatives. In *The Anatomy of Thatcherism* (1992), Letwin argued that Thatcherite policies had replaced the 'socialist consensus' with a healthier set of 'vigorous virtues', based upon personal independence, enterprise and the wider ownership of property.

One of the most important analyses on the left came from political scientist Andrew Gamble, author of *The Free Economy and the Strong State* (1994). He argued that Thatcher's market-driven reform of the economy was part of an attempt to establish Conservative dominance of the political scene, which entailed a significant, though incomplete, strengthening of the power of central government. Some of his conclusions have common ground with the less politically committed work of Simon Jenkins. In *Thatcher and Sons* (2006), he argued that the Thatcher government's transfer of many publicly owned industries and services to the private sector had replaced state ownership with centrally driven targets and regulation, a trend which continued under her Conservative and New Labour successors, John Major, Tony Blair and Gordon Brown. These criticisms also appeared in one of the first attempts to provide students with a critical analysis of the period, Eric Evans' *Thatcher and Thatcherism*, first published in 1997. Evans' overall judgement was negative, arguing that Thatcher's support for unrestrained capitalism had widened social divisions without achieving her much vaunted goal of reversing national decline.

There have also been a number of attempts to provide a full-length portrait of Thatcher herself. Several 'instant' biographies, mostly written by authors strongly sympathetic to their subject, appeared at the time of her election as Conservative leader, followed a few years later by a number marking her arrival in Downing Street and subsequent re-elections. The first significant critical biography was *One of Us* by *Guardian* journalist Hugo Young, first published in 1989, with the final revised edition appearing in 1993. Young took his title from the question which Thatcher was supposed to ask whenever it was suggested that she appoint a particular individual to a post, 'Is he one of us?' The book was widely acclaimed as an effective interim biography, which sought to explain as well as document the Thatcher phenomenon, and offered some tentative conclusions with regard to her wider impact. It was written with the advantages of its author's extensive contacts as a political columnist. More depth and detail was provided by John Campbell's two volume study, *Margaret*

Thatcher: The Grocer's Daughter and *The Iron Lady*, published in 2000 and 2003 respectively, with a single volume condensed version appearing in 2009. Like Young, Campbell had access to a wide variety of witnesses to Thatcher's career, although he was writing before the opening of the official archives relating to her premiership. He acknowledged Thatcher's courage and ability to dominate the political scene, whilst also highlighting the contradictions and limitations of many of her policies in practice.

No less thoroughly researched is Thatcher's official biography, written by former *Daily Telegraph* editor, Charles Moore. By agreement with his subject, the three-volume study did not start to appear until after her death. Moore was far from blind to Thatcher's defects though overall, as one might expect, the tone is more sympathetic than that of Young or Campbell. He had the advantage of access to a mass of documentation which had not been open to previous authors, and a number of Thatcher's contemporaries, who knew her both publicly and privately, clearly spoke to him with greater freedom because of the nature of his commission. Thatcher herself provided a number of interviews and also facilitated introductions to key figures from her past. The co-operation of the then Cabinet Secretary meant that government papers were made available to the author, before the date of their planned release into the public domain. Moore added greater understanding of Thatcher's early life in Grantham, Lincolnshire, before and during the Second World War. He was the only biographer to talk to Thatcher's sister Muriel, who died in 2004, whose recollections and surviving family letters shed some new light on her sibling's formative years. He also revealed details of hitherto unknown romantic involvements during his subject's time as an undergraduate at Oxford, and he covers her experience of Whitehall and Westminster in formidable detail. Indeed, all but the most dedicated reader may be daunted by its length – the text of the first volume alone, which ends with the aftermath of the Falklands crisis in 1982, runs to more than 700 pages.

Less detached was the single volume study by Robin Harris, one of her speech writers and policy advisers, which also appeared soon after Thatcher's death. By coincidence Harris chose for his title the phrase *Not for Turning*, which provides the subtitle for Moore's biography. The words are a direct reference to Thatcher's refusal to abandon or moderate her policies, in face of widespread criticism during her first government. In both cases the choice hints at an underlying sympathy for the subject's indomitable will and sense of purpose. Although he was not chosen as the official biographer, Harris' book was written with the active co-operation of its subject and is prefaced with a letter from Thatcher, stating that she could 'think of no one better placed than you to tackle the subject'.[18]

The present book seeks to provide, in one accessible volume, a balanced assessment of Thatcher as an historical figure. Written after her death, it has the advantage of greater distance from the controversies of her career. It traces the development of her personality, values and goals, and examines the ways in which she wielded power during the 1980s. It does not seek to present a comprehensive account of the policies of the Thatcher governments, still less a general history of Britain between 1979 and 1990. The focus throughout is on Thatcher as an individual, viewed in the context of her times, and on her impact on events. A biographical format enables us to explore the ways in which, far from remaining a static, unchanging figure, she grew and evolved over time. It will show how, with the passage of time, her face grew to fit the mask of the 'iron lady' – a persona which, with the assistance of her image-makers and her critics, she fashioned for herself. The book's approach is broadly chronological with the exception of three thematic chapters – on Northern Ireland, the Cold War and relations with the European Community – whose content ranges across the whole of her premiership. It also looks at the nature of her legacy – for her own party, the nature of government in Britain, and the making of public policy. As it becomes possible to see Thatcher in a longer-term historical perspective, the true significance of her achievements can be more fully grasped. We need to distinguish more clearly between the passion and conflict which she stirred up in her own lifetime, and the reality of how she acted, and the pressures with which she had to contend. It does not diminish Thatcher's importance to see her, in spite of her transformative rhetoric, as part of a broader continuity in post-war Britain – as a person who undoubtedly possessed a strong sense of mission but who also, for the greater part of her ascendancy, had a keen awareness of what was politically possible. A delineation of

Thatcher's personality, aims and achievements can only help to clarify our understanding of a critical period in British history.

Notes

1 *The Independent*, 9 April 2013, p. 2.
2 *The Times*, 9 April 2013, p. 8.
3 Interview for *Woman's Own*, 3 August 1982, quoted in John Campbell, *Margaret Thatcher: Volume Two: The Iron Lady* (London, Jonathan Cape, 2003), p. 474.
4 Alan Clark, *Diaries: Into Politics, 1972–1982* (London, Phoenix, 2001), p. 147, entry for 26 February 1980.
5 Peter Hennessy, *The Prime Minister: The Office and its Holders since 1945* (London, Allen Lane/Penguin, 2000), p. 403.
6 John Cole, *As It Seemed to Me: Political Memoirs* (London, Phoenix, 1996), p. 149.
7 Nicholas Ridley, *'My Style of Government': The Thatcher Years* (London, Hutchinson, 1991), p. 266. Reproduced by permission of The Random House Group Ltd.
8 Margaret Thatcher, *The Downing Street Years* (London, Harper Collins, 1993), p.14.
9 Margaret Thatcher, speech at Conservative European candidates' conference, 24 February 1979, www.margaretthatcher.org/document/103955 (accessed 11 December 2013).
10 Margaret Thatcher, speech at Monash University, Australia, 6 October 1981, www.margaretthatcher.org/document/104712 (accessed 11 December 2013).
11 Interview for *Woman's Own*, 21 May 1990, *Margaret Thatcher: Complete Public Statements 1945–1990 on CD-ROM* (Oxford University Press, 1999), 90_185.
12 Peter Hennessy, *The Prime Minister: The Office and its Holders since 1945* (London, Allen Lane/Penguin, 2000), p. 422.
13 Ronald Millar, *A View from the Wings* (London, Weidenfeld & Nicolson, 1993), p. 257.
14 http://www.conservativehome.com/thetorydiary/2013/09/watch-our-maggie-conference-film-tribute-to-margaret-thatcher.html (accessed 11 December 2013).
15 Ian Gilmour, *Dancing with Dogma: Britain under Thatcherism* (London, Simon & Schuster, 1992), p. 268.
16 Malcolm Rifkind, 'Britain restored in the world' in Subroto Roy and John Clarke (eds) *Margaret Thatcher's Revolution: How it Happened and What it Meant* (London, Continuum, 2005), pp. 35–6.
17 Peter Jenkins, quoted in *The Independent*, 9 April 2013, p. 4.
18 Robin Harris, *Not for Turning: The Life of Margaret Thatcher* (London, Bantam Press, 2013), p. 3. Reproduced by permission of The Random House Group Ltd and Thomas Dunne Books. All rights reserved.

1 From corner shop to cabinet room: 1925–1970

Growing up above the shop

Few British Prime Ministers can compare with Margaret Thatcher in the intense significance that she ascribed to her formative years. Her rise to power was one of the least likely of the twentieth century. She was born above her parents' corner shop in Grantham, an unremarkable market town in Lincolnshire, about a hundred miles north of London, on 13 October 1925. Her father, Alfred Roberts, was a self-educated grocer and sub-postmaster, whose own political career did not extend beyond participation in the affairs of the local town council. Thatcher certainly did not begin life with the social advantages which assisted those who led the Conservative Party in the years when she came to political maturity, in the era of Winston Churchill, Anthony Eden and Harold Macmillan. The male-dominated political culture of the period of course made her ascent all the more remarkable. When she entered Parliament in 1959, only three women had ever sat in a British Cabinet and only one of these, Florence Horsbrugh, Minister of Education in 1951–4, was a Conservative.

At the same time it is important not to exaggerate the obstacles that stood in Thatcher's way. The young Thatcher did not experience poverty as did, for example, the Labour Prime Minister whom she displaced in May 1979, James Callaghan, the son of a widowed mother in early twentieth-century Portsmouth. The Roberts family was higher in the pre-war social scale than that of Edward Heath, the man whom she was to supplant as leader of the Conservative Party in 1975, whose parents were a skilled carpenter and a former maid. Nor did the young Margaret Roberts know the economic insecurity suffered by another Labour leader whom she was to face across the floor of the House of Commons, Harold Wilson, whose industrial chemist father was unemployed during the slump of the 1930s. And, for all her championship of opportunity and social mobility, in old age she was privately to look down on her successor as Prime Minister, John Major, the 'boy from Coldharbour Lane'[1] – a reference to his father's descent from modest business success in Surrey to more straitened circumstances in Brixton.

Life in the Roberts household took its tone from the deeply ingrained values of its head. Alfred Roberts was an intensely active man, who extended his business interests with the purchase of a second shop in the town whilst also playing a part in local government. In 1943 he was chosen by his fellow councillors as an alderman, an office which has since disappeared but which carried considerable local distinction at the time. Two years later he served a term as mayor of Grantham. He did not dominate the borough in the manner of an urban political party 'boss', but he was without doubt a figure of some standing in his own community. He had accumulated his modest fortune through hard work and thrift, values whose importance he inculcated in his two daughters, Margaret and her elder sibling, Muriel. He imposed an austere life-style on them through deliberate choice rather than strict necessity. Their home lacked a garden, an indoor lavatory and even hot running water. Roberts' wife, Beatrice, was an efficient and economical household manager, who made the girls' clothes and was obsessive about cleanliness and tidiness. Holidays and outings were rare and there were few luxuries; the choice of films which the girls were allowed to see at the local cinema was strictly regulated and the family did not possess a radio for the first ten years of Margaret's life. The emphasis was on learning and self-improvement, reinforced through regular borrowing of educational books from the local library, and on the avoidance of waste and frivolity. Roberts actively supported her education at the local girls' grammar school, to which she won a scholarship at the early age of ten, helping her to develop a habit of intense study and an ability to think and to speak in public. Underpinning the Roberts family's values of self-discipline, duty and denial was their membership of the Methodist Church. Roberts was a lay preacher and attendance at chapel at least twice every Sunday was an established feature of his daughters' childhood routine.

Thatcher's upbringing was suffused with an emphasis on individual effort and independence. In her memoirs she recalled seeing queues of jobless people during the economic downturn of the 1930s, either seeking work or claiming benefits. It was typical of the emphasis that she placed on self-reliance that she noted 'how neatly turned out the children of those unemployed families were' – a recollected detail which perhaps sounds coolly distant to modern ears. Yet she also noted the way in which, through their own efforts and the voluntary support provided by others, the unemployed remained part of the community.[2] The notion that victims of misfortune should look primarily to their families and neighbours for assistance, rather than to the state, was one to which the mature Thatcher would return.

A straightforward sense of justice underpinned the Roberts family's view of international affairs. They were acutely conscious of the evils of the Hitler regime, and towards the end of the decade temporarily took in a teenage Jewish Austrian girl who had escaped from Nazi persecution. It seems likely that the seeds of Thatcher's later suspicion of continental Europe were sown in the era of appeasement, and in the Second World War which soon followed. Unlike many of her male near-contemporaries, with whom she was to serve in Cabinet in the 1970s and 1980s, she was a witness rather than a participant in the military conflict of 1939–45. She responded to the patriotism of Churchill's radio broadcasts, beginning a life-long devotion to Britain's wartime leader. In later life she would habitually refer to him as 'Winston', even though she was never personally acquainted with the great man. She also came to see the Atlantic relationship as the key to Britain's wartime survival and future security. The retired Conservative leader who was to embarrass her successors by writing in 2002 that 'during my lifetime, most of the problems the world has faced have come . . . from mainland Europe, and the solutions from outside it',[3] was no doubt thinking of the traumatic period that she knew as a teenager.

The adult Margaret Thatcher was deeply ambivalent about her childhood. She seems to have had limited rapport as a young adult with her mother. Certainly she spoke respectfully in later years of Beatrice's abilities as a homemaker, and she learned from her a number of practical skills of which she made use throughout her life. In later life her competence in a range of domestic tasks was part of her public persona, and it was noted that she continued to prepare her husband's breakfast after they moved into Downing Street. It is impossible to imagine any other Prime Minister, for example, sewing on a button for a policeman on guard duty at Number 10. The truth, however, was – as she acknowledged in later life – that as her own horizons broadened, she had less and less in common with her mother.

It was with her father that Thatcher had the more important bond. Some writers have speculated that Alfred Roberts focused his ambitions on his younger daughter as a substitute for the son he never had. From him she developed her earliest awareness of politics and her party loyalties. Following the convention of the time, which tended to keep party labels out of local government, he stood as an independent councillor rather than a Conservative. There can be little doubt, however, that he was a man of the political right. One of his foremost concerns was to keep the rates – the local taxes then paid by householders – as low as possible. It was the socialist group on the council which removed the rank of alderman from him nine years after his elevation, in a party political manoeuvre which caused his daughter great distress. When Margaret Roberts was adopted as the party's parliamentary candidate for Dartford in Kent, in February 1949, her father addressed the local Conservative worthies alongside his daughter. In his speech he declared that although his family had traditionally been Liberals, he now felt that the Conservative Party stood for much the same things as the Liberal Party of his youth. Such a transition was not unusual for middle-class Methodists and members of other nonconformist denominations in the interwar years, as the old Liberal Party both adopted increasingly collectivist social policies and continued to decline as a political force, opening up an opportunity for the Conservative Party to attract many of its supporters.

As a major political figure in the 1970s, Thatcher made much of her father's example when asked about her fundamental values. So well established was the popular image of the late Alderman

Roberts that, as she entered Downing Street after winning the May 1979 general election, more than nine years after his death, a reporter asked Thatcher for her thoughts 'about Mrs Pankhurst and your own mentor in political life – your own father'. Britain's first female Prime Minister sidestepped the reference to the celebrated leader of the pre-1914 campaign for women's voting rights, characteristically declining to be identified with any individual or organisation associated with feminism. Yet she answered without hesitation that 'I just owe almost everything to my own father. . . . He brought me up to believe all the things that I do believe. . . . And it's passionately interesting for me that the things that I learned in a small town, in a very modest home, are just the things that I believe have won the election.'⁴ In another interview, a few months before the 1983 election, she cited her father's belief in rugged individualism when challenged that her government showed insufficient compassion. 'Of course we have basic social services, we will continue to have those,' she assured her listeners, 'but equally compassion depends upon what you and I, as an individual, are prepared to do. I remember my father telling me that at a very early age.'⁵ Two years later Thatcher gave a fuller picture of her father's influence in an interview of a more personal kind. The dominant theme which emerged was of a parent who encouraged his daughter to stand up for what she believed in, without regard for the opinions of others: 'You first sort out what you believe in. You then apply it. You then must argue your case, but you do not say, "Well I am going to do it because someone else did it!" and always you do not compromise on things that matter.'⁶

The influence of Thatcher's father can be overstated. As she emerged into adulthood, she rebelled against the more restrictive aspects of her upbringing. She developed a taste for elegant clothes and, although work always remained her firm priority, she enjoyed parties and dancing. After her marriage she adopted her husband's Anglican faith, moving away from the Methodism of her youth. The hymns and readings used at Thatcher's funeral, which she had carefully chosen, reflected the personal tastes of someone who had come to love the traditional language of the services of the Church of England. She rarely returned to Grantham, and it is telling that her children did not have strong memories of their maternal grandparents. On one occasion she failed to remember the date of her father's death, inaccurately thinking that he had lived to see her appointment to Edward Heath's Cabinet in June 1970, whereas in fact he had died four months earlier. It appears that she attended his funeral service at Grantham but, oddly for a close family member, was not actually present at the subsequent cremation. Her official biographer excuses this absence on the grounds that she had to return to London in readiness for the next day's official engagements. He also points out that she had visited her father during his final illness, though it turns out that she stopped off *en route* to a meeting in Scotland, rather than making a purpose journey to the family home.[7] To make mention of this is not to condemn. It is not unusual for children to grow apart from their parents as a result of the new opportunities brought by education and a career. In any case to fit in regular visits home, whilst working and managing family responsibilities at a distance, is a challenge to even the most devoted offspring. At the same time, it does not suggest a great enduring personal closeness between father and adult daughter.

From Grantham to Oxford

Where Thatcher's background did have a genuinely important impact was in the way that it instilled notions of industry and ambition which stayed with her throughout her career. Her extraordinary capacity to focus on the task in hand; her insistence on being better briefed on any topic than her colleagues or opponents; her inability properly to relax – holidays seem to have induced a restless desire to return to work – all of this can be traced back to her early years and the example of Alfred Roberts. At school she demonstrated a high level of application and a consistently serious approach to everything, earning a reputation for asking penetrating questions of visiting speakers from a relatively early age. Drive and determination manifested themselves again in her desire to win a place at Oxford University so that, in the autumn of 1943, she became the first member of her family to go on to higher education. In preparing for entry she displayed early evidence of her readiness to defy others in pursuit of an objective on which she had decided. She refused to be discouraged by the rather negative attitude of her school's headmistress, Miss

Gillies, who – for reasons which have never fully been explained – was unwilling to support her application. Perhaps Miss Gillies wanted to take her thrusting young pupil down a peg or two; or she may have genuinely doubted her readiness for the rigours of the Oxford entrance process. One of the key requirements was knowledge of Latin, which Margaret Roberts acquired through coaching outside school. A less attractive side of her personality manifested itself many years later, when she publicly corrected the headmistress' use of Latin on a visit to the school as a recently elected MP. She was not a person who readily forgave or sought reconciliation with a former adversary.

Oxford took the young Margaret Roberts into a world far removed from the one in which she had grown up. It was not one in which she was particularly happy. Although she had rubbed shoulders with local grandees at civic events in Grantham, and her father was distantly acquainted with Lord Brownlow, a prominent Lincolnshire landed magnate, she was socially ill at ease with the more privileged members of the university. She was alienated from the prevailing politically liberal attitudes of the Oxford establishment. Nor did she possess the financial resources and personal contacts which provided easy access into the social world of the university. Her gender was, at that time, another obstacle to full participation in its activities. The prestigious debating society, the Oxford Union, was still closed to women. In time, however, she came to enjoy herself to some extent. We now know that at Oxford she had her first serious boyfriend, army cadet Tony Bray. Academically Margaret Roberts was able but not outstanding, gaining a respectable second class degree in her chosen discipline, chemistry. She graduated in the summer of 1947 after taking a fourth year to carry out a research project. Yet the subject did not enthuse her. She had opted for it because she was good at it at school, and after university it provided a means of earning her living – first in a plastics firm in Essex and then in the research department of the catering company, J Lyons, testing cake fillings and ice cream. Whilst still at Oxford her mind was turning towards studying for a degree in law, which would be a more appropriate preparation for her real career.

Outside her academic studies, Margaret Roberts' energies were mainly absorbed by membership of the Oxford University

Conservative Association (OUCA). Her sex was no barrier to advancement in university politics. By applying herself diligently to the administrative work of the association, in her final year at Oxford she became the third woman to serve as its president. OUCA by no means provided an automatic entry into national politics, but it did give Margaret Roberts valuable experience of arranging meetings and of 'networking' with well-known Conservative politicians, who visited the university as guest speakers. The circumstances in which she first decided to seek selection as an MP are unclear. She seems to have first admitted that this was her ambition when the subject came up at a social gathering at a Lincolnshire friend's house, late in 1944. At the time this must have seemed a distant and somewhat implausible dream for someone of her background. The following summer, in the run-up to the general election which was to bring Clement Attlee's Labour Party to power with a crushing 146-seat majority, she delivered her first recorded political speech, on behalf of the Conservative candidate in Grantham. There is no evidence that the nineteen year old Margaret Roberts had in any way been touched by the leftward shift in public opinion during the Second World War. Like most Conservative supporters she was unmoved by the growing national demand for improved welfare services and greater social justice, which paved the way for the Labour landslide. She shared the dismay of other Conservative loyalists at Churchill's devastating rejection at the polls.

A partner and a seat

Margaret Roberts' fortunes began to change as a result of two chance encounters. The wealthy MP for Maidstone in Kent, Alfred Bossom, who was noted for encouraging aspiring young members of the party, 'talent-spotted' her in the summer of 1948 when she gave a speech at a Young Conservative conference in Kent. Through his influence she attended the party conference at Llandudno in the autumn of 1948, where a second unexpected meeting enabled her to take the next step in her embryonic political career. Present at the conference was John Miller, chairman of the Dartford Conservative Association, who was prevailed upon to consider her as the candidate for the seat. Dartford was a safe Labour seat, which Margaret Roberts had no realistic chance of winning, but her adoption for the two closely fought general elections of February 1950 and October 1951 was of great importance for her personal and professional life. Her vigorous campaigning, possibly combined with the fact that she was a young and photogenic female candidate, helped to reduce the sitting Labour MP's majority by 6,000 votes in the first election, and by a further 1,300 in the second one. It marked her out as someone with clear potential, even if she failed to share personally in the eventual success of the Conservatives in turning out Attlee's weakened Labour administration.

On a personal level, Margaret Roberts' involvement in Dartford Conservative politics proved no less significant. It was here that she first met her future husband, Denis Thatcher. A former army officer who had already been divorced following an unsuccessful wartime marriage, he was managing director of his family's paint manufacturing firm, the Atlas Preservative Company. It was not love at first sight. Margaret Roberts did not decisively break off another romantic involvement, with a doctor named Robert Henderson, until the summer of 1951. She seems initially to have bonded with Denis Thatcher through a shared political outlook and a common-sense appraisal of him as a potential partner. He was well off, with a liking for fast cars and an air of dash and sophistication. Ten years her senior, he provided the financial security which would enable her to concentrate on advancing her political career. Their marriage, which took place in December 1951, took her further away from her Grantham roots. Denis Thatcher gave Margaret access to the affluent world of the Home Counties – the 'gin and Jag' set which provided the core vote of post-war suburban Conservatism – as they moved during their early married life from his flat in Chelsea to the first of two substantial houses in Kent. Theirs was a notably successful marriage. As she became a public figure, he offered steady support and never embarrassed her by seeking a share of the limelight. He was not the henpecked subordinate figure of popular myth. Rather, the Thatchers pursued their own separate careers, at least until Denis was sufficiently secure to retire from business in 1975, the year that Margaret became party leader. He was typical of his generation in expecting his wife to manage the home and in playing a limited role in the upbringing of their children, the twins Mark and Carol, who were born in August 1953. His reasonably affluent position allowed them to employ a full-time nanny, which enabled his wife to make her long-contemplated career change, becoming a fully qualified barrister in January 1954.

Thatcher was unusual, as a married woman with a young family in the 1950s, in pursuing a full-time career. At this time she was working as a tax lawyer whilst actively seeking a parliamentary seat. The twins seem to have reached a slightly awed acceptance of the fact that their mother was unlike other children's. Their nanny recalled that Denis would remember to wave to them as he left for work whereas Margaret, already focused on the day ahead, would forget. Yet she played a more active part in the children's upbringing than their father, whose extended overseas business trips often coincided with school holidays. She was formidably well-organised as she 'juggled' her domestic and professional responsibilities. Carol Thatcher remembered her turning up to school functions after she had been elected to Parliament, 'often working on constituency papers in the car until the last minute and then ducking into the marquee for the Speech Day presentation'.[8]

Nonetheless, this same capacity to balance family and work, which would be considered unexceptional today, seems to have played a part in delaying Thatcher's entry into the Commons. Remarkably she failed to secure adoption as a Conservative parliamentary candidate in no fewer than five seats in the London area. In the mid-1950s, a working woman with a family was often viewed with suspicion by grassroots party activists seeking a new representative. Female members of selection committees in particular feared that such a candidate would be unable to reconcile her public and private commitments. To be turned down so often, however, may also hint at something more personal. It is possible that Thatcher came across as formidably competent and well informed, but as lacking in the warmth and humour which might have enabled her to develop a rapport at a human level. At any rate, it was not until July 1958 that Thatcher secured adoption as the candidate for Finchley, a well-to-do north London constituency. Even here she had to contend with opposition from an unreconstructed chauvinistic element in the local association, which staged an unsuccessful last-ditch attempt to block the nomination of a woman.

There were some difficulties to be ironed out in readiness for the next general election. The organisation of the local party in Finchley, which had been allowed to ossify under Thatcher's lack-lustre predecessor, Sir John Crowder MP, had to be revived. In addition, the new candidate had to deal with an unfortunate perception, which local Liberals were seeking to exploit, that there was a degree of anti-Semitic feeling lurking within the local Conservative Association. This was traceable to the attitudes of a small number of party activists prominent in the local golf club but, in a constituency where approximately 20 per cent of the electorate was Jewish, the anxiety was not without political significance. There was never any suggestion of anti-Semitism on Thatcher's part and she was soon able to correct the negative impression. She was assisted in this by a visit to the constituency by one of her party's most prominent Jewish MPs, Sir Keith Joseph, with whom she was later to build an important political partnership. Indeed she developed a respectful and harmonious relationship with the Jewish community, based upon a shared adherence to values of self-reliance and hard work. Finchley itself was a safe Conservative seat, whose population included a large proportion of upwardly mobile, managerial and professional people who were to remain archetypal 'Thatcherite' voters throughout her thirty-three-year period as its representative. It was no surprise that, in the October 1959 general election, called by Prime Minister Harold Macmillan at a time of rising post-war material prosperity, Thatcher was elected with a healthy 16,000 majority, an increase of more than 3,000 votes on her predecessor's last performance.

The party loyalist

What do we know of Margaret Thatcher's political outlook as she embarked on her parliamentary career? Some of her biographers have detected evidence of the ideology to be known three decades later as 'Thatcherism', with its emphasis on the free market, individualism and the restoration of national prestige, as early as her speeches in Dartford at the beginning of the decade. Thus Charles Moore cites her 1950 election address, in which she stressed the importance of sound finance and enterprise, and condemned the Labour government for allowing Britain's global standing in the Cold War to slip, as 'perhaps the first clear text of Thatcherism'.[9] If so, then 'Thatcherism' was perhaps less detached from mainstream Conservative thinking than some of its detractors – and a few of its supporters – were later to claim. With the euphoria of Labour's 1945 victory now a thing of the past, it was common for Conservative critics of Attlee's ailing government to draw attention to the allegedly enervating effects of 'socialism' on the economy, and to capitalise on the unpopularity of continued rationing and other forms of state control. Thus the 1950 Conservative manifesto claimed that 'Success has been penalised. . . . The crushing burden of public expenditure must be drastically reduced. Stronger effort, more enterprise and inventiveness, and greater thrift can only be encouraged by lower taxes.'[10] The manifesto on which Churchill was returned to power the following year stated that 'the attempt to impose a doctrinaire Socialism upon an Island which has grown great and famous by free enterprise has inflicted serious injury upon our strength and prosperity'. The nationalisation of industry, it maintained, had 'proved itself a failure which has resulted in heavy losses to the taxpayer, or the consumer, or both'.[11] The young Margaret Roberts may have stood out for the vehemence with which she expressed her views, but they were consistent with the official stance of the party leadership at this stage. She was in line with party orthodoxy in the 1950s, too, in her acceptance of the fundamentals of the welfare state created by the wartime coalition and the post-war Labour administration, and of the cross-party commitment to maintain full employment. She had read the text which was to become the inspiration of radical free market Conservatism, *The Road to Serfdom*, by Austrian political philosopher Friedrich von Hayek, shortly after its publication in 1944. The book argued that the concept of central planning, however good the intentions that lay behind it, was invariably a threat to personal freedom. Yet as she admitted in her memoirs, it was not until the mid-1970s that she digested its full implications for policy-making.[12] It was the breakdown of the post-war consensus, during that decade, which prompted Thatcher to rethink her position on the role of the state, and to take seriously the views of a thinker who was consciously an outsider to Britain's political elite. A generation earlier, there is little sign that she was out of step with the received wisdom of the opinion-makers in her party.

Nor was there anything particularly remarkable about Thatcher's views on international affairs at this stage. In stressing the importance of the empire to Britain's position in the world, and to its prospects of economic recovery, she was putting a view which found widespread support on the centre-right in the decade after the Second World War. As candidate for Dartford she was not exceptional in voicing support for imperial preference – the idea of reciprocal trade agreements between Britain and its colonies, which was not officially abandoned by the Conservative Party until its 1954 conference. The evidence for her response to the 1956 Suez crisis, which followed Prime Minister Anthony Eden's attempt to recover control of the canal from Egypt by force, is less clear-cut. Sir John Coles, one of her foreign policy advisers during her premiership, relates a story which suggests that she had qualms about the legality of the military operation. Seeing a newspaper placard bearing the headline 'Eden goes into Egypt' she is supposed to have exclaimed, 'He has no right to.'[13] It is hard, however, to find any other suggestion that she was less than supportive of Britain's actions at the time. In her memoirs she recalls cancelling her subscription to the *Observer* newspaper because of its opposition to the expedition, and even forty years on she was not prepared to endorse the stance taken by two liberal-minded junior ministers, Anthony Nutting and Edward Boyle – the latter a personal friend – who had resigned from the Eden government in protest.[14] What distinguished Thatcher, however, was a refusal to look back in a spirit of sentimentality. She was far too pragmatic and hard-headed to join the diminishing band of right-wing imperial die-hards who maintained a determined yet ultimately futile opposition to the process of decolonisation, which gathered pace after she entered Parliament.

As a newly elected woman MP in 1959, the thirty-four year old Thatcher faced the challenge of winning acceptance in a still heavily male-dominated House of Commons. The sense of being an outsider was heightened by the fact that this was a generation of MPs who had acquired a degree of common ground through the shared experience of military service, from which Thatcher was clearly excluded. Many of those with whom she would serve in government, and a number of leading opposition figures, had distinguished war records. On the Conservative side, the majority of MPs still came from upper middle-class backgrounds and had attended the same private schools. There were some grammar school 'meritocrats' who were now making their way to the top of the parliamentary party, including some key figures of the next decade such as Edward Heath and Enoch Powell, the independent-minded right-wing MP for Wolverhampton South-West, but her relations with them were not close. As a backbencher Thatcher never belonged to a particular faction within the party and she did not have the advantage of an established network of contacts on which to draw. In addition, it must have been irritating as well as flattering to have her gender and physical appearance – she was by common consent the most attractive and best dressed of the twelve Conservative woman MPs in the House – so frequently remarked upon. She was always impatient with media or party requests to give a view on an issue from a 'woman's perspective', rather than simply being taken on her own merits as a politician. Nor did she seek to make common cause with other female MPs. The reluctant admiration that she drew from Labour's rising star, Barbara Castle, who was to serve in Harold Wilson's Cabinets in the 1960s and 1970s, was not reciprocated.

It was extremely helpful to Thatcher to find herself allocated, entirely at random, second place in the annual ballot to introduce a private member's bill. The topic which she chose, after two earlier ideas had fallen on stony ground, was a proposal to prevent local councils from excluding press reporters from their proceedings. One of Thatcher's biographers, John Campbell, has argued that her selection of this issue was part of a belated rebellion against her father, whom she identified with the system of local government which she sought to attack. Campbell speculates that although no record of his views survives, Alfred Roberts himself may have regarded the measure as 'a clumsy interference with the right of local authorities to conduct their own affairs'.[15] Such a theory is incapable of definitive proof. Her decision to bring forward the bill can surely be explained more mundanely in terms of straightforward political partisanship. As Campbell himself notes, some Labour councils had been restricting access to journalists who had broken with expectations of trade union solidarity by providing so-called 'blackleg' labour during a newspaper dispute. The issue had been highlighted in the 1959 Conservative election manifesto, and the only real difference between Thatcher's approach and the official line was that she wanted to introduce legislation to curb the practice, whereas the government favoured the less confrontational approach of a new code of conduct for councils. Certainly, a lack of full co-operation from Whitehall meant that Thatcher's bill lacked the force that she wished it to have. Nonetheless the experience of researching the issue, making contacts with relevant ministers and civil servants, and then bringing forward the measure and rallying parliamentary support for it, helped her learn the ropes. The speech with which she introduced it won general acclaim.

At this stage in her parliamentary career, Thatcher wisely concentrated on gaining a reputation for competence. She rebelled only once, in support of an abortive measure to reintroduce corporal punishment for young offenders, which had been abolished by the Labour government in 1948. Some considered that in identifying herself with a lost cause of the atavistic Tory right, she risked damaging her career prospects. After all, the dominant philosophy of the Conservative leadership at the time was one of benevolent liberalism on moral and social issues, which went hand in hand with a slightly patronising attitude towards the more clear-cut instincts of the party's core supporters. R.A. Butler, for example, who as Home Secretary bore the brunt of calls for the restoration of tougher penalties from the so-called 'hangers and floggers' at successive party conferences, recalled his clashes with the 'Colonel Blimps of both sexes – and the female of the species was more deadly, politically, than the male'.[16] Thatcher's dissent from the government line may, in fact, indirectly have helped her chances of promotion. By demonstrating a willingness to take an independent approach – whilst avoiding being stereotyped as an obstructive right-winger – she may have encouraged the party whips to think of offering her minor office. At any rate, in October 1961, shortly before her thirty-sixth birthday, Macmillan asked her to join the government as parliamentary under-secretary at the Ministry of Pensions and National Insurance. Another reason for the invitation may have been that the previous incumbent, Patricia Hornsby-Smith, had been a woman. Even at this time, when the levers of power were indisputably in the hands of a male elite, it is likely that the Prime Minister recognised the need to give some token representation to women in the government. In this way Thatcher joined the front bench, scarcely two years after her arrival in the House.

Junior office and shadow cabinet

The work of the Ministry of Pensions and National Insurance was decidedly unglamorous, especially the heavy burden of decisions on individual benefit application cases which was the lot of its most junior office-holder. It says a great deal about the attitudes of the party leadership that, although Thatcher soon established herself as a competent and conscientious minister, she was not offered promotion or even a sideways transfer, which might have broadened her experience of government, when Macmillan was succeeded as premier by Sir Alec Douglas-Home in October 1963. Indeed she continued to shadow the department for the first nine months in opposition after the Conservatives lost the October 1964 General Election. If Thatcher privately resented being kept in her ministerial backwater, she did not betray any hint of it in public. Although, a decade earlier, she had speculated that a woman might aspire to serve as Chancellor of the Exchequer or Foreign Secretary,[17] she was realistic enough to know the likely boundaries to ambition for a woman at that time. Both then and in her memoirs, she evinced no criticism of the so-called 'magic circle' of upper-class Tory grandees which, in the days before the party adopted a formal process of leadership elections, brought about the aristocratic Douglas-Home's succession to Macmillan. Perhaps surprisingly for one who had risen through merit and good fortune, rather than through any sense of inherited entitlement, she expressed affection for Douglas-Home as a gentleman of the old school. She admired his robust approach to the Cold War as Foreign Secretary in 1960–3, and later described herself as 'stunned and upset'[18] when he was ousted from the party leadership in July 1965.

At the level of policy, too, Thatcher continued to show no real sign of divergence from current orthodoxy. In her memoirs she stated that she had become uneasy about the direction of economic policy by 1961–2, criticising the government of which she had been a member for resorting to an incomes policy in a bid to curb inflation, instead of tackling the fundamental problem of trade union power.[19] The Macmillan government's attempts to control wages and price increases through government consultation with management and unions was later to be seen by Thatcherites as the beginning of the Conservative Party's departure from sound economic principles. At the time, however, Thatcher failed to develop anything approaching a coherent critique of government policy. Her isolated public warning, at a meeting in Finchley in March 1962, that the country was paying itself more than it earned, leading to a rise in prices, and that the maintenance of current living standards depended on competitiveness in world markets, was not followed up.[20] She also supported Macmillan's decision to apply for membership of the body which was then known as the European Economic Community or, in everyday parlance, the Common Market. Like most people, both within the Conservative Party and outside, at this stage she saw 'Europe' as primarily a trading organisation, which presented no threat to Britain's political sovereignty. There was as yet no hint of the anxieties on this issue which would play such a prominent part in her later career. In short she toed the party line on both home and foreign policy. It would have been surprising for a young and aspiring minister, with so many demands on her time, to have done otherwise.

Indeed, had Thatcher felt so strongly about the direction of policy at the time, it is hard to understand her initial reaction to the leadership contest which took place when Douglas-Home stepped down – the first in which Conservative MPs formally voted, rather than the leader emerging through backroom machinations. Her first preference was for the breezily expansionist figure of Reginald Maudling, who had engineered the so-called 'dash for growth' as Chancellor of the Exchequer in the run up to the 1964 election. It was Keith Joseph who persuaded her to transfer her support to Edward Heath, whom he regarded as a more serious potential leader. Significantly, Thatcher never considered backing the candidate of the outside right, Enoch Powell, who alone of the three leadership contenders stood for an unequivocally radical, free market approach. In shunning Powell, who garnered only 15 votes from the parliamentary party, to Heath's 150 and Maudling's 133, she showed once again her keen sense of political realism.

Heath was to hold the party leadership for almost ten years, until he was displaced by Thatcher in February 1975. They had known each other since the latter's candidacy in Dartford in 1950, when Heath was elected MP for the neighbouring seat of Bexley. Relations between the two, however, were never easy. Aloof and business-like, Heath was a confirmed bachelor who was rarely comfortable in the company of women. Thatcher was not his first choice when it came to appointing the shadow cabinet's so-called 'statutory woman'. According to James Prior, who was to serve in Thatcher's first Cabinet, Heath and his Chief Whip, Willie Whitelaw, recognised her ability but feared that 'once she's there we'll never be able to get rid of her'.[21] Nonetheless Heath clearly respected her capacity to master a brief, giving her experience of a variety of portfolios in opposition. She shadowed the Ministry of Housing and the Treasury in a junior capacity. Finally, as a member of the shadow cabinet from October 1967, she covered in turn the departments of Power, Transport and Education.

Thatcher found membership of Heath's shadow cabinet a frustrating experience. Although his election as leader was heralded as marking a dynamic new approach, Heath was essentially a technocrat – a 'Permanent Secretary *manqué*'[22] – who saw politics in terms of management. Not only did he tend to avoid debate on matters of principle, he also gave Thatcher little encouragement to contribute to discussion. Ironically the two had more in common than either would have cared to acknowledge. Both favoured an authoritarian style of chairmanship in which there was little tolerance of time-wasters. Both were lower middle-class grammar school pupils who had won places at Oxford University on their own merits. Here, however, the similarities ended. Nine years older than Thatcher, Heath had travelled widely in Europe in the 1930s before enlisting in the army in the Second World War. His experience left him with a profound sense of the need for a political union to overcome the deep divisions which had scarred the continent. Elected to Parliament almost a decade before Thatcher, he rapidly assimilated himself into the Conservative Party's ruling group. As a trusted Chief Whip and senior minister he expunged most traces of his humble background. Whilst Thatcher was still struggling to establish herself at Westminster, Heath was a secure member of the political establishment, whose inclusion in Macmillan's circle marked him out for still greater things.

Partly because of her sex, Thatcher was an often isolated member of the shadow cabinet. Her colleagues' memoirs contain relatively few references to her from this period. Lord Carrington, who was to serve as her Foreign Secretary in 1979–82, later recalled that 'I don't think she was much noticed at Ted [Heath]'s shadow cabinet. She made no mark at all.'[23] An exception was James Prior who, although he was to be one of Thatcher's strongest opponents within the party after 1979, felt that she deserved a place on merit: 'She was of the right, but not excessively so. She was by far the best of our women MPs and was beginning to build a following in the country.'[24] Thatcher was now slowly emerging as a national figure. Her frequent changes of shadow post meant that she had to immerse herself in a great deal of rapidly changing policy detail, but she learned fast and, especially as understudy to Heath's Shadow Chancellor, Iain Macleod in 1966–7, she took on her Labour counterparts in the Commons with relish and some skill. Although Macleod was by conviction a figure of the party's centre-left, and thus an unlikely role model for Thatcher, she learned a great deal from him, later acknowledging his skills as a quick-thinking and combative debater and an effective communicator. In these years she was gaining a favourable reputation among Conservative MPs for her robust attacks on the economic policies of Harold Wilson's government. She even earned an admiring headline in the *Sun* – not yet the Conservative-supporting newspaper of the 1980s – for her speech at the 1966 party conference, in which she berated Labour for increasing taxes: 'A Fiery Blonde Warns of the Road to Ruin'.[25]

By now there were indications of a willingness on Thatcher's part to question aspects of the post-war consensus. She was critical of the effects of nationalisation and, in a lecture to the Conservative Political Centre at the October 1968 party conference, she identified control of the money supply as a key requirement of government. Most of the lecture, however, comprised an attack on the growth of over-powerful government and excessive bureaucracy – sentiments which were widely held across the right of British politics in the late 1960s, and which in no way drove a wedge between her and her shadow cabinet colleagues. She would not allow her instincts on policy to inhibit her advance through the party's ranks. When Enoch Powell made his so-called 'rivers of blood' speech in April 1968, in which he argued in inflammatory language that continued large-scale Commonwealth immigration would produce racial conflict in Britain, Heath telephoned his colleagues to inform them of his decision to sack him from the shadow cabinet. Thatcher's was a lone voice urging the leader to stay his hand, but she did not press the point, and she was careful not to identify herself with Powell in public. Although she later acknowledged Powell as a pioneer of the approach to economic policy that she was to take as Prime Minister, self-preservation dictated a prudent distance from his politically toxic views on race and immigration, and from the solitary feud that he was to pursue against Heath's leadership over the next six years.

In October 1969 Thatcher moved to shadow Education, the department that she was to head when the Conservatives returned to office. Once again instinctive caution asserted itself in relation to the central issue facing Thatcher in her new role. This was the impetus being given by the Wilson government to the creation of comprehensive schools. Thatcher's sympathies lay with the grammar school model through which she had herself made her way. She recognised, however, that the current was flowing strongly against the principle of academic selection in secondary education. It was not merely that comprehensive schools commanded growing support in the educational establishment. Many Conservative voters favoured the idea because they did not wish to see their children consigned to the poorer quality secondary moderns, if they failed the 'eleven plus' test which gave access to the grammar schools. Moreover, few members of the Conservative establishment would die in the last ditch for the grammars; they tended to use the private sector and so selection in the state sector was an issue of limited concern to them. By 1970, almost three-quarters of secondary schools would become comprehensives. In these circumstances, as the next general election approached, Thatcher and her colleagues settled on a pragmatic compromise. An incoming Conservative government would leave it up to local authorities to decide which model would apply in their own area. There would certainly be no attempt to turn back the clock.

As the Conservatives returned to power in the June 1970 General Election, there was little to distinguish Thatcher's general political stance from that of most of her colleagues. Although undoubtedly to the right of the party, she had demonstrated under a series of leaders that she would not jeopardise her prospects by rocking the boat. This was partly the result of a keen sense of self-interest. It was also because her ideas were not yet fully formulated. It would take the experience of office under Heath, his defeat in 1974 and the subsequent turmoil in the Conservative Party, to transform Thatcher into the distinctive and dominant figure of later years.

Notes

1 Jonathan Aitken, *Margaret Thatcher: Power and Personality* (London, Bloomsbury, 2013), p. 664.
2 Margaret Thatcher, *The Path to Power* (London, Harper Collins, 1995), pp. 23–4.
3 Margaret Thatcher, *Statecraft: Strategies for a Changing World* (London, Harper Collins, 2002), p. 320.
4 'Remarks on becoming Prime Minister', 4 May 1979, www.margaret thatcher.org/document/104078 (accessed 29 December 2013).
5 TV Interview for London Weekend Television *Weekend World* ('Victorian Values'), 16 January 1983, www.margaretthatcher.org/document/105087 (accessed 29 December 2013).
6 TV Interview for Yorkshire Television *Woman to Woman*, 2 October 1985, www.margaretthatcher.org/document/105830 (accessed 29 December 2013).
7 Charles Moore, *Margaret Thatcher: The Authorized Biography: Volume One: Not for Turning* (London, Allen Lane, 2013), pp. 206–7.
8 Carol Thatcher, *Below the Parapet: The Biography of Denis Thatcher* (London, Harper Collins, 1996), pp. 71 and 86.
9 Moore, *Margaret Thatcher: Volume One*, p. 98.
10 'Conservative Party 1950: This is the Road', www.politicsresources. net/area/uk/man/con50.htm (accessed 31 December 2013).

11 'Conservative Party 1951', www.politicsresources.net/area/uk/man/con51.htm (accessed 31 December 2013).

12 Thatcher, *Path to Power*, p. 50.

13 MT: Appreciation of Margaret Thatcher (contemporary recollection by Private Secretary for Foreign Affairs), 14 June 1984, www.margaret thatcher.org/document/135761 (accessed 4 October 2014).

14 Thatcher, *Path to Power*, p. 89.

15 John Campbell, *Margaret Thatcher: Volume One: The Grocer's Daughter* (London, Jonathan Cape, 2000), p. 133.

16 R.A. Butler, *The Art of the Possible: The Memoirs of Lord Butler* (London, Penguin, 1973), p. 202.

17 Article for *Sunday Graphic* ('Wake up, Women'), 17 February 1952, www.margaretthatcher.org/document/100936 (accessed 1 January 2014).

18 Thatcher, *Path to Power*, p. 133.

19 Thatcher, *Path to Power*, pp. 116 and 126.

20 Speech to Finchley Conservatives (Association AGM), 19 March 1962, *Margaret Thatcher: Complete Public Statements 1945–1990 on CD-ROM* (Oxford, Oxford University Press, 1999), 62_015.

21 James Prior, *A Balance of Power* (London, Hamish Hamilton, 1986), p. 42.

22 John Campbell, *Edward Heath: A Biography* (London, Jonathan Cape, 1993), p. 490.

23 Aitken, *Margaret Thatcher*, p. 116.

24 Prior, *Balance of Power*, p. 53.

25 *Sun*, 13 October 1966, quoted in Campbell, *Grocer's Daughter*, p. 173.

2 The unexpected leader: 1970–1979

Education Secretary

Margaret Thatcher's appointment as Education Secretary was a logical choice, as it was the department which she had shadowed most recently. It was regarded as one of the more junior Cabinet posts, and as a natural ceiling for a female politician in the post-war decades. The position had been held by two of the four women before Thatcher to reach Cabinet rank, Ellen Wilkinson and Florence Horsbrugh, and was to be held by Shirley Williams in James Callaghan's government. Although Thatcher held the portfolio throughout the three years and eight months of the Heath government, she had a limited opportunity to make her mark. The department had little direct control over education policy. The key decision-making bodies were the local education authorities of the county and borough councils, and any major change was usually the outcome of consultation within a close-knit community of civil servants, local administrators, teachers' unions and educational theorists.

The new minister won her officials' respect with her decisiveness, and her success in securing resources from the Treasury. The relationship, however, had its tensions. Thatcher was suspicious of the liberal educational ideas which had been gaining ground since the 1960s, and showed a preference for the grammar school culture in which she had been brought up. She did not, however, appear to have a coherent programme in mind. The Heath government has often been described as one of the most thoroughly prepared of the century, but the new Education Secretary's arrival with a series of action points, written on a page torn from an exercise book, scarcely suggests detailed advance planning. She challenged conventional thinking by reversing the outgoing Labour government's attempt to compel local authorities to introduce comprehensive schools. Even here she was apparently unaware of the correct procedure, having to be told by her civil servants that in order to cancel a circular issued by a previous government, it was necessary to draft a new one.

In practice, although her departure from the emphasis of Labour's policy was condemned by progressive educationalists, Thatcher's impact on the overall shape of the secondary sector was limited. The most that she did was to insist on scrutinising individual local education authorities' plans for reorganisation, and to encourage supporters of selection at local level to maintain support for grammar schools. During her term of office the proportion of secondary pupils in comprehensives rose from 32 to 62 per cent. Commentators have frequently drawn attention to the fact that she approved more plans for comprehensive schools than any other Education Secretary, rejecting only 326 of the 3,612 proposals which landed on her desk. In fairness, as the longest serving occupant of the office between 1964 and 1979[1] – the period when the move towards non-selective education was at its height – she would almost certainly face a greater number of submissions from local authorities than any of her predecessors or successors. The fact was that Thatcher was realistic enough not to swim too hard against a tide which was already flowing strongly.

Thatcher's lukewarm defence of the grammar school system does not really explain the antagonism that she aroused on the centre-left of the political spectrum. It was partly a matter of her image as a well-to-do Home Counties Tory lady, always immaculately turned out and with a cut-glass accent – later to be moderated by her public relations advisers as party leader – which grated on some hearers. Her portrayal in a BBC TV *Panorama* documentary, early in her term of office, did her no favours. Admittedly, the programme contained a generally positive assessment of Thatcher from Shirley Williams, who commended her for her intelligence and toughness. The overall message of the programme, however, was to emphasise the gulf between the privileged Thatcher life-style and that experienced by the majority of the population. As images of the family residence in Kent appeared on the screen, the commentator noted dryly that 'after the week spent in the Chelsea house, it's good to have a second home'. Viewers learned that the new minister did not use the state education system over which she presided, as her son, 'on holiday from boarding school at Harrow', was shown cleaning the swimming pool.[2]

A more serious blow to Thatcher's reputation was dealt by her association with the withdrawal of free school milk for eight to eleven year old schoolchildren. The outcry which greeted the move, on the opposition benches and in the tabloid press, was out of proportion to the magnitude of the deprivation. Free milk was an outdated legacy of the wartime period, when child nutrition was a much more pressing concern for government, and was no longer strictly necessary in the more affluent 1970s. The Wilson government had already withdrawn the service from older children. Moreover Thatcher was implementing a modest spending cut required by the Treasury as the price of making funds available for investment in other, more important areas of education.

Perhaps the bitterness of the attacks is to be explained by the fact that the Education Secretary was a woman, who was seen to be acting against the nurturing, compassionate stereotype associated with her sex. The label 'milk snatcher', coined by a speaker at the Labour Party conference, typified the venom with which she was assailed. It was unfortunate that the move coincided with another unpopular announcement, of a rise in charges for school meals, and a politically unwise decision to pick a fight with the student unions over the way in which they were funded through grants from local education authorities. The ensuing protests against the minister on university campuses betrayed a disturbing undercurrent of personal hatred, mixed with misogyny. At Coventry in February 1971, for example, hostile demonstrators shouted, 'Thatcher out, Tories out, fascist pig, get her f******
knickers off!'[3] The experience rattled Thatcher and helped to develop the hard carapace which she was to exhibit as she climbed higher. 'Iron entered my soul,' she later said.[4] It confirmed her suspicion of the officials in her department, who she felt could have done more to protect her. It also left her with a career-long aversion to reading the press; in Downing Street after 1979, she would rely instead on a digest of newspaper comment prepared by her trusted Press Secretary, Bernard Ingham.

Yet in spite of these controversies, Thatcher's period of office did not see the implementation of a distinctive right-wing agenda. Although she had sympathy for the views of group of traditionalist thinkers, who argued in the so-called 'Black Papers' for a return to old-fashioned teaching methods and standards, she made little effort to put their ideas into practice. In her memoirs Thatcher expressed regret that she had been more interested in the 'inputs' – investment in new school buildings and more teachers – than the 'outputs' of education, by which she meant an emphasis on quality and attainment.[5] At the time, she rejected the radical right's favoured means of extending parental choice of schools, education vouchers which could be exchanged in either the state or the private sector. She did not attempt to replace student grants with loans. On the contrary, she impressed many of those with whom she worked as a minister whose main concern was to protect her department's budget. Thatcher successfully defended the embryonic Open University, which had been launched towards the end of the Wilson government but had been marked down for the chop by the incoming Conservative Chancellor, Iain Macleod. She also ensured that the long delayed raising of the school leaving age, from fifteen to sixteen, took effect from 1972. James Prior recalled the delicious irony that she and the Secretary of State for Health and Social Security, Sir Keith Joseph, who was later to join her in advocating a tough approach to public spending, were 'the big spenders in the Heath Administration. They were always asking for more.'[6] The high point of the post-war expansionist approach to education spending came with Thatcher's December 1972 White Paper, which promised free nursery places for all who required them, the employment of a further 130,000 teachers, the renewal of outdated school buildings and plans to increase participation in higher education from 15 to 22 per cent of young people. When deteriorating economic circumstances forced the government to announce cutbacks a year later, she accepted the curtailment of her plans with reluctance.

The trials of the Heath government

As Education Secretary, Thatcher played a minor role in the wider political and economic issues with which Edward Heath's government had to grapple. After she became Prime Minister in 1979, her followers would contrast her single-minded dedication to a free market agenda with Heath's alleged willingness to abandon the principles on which he had originally been elected. The 'new right' interpretation was that Heath had betrayed true Conservatism by offering subsidies to declining industries, attempting to control prices and incomes by government action – in contradiction of pledges made when he took office – and failing to overcome the challenge of militant trade unions. His eventual electoral defeat in February 1974 was regarded as just retribution for a succession of lamentable 'U-turns'. In her memoirs Thatcher did not spare the government for its failures, and she was at pains to point out that she had neither belonged to the key Cabinet committee on economic policy, nor been a member of Heath's inner circle. Nonetheless she accepted her share of the blame, under the doctrine of collective Cabinet responsibility, for the government's policies: 'his errors – our errors, for we went along with them – did huge harm to the Conservative Party and to the country'. She was unexpectedly generous in her description of the premier as 'an honest man whose strength of character made him always formidable, whether right or wrong'.[7]

There is a danger of reading the relations between Heath and Thatcher as Education Secretary in the light of the vendetta which developed after she replaced him as Conservative Party leader. Stories of Heath's irritation at her interventions in Cabinet meetings first began to circulate after she had displaced him. Their relationship in government was coolly professional rather than mutually antagonistic. Heath briefly considered removing Thatcher in the wake of the 'milk snatcher' uproar, but then decided to retain her. In January 1972 he held a seminar on education with Thatcher at Chequers, which was followed by an unequivocal defence of her record in the Commons. He thought of moving her to Consumer Affairs in November 1972 and, a year later and more surprisingly, he seems to have had her in mind as a possible Minister for Europe. Nor is there any indication of serious divergence between Heath and Thatcher over the general direction of government policy. She accepted the rescue of Rolls Royce in February 1971 – the first departure from the government's initial policy of leaving 'lame duck' industries to the mercy of market forces – on the grounds that the company's manufacture of aero-engines was of strategic importance. She was more uneasy about the subsequent intervention in Upper Clyde Shipbuilders but took no action. The idea that government should hold aloof from the difficulties facing industry was held at the time by a small minority of free market ideologues. One of these was Nicholas Ridley, who resigned from the government in protest at Heath's 1972 Industry Act, which made available public money for the succour of failing companies. In his memoirs he recalled Thatcher telling him that she wished she could join him and MP, John Biffen, another rebel. Ridley believed that she declined his advice to resign and work with them because she did not then realise the gravity of the situation, and she felt it would have been 'disloyal' to leave the government.[8] Peter Walker, a minister who was close to Heath, later wrote that he 'liked Margaret a great deal and there were no policy differences between us'. As the government embarked on greater intervention in the economy, he recalled, there was 'no free market voice in the Cabinet' and there was unanimous support for Heath's 45 attempts to control wages and prices.[9] Nor did Thatcher voice any concerns over Heath's most important achievement, Britain's entry to the European Economic Community in January 1973. Even if her own, infrequent statements on Europe lacked passionate commitment, she was with the Conservative mainstream in welcoming the economic opportunities offered by the Common Market.

Perhaps Thatcher was too heavily absorbed in departmental matters and, from her relatively isolated position at Education, too unsure of the detail of other policy areas, to voice dissent. In her memoirs she recalled feeling uneasy about the growing intervention in industry, but stated that she had not yet worked out an alternative analysis. She added realistically that had she resigned from her relatively junior Cabinet post, it would have made little difference.[10] Moreover, as an ambitious politician Thatcher recognised that as long as Heath remained premier, resignation on policy grounds was a certain route to oblivion. As the government came into conflict with the miners over the issue of pay restraint, solidarity with her colleagues outweighed any private misgivings she may have had about the corporatist flavour of Heath's approach to industrial relations. In the confrontation with the miners which reached a crisis in the winter of 1973–4, Thatcher loyally supported the government's imposition of a three-day week in industry to conserve energy. As the miners progressed in January 1974 from an overtime ban to a full-blown strike, she was one of a small group of ministers who favoured an early general election, enabling the Conservatives to take their case against excessive union power to the country. She betrayed no criticism of Heath's strategy when he decided to delay the election until the end of February, whilst referring the miners' wage claim to the judgement of a Pay Board set up by the government. At her adoption meeting in Finchley she echoed the Prime Minister's appeals for national unity. The election, she stated, was 'a chance for the British people to show the world that at a time of crisis the overwhelming majority of us are determined not to tear ourselves apart, but to close ranks'.[11]

Thatcher maintained her stance of loyalty to Heath until the general election, and beyond. After failing to win a majority, the Prime Minister engaged in talks with the Liberals with a view to forming a coalition, and raised the possibility of adopting the smaller party's favoured policy of proportional representation as the price of an agreement. According to a source quoted by historian Vernon Bogdanor, the episode crystallised Thatcher's hostility to Heath, as it demonstrated his willingness to give up the prospect of a future overall majority for the sake of a temporary continuation in office.[12] If so, it makes it all the more surprising that she was also the only minister, at the final meeting of the Cabinet, to pay a fulsome tribute to the sense of team spirit that had prevailed since 1970.

Seizing the party leadership

There was nothing predetermined about Thatcher's succession to the Conservative leadership. Even Norman Tebbit, who was to earn a reputation as a diehard Thatcherite, recalled that like many others, he hardly knew her before the leadership contest: 'indeed I think I had only ever exchanged a dozen words with her and had never thought of her as a potential leader of the Party'.[13] In the aftermath of the February 1974 defeat, an immediate challenge to Heath's leadership was unlikely from any quarter. Harold Wilson had formed a minority government and would undoubtedly seek an early opportunity to consolidate his position by calling a further general election. Whatever their misgivings about Heath, this was no time for Conservative MPs to change their leader. In any case Thatcher had her hands full, getting to grips with the new post to which Heath appointed her, that of Shadow Environment Secretary. Under strong pressure from Heath, who was desperately seeking populist policies with which to face the electors in a few months' time, she adopted a programme about which she had significant private reservations. One proposal was to hold mortgage interest down to a figure of 9.5 per cent, by granting tax relief to building societies – a piece of interventionism which was alien to Thatcher's instincts. Perhaps more surprisingly, she was at this stage reluctant to endorse a policy which would be a centre-piece of the Thatcherite programme in the 1980s, a plan to allow council tenants to purchase their homes cheaply. Thatcher feared that this would be resented by private householders who received no such assistance in becoming property owners. She was also uneasy about Heath's insistence on a pledge to scrap the rates, the property-based system of local government funding, without clearly thinking through the alternatives. Nonetheless Thatcher presented this uncomfortably radical package when Wilson asked the electorate to confirm his mandate in October 1974. In fact it did her no harm with the party's natural middle-class supporters, who were affected by rising mortgage payments and rate increases. Perhaps, too, she knew that with the Conservatives highly unlikely to win, she would not be responsible for implementing the proposed changes.

Although Labour gained a majority of only four, the outcome of the election raised Conservative MPs' discontent with Heath's leadership to fever-pitch. It was not only the right, who loathed him for the U-turn of 1972, who wanted him out. He was opposed by a much broader band of non-ideological Tories, who saw him as an electoral liability. In the space of nine years Heath had lost three general elections out of four. By clinging to the leadership he deepened their antagonism, whilst making it impossible for one of his trusted lieutenants to replace him and keep the party in the centre ground. The most eligible senior Conservatives, such as party chairman Willie Whitelaw, were inhibited from standing by a lingering sense of loyalty to their chief.

Heath's critics now began to look round for a credible alternative. For a short time in the autumn of 1974, the most likely candidate seemed to be Thatcher's closest associate in the late government, Sir Keith Joseph. That such an unlikely figure should be canvassed as a possible leader indicates the turmoil in which the party found itself. Joseph was unusual in high politics for the intellectual honesty with which, after the Conservatives' ejection from office, he had begun to reappraise the whole trend towards collectivism since 1945. His willingness to agonise about first principles earned him suspicion, ridicule and admiration in equal measure. The nickname 'the mad monk', thought to have been conferred on him by Chris Patten, director of the Conservative Research Department, captured the combination of masochistic austerity and obliviousness to sordid political reality which typified his reinvention of himself. Under the influence of Alfred Sherman, a former communist who had become an uncompromising advocate of free market economics, in March 1974 Joseph co-founded a research institution, the Centre for Policy Studies.

In a series of speeches Joseph proclaimed his new-found attachment to the doctrine of monetarism, the idea that the root cause of inflation, and of the country's economic problems, was the failure of successive governments to restrain the growth of the money supply. He rejected prices and incomes policies, and the growth of state intervention and taxation which, he argued, had stifled the wealth-creating private sector. These ideas were commonplace in so-called 'new right' circles in the mid-1970s. A number of intellectuals, influenced by the Austrian philosopher Friedrich von Hayek and the leading 'Chicago school' economist, Milton Friedman, had been developing a critique of the post-war consensus in discussion groups such as the Institute for Economic Affairs. What was striking, however, was for a front-rank politician to adopt such an analysis so publicly, and in the process implicitly to condemn the record of the Conservative government to which he had recently belonged. Enoch Powell had articulated similar economic views but he had long been disqualified by his hard-line views on immigration, and in February 1974 he had placed himself even further beyond the pale by calling on the voters to reject Heath, a preliminary to his own departure to join the Ulster Unionists.

Thatcher shared Joseph's fascination with ideas and thrived on discussion and debate. She accepted the vice-chairmanship of the Centre for Policy Studies. They were, however, quite different personalities. Joseph himself later acknowledged that whilst he had reached his conclusions 'with the help of friends', she 'came to it by her own common sense and instinct'.[14] His role was to buttress her beliefs with arguments drawn from his voracious theoretical reading. She was never tempted to emulate Joseph by exposing her innermost thoughts, still less to seek to atone publicly for the errors of the past. Thatcher admired Joseph's intellect, and felt personal warmth for him, but was always a far more practical politician. This was demonstrated when Joseph made a poorly thought-out speech in Edgbaston on 19 October, in which he appeared to advocate compulsory birth control for the most disadvantaged social classes. The speech provoked a chorus of condemnation which, a month later, led him to pull out of the leadership race. Thatcher's response, when he told her of his withdrawal, has become well-known as a statement of her greater decisiveness and willingness to take risks: 'Look, Keith,' she later remembered telling him, 'if you're not going to stand, I will, because someone who represents our viewpoint *has* to stand.'[15] Quite simply, Joseph was not cut out for the role. Thatcher no doubt felt obliged to support him for as long as he remained in contention. Yet she had begun to see herself as leadership material before he destroyed his own chances. In an interview given before the Edgbaston speech, she disowned an earlier remark, that it would be ten years before either the party or the country accepted a female leader – 'the prejudice against women is dropping faster than I expected, and I think a woman may succeed before that time'. She also indicated second thoughts on the need for a prospective leader to have first occupied one of the three most senior Cabinet posts.[16] It could not have been clearer that she was indicating her own availability.

A lucky combination of circumstances now came together to help Thatcher secure the leadership. For a short time it looked as if another 'fresh start' candidate would attract the votes of those who were discontented with the incumbent. Sir Edward du Cann, a wealthy financier and MP, was the influential chairman of the backbench 1922 Committee. He loathed Heath, who had removed him from the party chairmanship seven years earlier, and was untainted by membership of his Cabinet. In spite of his limited governmental experience, in a party where establishment connections still counted for a great deal he was a credible right-wing contender. His withdrawal from the contest in mid-January 1975, for personal reasons, must therefore have come as a great relief to Thatcher.

Another piece of good fortune was when one of the most gifted parliamentary conspirators of the day offered his services as her campaign manager. Airey Neave was not identified with any wing of the party, and he seems to have been motivated primarily by a personal dislike of Heath, for he had already made approaches to Whitelaw and du Cann. Well known for his wartime escape from Colditz, Neave inhabited the shadowy area where the political world overlapped with the intelligence community. He was a natural intriguer who, in the words of his biographer, 'moved with an almost feline grace, seeming to drift along rather than walk'.[17] Neave's capacity for dissimulation was to prove indispensable to Thatcher's cause. Many MPs wanted Heath out, not only because of his track record of failure but also because for years he had loftily disdained to use his prime ministerial powers of patronage to win their support. This was critical at a time when only Conservative MPs were entitled to participate in leadership elections. Meanwhile Thatcher had impressed many of her parliamentary colleagues in the latest role to which Heath had appointed her, as Shadow Treasury spokeswoman, which enabled her to land some crushing blows on Labour's heavyweight Chancellor, Denis Healey. This did not necessarily mean that a majority actively wanted her as leader. There was still considerable prejudice against her as a woman, and as someone who lacked high level experience. Neave, therefore, deliberately downplayed her chances of success when canvassing MPs, so that waverers would vote for her to ensure Heath's downfall, in order to make it possible for more appealing candidates to take part in a second round. In any case, a recent change to the rules governing Conservative leadership competitions had raised the bar that the leader needed to clear. In order to win outright on a first ballot, he had to win a majority plus 15 per cent of all those entitled to vote. It was a qualification which in November

1990 would help to cripple Thatcher's chances of carrying on as leader; now it helped her as the challenger. In the first round, held on 4 February, she won convincingly, gaining 130 votes to Heath's 119. An unexpected intervention by a maverick right-winger, Hugh Fraser, who received a paltry 19 votes, failed to affect the outcome.

This is not to say that Thatcher did not deserve to win through her own efforts. Ironically, for someone who was later to be every bit as remote and autocratic as her predecessor, she went to great lengths to make herself available to backbenchers, listening to their concerns where Heath had spurned them. In spite of the warning issued by one of her sourest critics, Ian Gilmour, that the party must not 'retire behind a privet hedge',[18] she did not come across as the one-dimensional champion of a narrowly middle-class, right-wing faction. Those who had hitherto held back finally came forward – too late to sway support away from the front-runner. Even the most credible representative of the old Heathite establishment, Whitelaw, managed to win only 79 votes to Thatcher's 146 in the second round, which followed a week later. The other candidates received derisory totals: Sir Geoffrey Howe and James Prior 19 each, and John Peyton, another former Heath minister, a mere 11. Thatcher benefited from the momentum which had built up behind her in the first round, whilst her new opponents gained no credit for putting their heads belatedly above the parapet. She had won against the expectations of the press and the political establishment. With its customary loyalty to a sitting leader, the party in the country favoured Heath. According to Alistair McAlpine, whom Thatcher appointed as party treasurer in July 1975, the activists, especially the women members, were slow to take her to their hearts. 'Traditional Tories hated Margaret Thatcher's hair, hated her voice, hated her accent and, indeed, many of them hated the whole idea of her.'[19] Thatcher owed her victory to the determination of enough Conservative MPs to reject an individual, and an approach, which had proved unable to deliver power. Her elevation was not the triumph of an ideology, but the decision of a group of worried and dispirited backbenchers who had decided to break with a failed past. Thatcher still had everything to prove as she savoured her victory on 11 February 1975.

Leader of the Opposition

Thatcher's first task as leader was to assemble a front-bench team. It was a mark of her insecurity, as well as an indication of the dearth of talent on the party's right wing, that she made few changes to the shadow cabinet that she inherited from Heath. It was vital to buttress her position by conciliating the party's grandees. The only significant casualties were Peter Walker and the Shadow Chancellor, Robert Carr, although the former was to return when the party regained office in 1979. To Thatcher's relief – although she had to go through the motions of offering him a senior post – Heath himself refused to serve. Whitelaw agreed to play the part of deputy leader, a role in which he gave loyal service for more than a decade. Keith Joseph took on a broader policy formation role whilst Sir Geoffrey Howe was perhaps a safer choice for the key post of Shadow Chancellor. Closely associated with Heath's corporatist approach in 1970–4, he now professed a belief in the free market, though he did not announce it with the evangelical zeal of Thatcher and Joseph. Other surviving Heathites – James Prior, Francis Pym, Lord Carrington, Ian Gilmour – were pragmatists who agreed to serve without abandoning their centrist instincts. Some accepted appointment in the belief that Thatcher's economically liberal ideas would be tempered by the compromises of government. Others gritted their teeth, expecting the leader not to last long and hoping for a return to middle of the road normality under one of their own number. One unexpected though successful appointment was that of Lord Thorneycroft, who had left the Commons as long ago as 1966, to the key post of party chairman. His return to the political foreground was an acknowledgement of his symbolic role in blazing the trail for Thatcherism with his 1958 resignation as Macmillan's Chancellor of the Exchequer, in protest at rising levels of public expenditure. As with her recall of Angus Maude, a free marketeer who had been sacked by Heath almost a decade earlier, to chair the Conservative Research Department, the appointment also indicated Thatcher's need to harness the experience of an older generation. The same motive seems to have influenced a less happy appointment of a senior figure from the past, that of Reginald Maudling as Shadow

Foreign Secretary. By the autumn of 1976, however, Maudling's lazy style, together with his evident distaste for Thatcher's confrontational style, ensured a second and final return to the backbenches for this world-weary survivor.

The shadow cabinet was far from united at the outset on the most important domestic issues – how to tackle inflation and deal with the trade unions. Thatcher was at one with the party's right wing in instinctively wanting to pass tough legislation to restrict union powers; memories of the Heath government's humiliation at the hands of the miners were still fresh. More controversially, she favoured outright rejection of incomes policies as a means of dealing with inflation. Tight control of the money supply was the most effective way to resist unreasonable wage demands. If unions persisted in making excessive pay claims, unemployment would enforce its own discipline; workers would have effectively 'priced themselves out of a job'.[20] She was supported by her more hawkish allies, notably Joseph, but could not count on carrying a majority of her colleagues on every aspect of economic policy. Howe, for example, wanted a tough line on the unions, and was persuaded of the monetarist case for controlling public expenditure. He was, however, sympathetic to the kind of corporatist planning to control wages and prices, which he believed had helped to bring about West Germany's post-war economic recovery. At the opposite end of the spectrum from Thatcher was her Employment spokesman, James Prior, an instinctive supporter of consensus politics, who remained attached to incomes policies and believed in conciliating the unions. Prior's standing within the party's higher echelons made his retention politically advisable, yet at a cost of continuing friction. Matthew Parris, who worked in the leader's office in opposition, recalled Thatcher's response to an evasive draft letter written by Prior's department, following an enquiry about Conservative policy from a man who had lost his job as a consequence of the closed shop – the practice whereby, in certain industries, it was legal for trade unions to oblige all employees to be union members. Thatcher crossed out the offending text and wrote against it, 'I HATE (underlined three times) the Closed Shop'.[21]

Although Thatcher revealed her true feelings in private, she was realistic enough to appreciate the need for compromise in public. The first major statement of Conservative policy after she became leader, entitled *The Right Approach*, appeared shortly before the 1976 party conference. It fudged the issue of incomes policies, stating that they did not offer a long-term solution to inflation, but failed to rule them out. Neither in this document nor in its more detailed successor, *The Right Approach to the Economy*, published in October 1977, did the party commit itself to legal measures against trade unions. The omission was the more remarkable for the fact that it was published against the backdrop of a well-publicised dispute over union recognition at a film-processing factory in Grunwick, North London. The appearance of large numbers of pickets – supported at one point by two Labour Cabinet ministers – provoked the ire of rank and file Conservatives, who wanted the removal of the legal immunities which made this kind of mass industrial action possible. Nonetheless Thatcher stood by the cautious compromise position worked out by the Shadow Cabinet.

In this period Thatcher walked a political tightrope, maintaining a broadly moderate public stance, whilst indicating her own beliefs to those who wanted a more robust approach. She began to balance the influence of the Heathite old guard by appointing more hard-line private advisers, including Norman Tebbit and Nigel Lawson, who were later to hold high office. On foreign policy issues she garnered advice from academic specialists who stood outside the official consensus, such as the independent-minded anti-communist historian, Robert Conquest. After a January 1976 speech warning of the military threat posed by the USSR, a Soviet media outlet dubbed her the 'iron lady'. Although it was intended as an insult, Thatcher embraced the label as an indicator of her willingness to wage the Cold War. The phrase was rapidly picked up by her supporters in the press and Parliament to evoke her growing reputation as a hard-liner. One Conservative backbencher, for example, contrasted Thatcher with Harold Wilson, claiming that the Soviets 'will respect Britain more if we are led by an iron lady rather than by a plasticine man'.[22]

On other issues, too, Thatcher dropped broad hints that she shared the anxieties of her core supporters, without making commitments which might embarrass her in office. A good example was her statement on television in January 1978 about immigration, in which she identified herself with white Britons who were 'really rather afraid that this country might be rather swamped by people with a different culture'.[23] The sound-bite led to protests from her more liberal-minded colleagues, and was not followed up, but the message had been conveyed to those who chose to hear it. Thatcher had begun to develop a rapport with those she called 'our people', the voters and activists who shared her sense of dismay at the state of the country in the mid-1970s. This was a time when there was widespread middle-class unease on a range of fronts. On the economy, there was concern at the way in which inflation eroded incomes, and at the influence that trade union leaders enjoyed with Labour governments. Deeper fears and resentments – of a state unable to control strikes led by militant shop stewards, and tolerant of 'welfare scroungers', mass immigration, sexual permissiveness and student demonstrations – were also at work. To some, the country was becoming ungovernable. Rumours circulated of ex-military figures, waiting in the wings to intervene in the event of a wholesale collapse of public order. The foundation of the right-wing pressure group, the National Association for Freedom, in 1975, was one response to these concerns. Although she never explicitly identified herself with the more extreme manifestations of right-wing paranoia, Thatcher benefited politically from the sense of national decline. In the words of former Labour minister Lord Chalfont, she 'struck a chord which was waiting to be struck . . . all these fears of bureaucracy, of too much government, of the erosion of freedom of the individual, fears of anarchy . . . she just came at the time when all these fears began to coalesce'.[24]

Nonetheless, it took time for Thatcher to make her mark as a potential national leader. The downside of the vital energy and application which she exhibited was a tendency to be bossy, to fail to delegate, not to differentiate between issues of minor and major importance. There are numerous stories of her incessant rewriting of speeches, a characteristic which she took with her into Number 10. Chris Patten commented that 'she will be found at two o'clock in the morning rewriting a badly drafted letter to some ordinary voter in Sunderland'.[25] Her staff noted the certainty with which she articulated her essential goals and values but the more methodical ones despaired of her apparent inability to plan ahead. John Hoskyns, a former army officer and businessman who worked in her private office, tried to bring the insights of systems analysis – the scientific study of how an organisation functions – to bear on the issues facing policy makers. He was irritated to learn that, when shown a complex diagram he had produced, which illustrated Britain's economic problems, 'she had apparently giggled and said it looked like a piece of chemical engineering'. Although he admired her courage and determination, he found her no better than other politicians in her disinclination to think strategically, and much too focused on detail: 'I never find her a very satisfactory person,' he confided to his diary in October 1977, 'too carping, too much line-by-line drafting instead of seeing the wood for the trees.'[26]

More serious in the short term was the difficulty Thatcher found in establishing herself as Leader of the Opposition in the House of Commons. In her diaries Labour's most successful female minister, Barbara Castle, recorded a series of indifferent parliamentary performances, even if her criticisms were tempered by sympathy for Thatcher as a woman. Thatcher seemed uncomfortable in her new role, relying too much on detailed preparation and unable to react quickly to the changing atmosphere of debate. More than once Castle describes Thatcher visibly tensing herself before an intervention in the chamber and then failing to make an impression. Thatcher, she wrote in July 1975, 'with her prim and carefully modulated diction flopped'. On another occasion Castle noted Thatcher sitting, 'as she usually does before a parliamentary effort, head down and lips pursed'. When the Conservative leader finally spoke, a Labour MP dismissed her contemptuously: 'She can't rise to an occasion.'[27] Thatcher struggled to make an impression facing Harold Wilson, a past master of debate. The succession of James Callaghan in April 1976, if anything, placed her at a greater disadvantage. Formidably experienced – he was the only premier to have also served as Chancellor, Home Secretary and Foreign Secretary – Callaghan gave the impression of swatting away an irritating upstart as he faced her across the despatch box. The advent of radio broadcasting from the chamber highlighted the contrast between the Prime Minister's easy confidence and his opponent's struggles to gain a hearing in the bear-pit of the Commons. In July 1978, for example, Bernard Donoughue, head of the Number 10 Policy Unit, heard his boss score a notable victory over Thatcher, whose 'reply was all economic, full of statistics and completely missed the mood of the House'.[28]

Power at last

Within months, however, a new opportunity had opened up for Thatcher, partly as a result of a serious miscalculation on Callaghan's part. In the autumn of 1978 he was widely expected to call a general election. Yet, for reasons which remain unclear, the Prime Minister backed away from an early dissolution. Perhaps, having headed a minority government for two years, he feared that a contest might deliver another hung parliament, followed by endless negotiations with minor parties as the price of retaining office. Alternatively he may have been deterred by the publicity given to an inspired Conservative poster, which reminded people that unemployment remained stubbornly high at 1.5 million. The image of a snaking dole queue, over the slogan 'Labour isn't working', was a breath-taking piece of opportunism, given the near-certainty that unemployment would continue to rise under the economic policies advocated by the opposition. This was unimportant, as was the fact that the so-called unemployed people were actually young Conservative activists. The poster's release damaged the Labour leadership's confidence at a time when other economic indicators, notably inflation, were beginning to appear more positive, and when opinion polls showed that Callaghan was consistently more popular than his rival. The premier's decision to delay the contest came as a relief to Thatcher, as she later admitted in her memoirs. She might well have lost an October 1978 election. Had she won narrowly, she would have faced the same industrial problems which were soon to overwhelm Callaghan's government.

The winter of 1978–9 was to mark a decisive turning point for Thatcher's still fragile leadership. The government's attempt to impose a 5 per cent limit on pay increases led to a series of strikes by a range of groups, from Ford car workers to lorry drivers, health service employees and refuse collectors. Against a backdrop of harsh weather, the tabloid press aided the Tory cause with a series of emotive headlines – 'No Mercy', 'The Road to Ruin' – which created an impression of widespread social break-down. In what became known as the 'winter of discontent', television images of picket lines outside hospitals and piles of rubbish in London squares reinforced the sense of chaos. The notion of working-class solidarity, central to trade unionism, appeared to have been replaced by an ugly militancy, as shop-floor activists encouraged their members to advance their wage claims without regard for the common good. Callaghan seemed uncertain how to respond. In January he was pictured on TV relaxing with other heads of government at a Caribbean island summit. On his return he seemed dangerously out of step with public opinion when challenged by an interviewer, asking him what he intended to do about the 'mounting chaos'. His response, an ill-judged attempt to play down the gravity of the situation, was reduced to a memorably damning headline in the *Sun*, 'Crisis? What crisis?'

These developments turned public opinion against the unions, vindicating the hard line Thatcher had always favoured but had suppressed in the interests of party unity. The key moment was a party political broadcast delivered on 17 January, in which she offered to support the government in taking legal action to curb damaging strikes. Characteristically, she was doubtful about a strategy which was not explicitly partisan; her advisers persuaded her that she stood to gain from showing a willingness to put country before party. By making Callaghan an offer which he was bound to refuse, she moved the debate on to ground which was much more favourable to her own side. In a speech in Glasgow she pressed home the attack on the 'wreckers in our midst', whom she was at pains to distinguish from the mass of responsible trade unionists, and highlighted the powerlessness of the Labour administration by asking, 'What sort of Government is this which sees its authority pass to strike committees?'[29]

Events continued to move in Thatcher's favour. The government's failure to win support for its plans for Scottish and Welsh devolution enabled the Conservatives to bring forward a motion of no confidence on 28 March, which they won by just one vote. With a general election scheduled for 3 May, the Conservatives at last had the opportunity to make their case to the country. Thatcher's campaign frustrated Labour's attempts to depict her as an extremist. The Conservative manifesto was studiously moderate, with prices and incomes policies not explicitly ruled out, and no indication of plans for significant public spending cuts or the indiscriminate removal of state subsidies from ailing firms. Only industries recently nationalised by the Labour government were to be returned to the private sector. The promise to offer council houses for sale to their tenants was hardly unique to the radical right. There were references to the need to control the money supply in the battle against inflation, and to shift the emphasis from direct to indirect taxation, but no specifics. In the course of the campaign Thatcher even promised to honour the findings of a commission on public sector pay headed by Professor Hugh Clegg, which had been appointed by the Labour government.

In short, ideology was ruthlessly subordinated to the task of winning the election. Traditional, uncontroversial Tory themes of freedom under the law, respect for the individual and strong defence were emphasised. On trade union law there were proposals to limit secondary picketing, to compensate workers who were dismissed as a result of the closed shop, and provide postal ballots for the election of union officials. Unions would be expected to pay a greater share of the cost of supporting members who went on strike. Nonetheless the Conservatives would also consult unions and employers on economic strategy. Thatcher denied that she expected a confrontation with the unions; the Conservatives would govern in a common-sense way, in the interests of ordinary trade unionists, who were assumed to be appalled by the Labour government's failure to prevent anarchy during the winter of discontent. Like the Conservatives, they wanted a fresh start: 'we find an echo in the hearts and minds of people. . . . They say, "We can't go on as we are, we can't go on like this."'[30] It was an unabashed appeal to those skilled workers and lower middle-class people who would not normally have considered supporting the Conservative Party. In pitching the campaign to these voters she received the invaluable support of a substantial section of the popular press. The *Sun*, with a circulation now approaching 4 million, cast its verdict for the first time decisively against Labour:

'Vote Tory This Time,' it urged its readers. 'It's The Only Way to Stop The Rot.'[31]

Thatcher was undoubtedly the dominant figure in the Conservative campaign. At press conferences she was pictured briskly marshalling her Shadow Cabinet colleagues. In one film sequence, party grandees were photographed arriving at Thatcher's Chelsea home for a meeting. 'What brings you here?' asked a reporter of Lord Carrington, whose reply, 'the Boss', drew laughter from the waiting press pack. 'Like coming out of the bloody zoo,' remarked a mildly irritated Prior as Thatcher busily paraded them for the TV cameras.[32] She proved herself an assured and indefatigable campaigner, whose image had already benefited from the guidance provided by two experienced publicity experts. Gordon Reece, a flamboyant former TV producer who had first met Thatcher before the party leadership contest, had supplied voice coaching to make her sound less shrill, and advised her on her wardrobe. Tim Bell, a gifted advertising executive, was also enlisted to help project a winning public image. Thatcher rapidly grasped the importance of their specialist skills and warmed to their natural ebullience and directness. The highly individualistic Bell – the only Conservative supporter working at a senior level in the Saatchi and Saatchi advertising agency – responded positively to a Tory leader whom he regarded as an outsider like himself: 'I think there was an unspoken awareness between us that we were both trying to make our way through a scowling establishment that did not really recognise either of us as one of its own'.[33] During the campaign Thatcher took their advice to decline the offer of a televised debate with the Prime Minister, fearing that she might be placed at a disadvantage by Callaghan's greater experience. This was wise since, even though Labour invariably lagged behind the Conservatives in the opinion polls, Callaghan enjoyed an average lead of twenty points when voters were asked which of the two party leaders would make the better Prime Minister. In any case, as such a debate had never been held before, her refusal did her no harm with the electorate. Thatcher also gamely played along with the relentless schedule of photo-opportunities arranged for her, from tasting tea to holding a new-born calf on an East Anglian farm. She did, however, firmly reject a proposal by Thorneycroft that she should seek to broaden her appeal by sharing a platform with Heath.

The Conservatives won an overall majority of 43, having taken 51 seats from Labour and gained almost 44 per cent of the popular vote. The swing to the Conservatives was particularly marked among the C2 social class – the upwardly mobile workers who had been deliberately targeted by the Conservative campaign. In a remark that later became famous, Callaghan observed in private that 'there are times, perhaps once every thirty years, when there is a sea-change in politics. . . . I suspect there is now such a sea-change – and it is for Mrs Thatcher.'[34] It was undoubtedly a moment of triumph. Yet it was far from a landslide, and although it was clear that a new direction had been taken, it was not obvious that Thatcher would permanently stamp her impress on the country. It would have taken an exceptionally far-sighted commentator to predict that the coming decade would come to be so indelibly associated with the personality and policies of this one woman.

Notes

1 There were no fewer than four Education Secretaries during the Wilson governments of 1964–70, and a further three under the Labour governments of 1974–9, which followed the fall of Heath.

2 A clip from the programme can be viewed at 'Margaret Thatcher Education Secretary 1970 – Youtube', www.youtube.com/watch?v=h3CSpjyp-44 (accessed 10 February 2014).

3 Robin Harris, *Not for Turning: The Life of Margaret Thatcher* (London, Transworld Publishers, 2013), p. 83. Reproduced by permission of The Random House Group Ltd and Thomas Dunne Books. All rights reserved.

4 Hugo Young, *One of Us* (London, Macmillan, 1989), p. 74.

5 Margaret Thatcher, *The Path to Power* (London, Harper Collins, 1995), p. 184.

6 Hugo Young and Anne Sloman, *The Thatcher Phenomenon* (London, BBC, 1986), p. 27.

7 Thatcher, *Path to Power*, p. 195.

8 Nicholas Ridley, *'My Style of Government.' The Thatcher Years* (London, Hutchinson, 1991), p. 6. Reproduced by permission of The Random House Group Ltd. and Peters Fraser Dunlop (www.petersfraserdunlop.com) on behalf of the Estate of Nicholas Ridley.

9 Peter Walker, *Staying Power: An Autobiography* (London, Bloomsbury, 1991), pp. 92 and 123–4.

10 Thatcher, *Path to Power*, p. 221.
11 Margaret Thatcher, speech at adoption meeting, 11 February 1974, www.margaretthatcher.org/document/102337 (accessed 20 January 2015).
12 Vernon Bogdanor, 'The fall of Heath and the end of the postwar settlement' in Stuart Ball and Anthony Seldon (eds) *The Heath Government 1970–74: A Reappraisal* (London, Longman, 1996), p. 373.
13 Norman Tebbit, *Upwardly Mobile* (London, Futura, 1989), p. 177.
14 Andrew Denham and Mark Garnett, *Keith Joseph* (London, Acumen, 2001), p. 322.
15 Thatcher, *Path to Power*, p. 266.
16 Interview for *Sunday Express*, 17 October 1974, *Margaret Thatcher: Complete Public Statements*, 74_165.
17 Paul Routledge, *Public Servant, Secret Agent: The Elusive Life and Violent Death of Airey Neave* (London, Harper Collins, 2002), p. 9.
18 *The Times*, 31 January 1975, quoted in John Campbell, *Margaret Thatcher: Volume One: The Grocer's Daughter* (London, Jonathan Cape, 2000), p. 287.
19 Alistair McAlpine, *Once a Jolly Bagman* (London, Weidenfeld & Nicolson, 1997), p. 211.
20 E.H.H. Green, *Thatcher* (London, Hodder Arnold, 2006), p. 63.
21 Matthew Parris, *Chance Witness: An Outsider's Life in Politics* (London, Penguin, 2013), p. 195.
22 House of Commons Prime Minister's Questions, 27 January 1976, www.margaretthatcher.org/document/102942 (accessed 20 January 2015).
23 TV interview for Granada *World in Action* ('rather swamped'), 27 January 1978, *Margaret Thatcher: Complete Public Statements*, 78_026.
24 Phillip Whitehead, *The Writing on the Wall: Britain in the Seventies* (London, Michael Joseph, 1985), p. 216.
25 Ion Trewin (ed.), *The Hugo Young Papers: Thirty Years of British Politics – Off the Record* (London, Allen Lane, 2008), p. 94, interview with Chris Patten, 21 April 1976.
26 John Hoskyns, *Just in Time: Inside the Thatcher Revolution* (London, Aurum Press, 2000), p. 18, pp. 43–4.
27 Barbara Castle, *The Castle Diaries 194–76* (London, Book Club Associates, 1980), p. 458, entry for 11 July 1975; p. 692, entry for 16 March 1976.
28 Bernard Donoughue, *Downing Street Diary: With James Callaghan in No. 10* (London, Pimlico, 2009), p. 349, entry for 25 July 1978.
29 Speech to Glasgow Conservatives, 19 January 1979, *Margaret Thatcher: Complete Public Statements*, 79_015.
30 General election press conference, 2 May 1979, *Margaret Thatcher: Complete Public Statements*, 79_223.
31 *Sun*, 3 May 1979, quoted in Campbell, *Margaret Thatcher: Volume One*, p. 444.

32 TV interview for BBC Campaign '79, 27 April 1979, *Margaret Thatcher: Complete Public Statements*, 79_195.
33 Tim Bell, *Right or Wrong: The Memoirs of Lord Bell* (London, Bloomsbury, 2014), p. x.
34 Bernard Donoughue, *Prime Minister: The Conduct of Policy under Harold Wilson and James Callaghan* (London, Jonathan Cape, 1987), p. 191.

3   The challenges of office: 1979–1982

Thatcher takes the helm

The watching public had its first glimpse of Prime Minister Thatcher as she stepped from her car in Downing Street on 4 May 1979. Speaking against a noisy background – the boisterous crowd were mostly, though not all applauding – she delivered a brief statement to the television cameras. She and some of her advisers had had reservations about the text recommended by her speech writer, Ronald Millar, for her to read out a prayer attributed to St Francis: 'Where there is discord may we bring harmony, where there is error may we bring truth, where there is doubt may we bring faith, and where there is despair may we bring hope.'[1] The opening phrase in particular would be derided as bitterly ironic by her critics, who viewed her as deliberately seeking conflict. James Prior, who served uneasily as her Employment Secretary in 1979–81, described the words as 'the most awful humbug . . . totally at odds with Margaret's belief in conviction politics and the need to abandon the consensus style of government'.[2] Even a broadly sympathetic backbencher like Jonathan Aitken later wrote of 'an ill-judged lurch into uncharacteristic hypocrisy',[3] which did not represent her true instincts. Thatcher's own rationalisation of this choice of words, however, focused on the need to vanquish 'the forces of error, doubt and despair', whose hold on British society had just been demonstrated by the winter of discontent, and whose defeat 'would not be possible without some measure of discord'.[4]

There was no doubt in Thatcher's mind that the country required a new approach. This would comprise responsible national housekeeping, strict control of public spending, reduced government support for industry – if not yet a full-blown strategy of privatisation for state-owned assets – and a refusal, unlike some previous administrations, to be blown off course by trade union pressure. To shape policy as she desired would, however, present her with a daunting set of challenges. In opposition she had told an interviewer that 'as Prime Minister I couldn't waste time having any internal arguments' with Cabinet colleagues, and that she would form a 'conviction' government.[5] In practice, however, the first two and a half years would be marked by almost continuous conflict. To some extent Thatcher thrived on argument, which probably helped to clarify her own thinking, although her need to win each contest would take its toll on her and her fellow ministers.

Internal division was an almost inevitable consequence of Thatcher's decision to appoint to key Cabinet positions a number of individuals who were certainly not her soulmates. In 1979 she had in truth limited room for manoeuvre. The upper echelons of the party were still dominated by former Heathites, who favoured compromise with the unions and feared the social division which, they warned, would result from a severe programme of spending cuts. However uncongenial their views might be to Thatcher, these representatives of the old guard could not be excluded from office without provoking open unrest. The promotion of like-minded figures such as Norman Tebbit, Nigel Lawson and Cecil Parkinson would have to be delayed until she felt more secure as Prime Minister. She certainly felt the absence of another loyal colleague, Airey Neave, who had been killed by an Irish republican car bomb at the outset of the general election campaign.

The new Home Secretary, and unofficially the Deputy Prime Minister, was Willie Whitelaw. His standing, based on decades of service and a reputation for calm and common sense, made him an indispensable support, both in Cabinet and in the parliamentary party. Whitelaw's presence helped to keep dissent from the party's centre-left within bounds, although the Prime Minister's strongest Cabinet critics resented what they saw as his weakness in subordinating his moderate instincts to her priorities. Another prominent survivor from the post-war consensus era was Lord Carrington, who was appointed as Foreign Secretary. His aristocratic pedigree and worldly air of self-assurance – he had first served in government under Churchill in the early 1950s – enabled him to treat the Prime Minister almost as an equal. Knowing relatively little of foreign affairs at this stage, she was generally happy to trust Carrington's judgement in his field of expertise, in return for his tacit support in areas of domestic policy, where he was much less at home. The same could not be said of his deputy in the Commons, Ian Gilmour, whose disdain for what he regarded as Thatcher's adherence to mistaken economic dogma was barely concealed. Nor did Thatcher establish an easy working relationship with James Prior, who was appointed to Employment on grounds of his experience and as a sign that the government did not plan an early confrontation with the unions. In her memoirs she was to excoriate him as a kind of 'false squire' whose bluff manner concealed a philosophical inclination to retreat in face of the advances made by the political left.[6] On the same wing of the party were Peter Walker – recalled from exile on the backbenches to be Minister of Agriculture – Francis Pym as Defence Secretary and Lord Soames as leader of the upper house. Another potential dissident, though too wily and independent-minded to be pigeon-holed as a member of a particular faction, was Michael Heseltine, who became Environment Secretary. Flamboyant, ambitious and a keen advocate of government intervention to support industrial and urban regeneration, he was never trusted by Thatcher. His presentational skills and popularity with the party rank and file, however, meant that she could not afford to exclude him from the Cabinet.

A great deal has been made of Thatcher's decision to place most of the key economic ministries in the hands of more ideologically sympathetic colleagues. Sir Geoffrey Howe was a logical choice as Chancellor of the Exchequer. Mild-mannered, dogged and quietly competent, he was first-rate at assessing different sources of information and reaching a reasoned solution to problems. He shared the Prime Minister's commitment to bringing inflation under control, and was inclined to take a hard-line approach to the curbing of union power. Alluding to their growing differences after his move to the Foreign Office in June 1983, Thatcher described Howe's time at the Treasury as 'in my view . . . his best political years'.[7] There was an element of conditionality, rather than genuine comradeship, in their relationship from the start. Referring to the phalanx of grey bureaucrats who formed the governing body of the Soviet Union, one backbench Conservative MP disparagingly said of Howe: 'no personal loyalties – durable politburo man, will serve under anyone'.[8] Indeed Howe's appointment was not a foregone conclusion. His indifferent parliamentary performances in opposition, confronting Labour Chancellor Denis Healey – who famously likened his shadow's debating tactics to 'being savaged by a dead sheep'[9] – had not inspired unbounded confidence. Surprisingly, it appears that Thatcher briefly considered inviting a former Labour Chancellor, Roy Jenkins – then serving as President of the European Commission and known to be increasingly out of sympathy with his former party colleagues – to occupy the Treasury. Although this idea was not pursued, no doubt because it would have caused great resentment within the Conservative Party – and it seems unlikely that Jenkins would have accepted anyway – it does indicate that Howe's position was not beyond challenge.

Although Thatcher and Howe worked together quite constructively in her first term, some ministers who would later be described as Thatcherites turned out to be rather disappointing. Sir Keith Joseph – apparently denied the Exchequer on the urging of Whitelaw, who seems to have doubted his political judgement and stamina – proved a weak departmental minister as Industry Secretary. Although in theory dedicated to making business stand on its own feet, in practice he gave in to pressure for continued government support for failing industries. Too sensitive to make difficult decisions, he was retained out of regard for his past services to the reconstructing of Conservative thinking. Two other figures, Sir John Nott at the Department of Trade and John Biffen as Chief Secretary of the Treasury, turned out to be less committed to free market ideology when the government encountered growing resistance to its policies in the summer of 1981.

Thatcher compensated for the difficulties she faced with her Cabinet by working excessively hard and seeking to gain personal dominance over her colleagues and officials. In the early years in Downing Street, visits to Whitehall departments were one of her chosen methods of keeping colleagues on their toes. Just as she had done in opposition, she sought to embarrass ministers by acquiring a more detailed mastery of the areas for which they were responsible. Thatcher became well known for her dedication to the job, taking few holidays and giving the impression that she attended social events out of duty rather than inclination. She was immensely energetic, and could manage with less sleep than those who worked with her, although she was not the super-woman of popular mythology. The second head of her Downing Street Policy Unit, Ferdinand Mount, recalled a late-night meeting at Chequers, at which the exhausted participants eventually excused themselves. Thatcher gave the impression that she would continue working alone but as Mount approached his bedroom he caught sight of 'the little figure below gathering up her things and going off to bed, her reputation for being indefatigable undented'.[10] She used verbal aggression as a management tech-nique, cross-questioning and harassing colleagues and showing no quarter to those who could not defend themselves. Perhaps unconsciously, she exploited the way in which upper middle-class men of her generation felt inhibited about arguing with a woman. One minister quipped that working with Thatcher was 'like leav-ing home and finding that Nanny was at the office'.[11] Michael Heseltine recalled that in order to withstand the flow of prime ministerial interruptions, he had to wait for a gap and then repeat, more than once if necessary, what he had to say. 'It was weary-ing, but those who shrank from it found themselves marginalised in the endless power struggle of Cabinet life.'[12]

Thatcher's closest allies were not spared discourteous treatment in front of other colleagues. Geoffrey Howe was the most senior figure who learned to live with this from an early stage. In his memoirs he also noted the Prime Minister's penchant for taking advice from unaccountable, hand-picked personal advisers, such as the committed free marketeer Professor Alan Walters, who began the first of two stints as her economic adviser in January 1981. Walters was one of the inner circle whom she termed 'my people'. 'It seemed sometimes,' wrote Howe, 'as if she was Joan of Arc invoking the authority of her "voices".'[13] Sir John Hoskyns, the first head of Thatcher's Policy Unit, found his boss's lack of system exasperating. After trying in vain to introduce a more methodical approach to problem-solving, he left Downing Street a frustrated man after less than three years in his post. After a session at Chequers in January 1981, for example, he recorded in his diary that the Prime Minister apparently expected a single meeting to offer 'an all-in-one, simple, painless and risk-free solution to a problem that had defeated every government of the past twenty years'.[14] In fairness, it seems unlikely that Hoskyns, whose obsession with thinking strategically always made him impatient of political realities, could ever have made a successful transition from the world of business management to that of Whitehall.

The truth was that Thatcher came to office with clear-cut ideas but with little idea of an overall strategy for their implementation. She was suspicious of the Whitehall mandarins as a class, seeing them as presiding grandly over Britain's relative decline, and as fundamentally unsympathetic to her radical instincts. Yet Thatcher took little interest in the structures of government. Perhaps the economic problems she faced were too pressing to allow her the luxury of thinking about long-term institutional change. Instead she worked through particular trusted individuals, with whom she built close working relationships. Her appointment in autumn · 1979 of Sir Robert Armstrong as Cabinet Secretary, a thoroughly professional career civil servant who had served Heath as his Principal Private Secretary, proved an inspired choice. His thirty years of Whitehall experience, appetite for work and considerable diplomatic skills were to prove extremely useful to Thatcher up to his retirement at the end of 1987. Another official who joined Number 10 during Thatcher's first year in office was her combative Press Secretary, Bernard Ingham. A blunt-spoken Yorkshireman, who had been associated with the Labour Party before entering public service, Ingham was to superintend the Downing Street news management operation for the rest of her premiership. He remained a civil servant who kept his distance from the Conservative Party machine, whilst exhibiting a fierce sense of loyalty to the Prime Minister. He became an enormously influential figure, providing Thatcher with a daily summary of news updates and acting as her mouthpiece in the print media. In the words of *Times* journalist Peter Riddell, he was 'his mistress's voice, intuitively understanding her instinct and moods . . . always the loyal retainer below stairs', whose role was not to advise on policy but to act as the interpreter of her vision.[15] Less positively, he was to be accused of using his press contacts to undermine ministers who fell out of favour with the premier, and of feeding her growing sense of self-sufficiency.

Nonetheless it is important not to exaggerate the extent, particularly in the first term, to which Thatcher departed from the practices of her recent predecessors. It was an established feature of central government by the 1970s that Prime Ministers would use their power of appointment to Cabinet committees, or convene *ad hoc* groups of ministers outside the formal Cabinet structure, in order to secure a desired outcome. This was particularly true of market-sensitive issues and defence matters where confidentiality was essential. Thus the decision to purchase the Trident nuclear weapons system was taken early in the life of the government by a Cabinet committee consisting of five people: the Prime Minister, Whitelaw, Howe, Carrington and Pym. This was one more than had served on the committee created by Callaghan before the 1979 election to consider the same question. Trident was not discussed by the full Thatcher Cabinet until the very day in July 1980 when the decision was due to be announced to the Commons. Nor did all ministers consider this to be an improper way of conducting government business. David Howell, who was never part of the inner circle as Energy Secretary and then Transport Secretary, considered that any Prime Minister would rely on the advice of a small group of colleagues: 'this country really since the sixteenth century has basically been run by five or six people'.[16]

Thatcher proved both flexible and ruthless in using the tools, and the personnel, to hand. One adviser recalled that 'she uses people and she spits them out when it suits her. . . . She eats people.'[17] There was a marked sense of urgency about the way in which she approached her task. Interviewed after he had left her Cabinet, John Biffen chose an analogy from the world of business to describe her as 'the Chief Executive as well as the Managing Director' of the government. Rather than giving each member of the board the opportunity to contribute to discussion, 'she was much more there saying, "The strategy is we've got to get twenty per cent of the market in the next eighteen months. Get on with it!"'[18] Yet although she remorselessly harassed those who worked with her, Thatcher was imbued with a strong sense of what was possible. She sought to enlarge the boundaries of what could be achieved, in a way which few could have predicted at the outset, but in doing so she was guided by a strong instinct for survival. Those who came into contact with her invariably noted her emphasis on practical results, her relentless focus on detail and her unsparing cross-examination of those who brought policy proposals to her. Ian Beesley, a civil servant tasked with improving efficiency in Whitehall in 1981–6, recalled that in preparing a submission it was important 'to keep things brief, to deploy evidence in support of the arguments and above all to use language which would resonate with her'.[19] She was an always demanding task mistress, at once exhilarating and infuriating to work for.

The struggle against inflation

The Thatcher government confronted a formidable set of economic issues in the spring of 1979. At the centre of the problem, in the minds of the Prime Minister and her closest advisers, was the need to control inflation, which was running at 10 per cent when the government took office. They regarded it as the main cause of poor productivity and low growth rates. According to the monetarist analysis to which they subscribed, it could only be reduced by controlling the growth of the money supply. This was to be achieved by altering the price of money using interest rates which, prior to May 1997, were directly determined by the Treasury rather than the Bank of England. Central to the strategy was the need to reduce the Public Sector Borrowing Requirement (PSBR), which required a steady reduction in the level of public spending. What made the government so unpopular was its seeming lack of concern for the fate of traditional industries, and the communities which had grown up around them, as the country slipped into recession in the early years of the new decade. In Thatcher's first term, Britain lost approximately one quarter of its manufacturing capacity. The government's withdrawal of subsidies from inefficient firms undoubtedly contributed to this process. To a great extent, the early 1980s were defined by television pictures of old factories, mostly in the north and the Midlands, being demolished to create bleak post-industrial wastelands. Critics attacked the government for its apparent indifference towards the human consequences of its policies. It seemed to Labour, the Liberals and a good many traditionalist Tories, along with spokesmen for the churches and a range of welfarist pressure groups, that Thatcher's principal goal was being pursued at the expense of wider social considerations. Her government's willingness to tolerate the rising unemployment rate, which neared the 7 per cent mark in the spring of 1980, offered the greatest affront to those who remained wedded to the ideals of the post-war consensus.

In implementing its policies the government had to contend with a variety of pressures, over many of which it had little control. For political reasons Thatcher was obliged to accept the recommendations of the Clegg Commission on public sector pay, which was to result in a number of wage settlements running ahead of inflation. The new government also inherited a commitment to increase defence spending by 3 per cent per year as part of Britain's membership of the NATO alliance. Moreover the Conservatives had promised during the election campaign to increase the pay of police and service personnel. Another constraint was provided by the exploitation of oil reserves in the North Sea, which was just beginning in the late 1970s. In the long run this would be a critical source of government revenue, but in the short term it increased the value of sterling as a 'petrocurrency', making British exports more expensive in overseas markets. This took place at a time when world oil prices were rising at an alarming rate as a result of the 1979 Islamic revolution in Iran. The ensuing problems facing British industry would unavoidably reduce tax revenues, whilst placing an additional burden on the social security budget, thus making it more difficult for the government to achieve its goal of reducing public spending.

Thatcher was not striking out in a wholly new direction in trying to curb the growth of the money supply. Callaghan and Healey had set targets for its expansion as part of their own anti-inflationary policies. Where Thatcher parted company from her predecessors was in the primacy that she gave to the monetarist analysis in her first term of office. The other strand in the Labour government's approach, the attempt to negotiate wage restraint in partnership with the trade unions, had been discredited by the winter of discontent. In any case Thatcher had never favoured such a strategy in principle. The monetarist diagnosis held that workers and management should be left alone to make their own decisions on pay, and should then be expected to live with the consequences. The attempt to control the growth of the money supply raised several practical problems. It was not capable of being easily measured and thus it was difficult for government to set appropriate targets for its restraint. The definition that the Treasury adopted, known as M3, comprising the amount of cash and bank deposits in the economy, was just one of several possible measures that were available. No less arbitrary was the Chancellor's announcement, in his June 1979 budget, of a money supply target of 7 to 11 per cent growth. In order to achieve this, Howe raised the Bank of England's minimum lending rate from 12 to 14 per cent, whilst seeking to reduce the PSBR by making £4 billion of public spending cuts.

The monetarist measures in the budget, however, were at odds with another Conservative priority. In line with the party's commitment to reducing the tax burden, especially on the entrepreneurs whom it regarded as the indispensable drivers of wealth creation, Howe reduced the top rate of income tax from 83 to 60 per cent, and the basic rate from 33 to 30 per cent. These measures conflicted with the need to lower the PSBR. In order to cover the resulting shortfall in revenue, the Chancellor increased VAT from 8 to 15 per cent – a switch from direct to indirect taxation, in his phrase from 'pay as you earn, to pay as you spend', which bore most heavily on those with the lowest incomes. The move was politically difficult to manage since, during the election campaign, the Conservatives had strenuously denied Labour Party allegations that they planned to double the rate of VAT. Thatcher accepted the argument that the decision was unavoidable, and was therefore best taken at the start of a new government. Nonetheless she was privately worried by the inflationary implications of the increase – a concern which was justified as the Retail Price Index reached 15 per cent in July. Her cautious instincts were also aroused by another example of Treasury radicalism, the decision to remove exchange controls from October 1979. The abolition of these outmoded restrictions on the flow of capital was entirely consistent with the spirit of free market Conservatism, and placed Britain at the forefront of the process of financial globalisation, which was to gather pace in the 1980s. At the time, however, Thatcher feared that the decision might lead to a damaging run on sterling, and had to be persuaded to go ahead by her more confident Chancellor.

Privately Thatcher continued to express anxieties about some features of government policy. Her political instincts as the self-appointed champion of the aspiring middle classes were sometimes at odds with the overall priorities of Treasury strategy. Thus she was concerned by the rise in interest rates, which reached an all-time high point of 17 per cent in November 1979, because of the adverse impact on home owners with mortgages. Howe's proposal, in his second budget, to increase the taxable value of company cars, provoked another challenge from Number 10 on behalf of those she termed 'our own people'.[20] On the fundamentals of government policy, however, she maintained a united front with her Chancellor. In public she continually pressed home the message, repeating the essential points with insistent simplicity. On a visit to Lancashire in August 1979, for example, she maintained that 'people in Britain had to understand that improved public services could only be paid for out of higher levels of productivity'. High interest rates were necessary because borrowing was still at a high level: 'the Government was determined not to print money to bring levels down as this would only lead to renewed inflation'.[21] Challenged by a Labour MP at Prime Minister's Questions in February 1980, as unemployment neared 2 million, she reiterated that 'if people continue to make excessive wage claims, those claims can, by pricing goods out of the market, lead to increased unemployment'. In response to an accusation that she had not lived up to the prayer she had quoted on taking office nine months earlier, she retorted that 'it is not easy to get a nation to live within its means when it has been living outside its means for a long time'.[22] At the same time, perhaps aware that the term 'monetarism' was viewed with suspicion as an overly intellectual abstraction, Thatcher began to offer more readily understandable alternatives. Addressing the Birmingham Chamber of Commerce, for example, she stated that monetarism 'used to be called "sound money"', and assured her audience that 'whatever you call it, is as fundamental to financial policy as the law of gravity is to physics'.[23]

As evidence of the success of government policy failed to materialise, Thatcher faced a real test of her willpower. The passing of the 'right to buy' legislation, which made it possible for council tenants to purchase their local authority-owned homes, was one of very few successes to appear during the government's first year in office. The March 1980 budget saw the introduction of the Medium Term Financial Strategy, an attempt to impose financial discipline by setting targets for the growth of the money supply for several years ahead. Yet M3 rose in the course of 1980 by 18 per cent, against a target of 6 to 10 per cent. Inflation reached a staggering 22 per cent in May before starting to fall; it stood at 13 per cent at the end of the year, which was higher than when the Conservatives had taken office. In spite of the government's rigorous approach to public spending, it proved impossible to bring the PSBR under control. This was in part a result of departmental overspending, high public sector wage claims – the Clegg Commission was not wound up until August 1980 – and the cost of subsidising the nationalised industries. It was widely expected that Thatcher would give in to pressure for a modification of the strategy. In these circumstances the Prime Minister's refusal to be swayed, in defiance of the economic facts that confronted her, was crucial. At the October 1980 conference she acknowledged the 'human tragedy' of joblessness but insisted that the attack on inflation – 'the parent of unemployment' as well as 'the unseen robber of those who have saved' – must remain the priority. In the most famous phrase of the speech she flatly repudiated the notion of a U-turn as practised by the Heath government eight years before: 'You turn if you want to. The lady's not for turning.'[24] It was a colossal gamble. Economic disaster might be the outcome of a refusal to change; but her outspoken public stance had made compromise practically impossible. From a political point of view the often repeated phrase, 'there is no alternative' – commonly reduced to the acronym 'TINA' – had a very real meaning for the beleaguered premier.

Trade unions and the industrial battlefront

In other policy areas, however, Thatcher proved more flexible. She showed a willingness to pick her battles and to settle for less than she really wanted when circumstances dictated. At the same time she was prepared to resort to indirect methods of pushing her own agenda when she encountered resistance. This was particularly the case in the area of trade union reform, where she allowed her own instincts for more far-reaching regulation to be overborne by the more moderate instincts of her Employment Secretary. Prior's bill, published in December 1979, was deliberately limited. It banned secondary picketing but left secondary strike action untouched. The closed shop was not banned outright; rather from now on, the approval of 80 per cent of the work force in a particular industry would be required for it to remain legal. Finally, the bill made available government money to fund secret ballots before a strike or to elect their officials, whereas right-wing MPs believed that unions should be obliged to bear the cost themselves. With the start of a strike in the steel industry the following month, the government came under growing pressure to widen the scope of the bill. Behind the scenes Thatcher's ultra-loyal parliamentary private secretary Ian Gow, her indispensable link to rank and file opinion in the Commons, was co-operating with the Solicitor-General, Sir Ian Percival, to stir up backbench dissent against the measure. The attempt to secure a more wide-ranging piece of legislation ended only after Prior mobilised a powerful group of Cabinet colleagues, headed by Whitelaw, Carrington and the Lord Chancellor, Lord Hailsham, in favour of his less confrontational approach. In response, Thatcher reassured the party's right wing with a unilateral announcement of a measure to reduce social security benefits for strikers' families, and by making clear that Prior's bill was only an instalment of reform.

Thatcher could afford to take a step by step approach to union law reform. Legislation was probably less important, in bringing about the long-term decline of union power, than her steadfast refusal to bring their leaders into the circle of policy-making, as recent Labour governments had done. She also knew that, following the winter of discontent, the unions no longer enjoyed the support of a tolerant public opinion, and their strength was being further sapped by the cumulative effects of unemployment. By appealing to ordinary trade union members, over the heads of their bosses, she could weaken the power of the militants. The strategy required her to avoid picking a quarrel with the more powerful unions until she was in a position to win. Thus in February 1981, faced with the threat of a miners' strike over a threatened closure of uneconomic pits, Thatcher backed away from confrontation. She appreciated that coal stocks must be built up at the power stations in order to withstand a renewed challenge in the future. In the short term, however, she had to face hostile comment from a normally sympathetic right-wing press, with the *Daily Express* running the headline 'Surrender to King Coal' and the *Sun* reproaching Thatcher directly with the charge that 'for the first time since you came to power your credibility is at stake'.[25] In addition the government was obliged to provide up to £400 million in subsidies to keep the reprieved collieries open. Yet however bitter the immediate consequences may have been, Thatcher knew that a tactical concession was better than the kind of defeat inflicted by the miners on the Heath government. As she wrote in her memoirs, 'all we could do was to cut our losses and live to fight another day, when – with adequate preparation – we might be in a position to win'.[26]

Thatcher's decision to continue supporting British Leyland provided another illustration of the triumph of pragmatism over ideology. BL was a major car manufacturing firm which was not only making heavy losses, in spite of generous subsidies introduced by the Wilson government, but was also plagued by poor labour relations. To the kind of free market ideologues who had gathered around Thatcher in the years of opposition, it was obvious that government support should be withdrawn. Characteristically, in a meeting shortly before the general election, Thatcher had bluntly asked the company chairman, Michael Edwardes, why a future Conservative government should 'pour further funds into British Leyland'.[27] In January 1981 the Cabinet was treated to the bizarre spectacle of Sir Keith Joseph presenting his department's case for additional support for the troubled enterprise, after which he pleaded with his colleagues to tear the proposal up and allow BL to go into liquidation. Not for the first time, however, Thatcher showed a more secure grasp of political realities than her conscience-stricken Industry Secretary. The large-scale losses which would have attended the closure or break-up of BL would have destroyed Conservative electoral prospects in the crucial West Midlands, where the firm was an important employer. In addition, whatever her personal reservations may have been, she judged that Edwardes' attempts to bring order to the troubled relationship between management and unions deserved her support. To withdraw support from a resolute manager of this kind would send the wrong signals to industry. In a homely phrase drawn from her Lincolnshire background, she declared that this was not the time to 'chop you [Edwardes] off at the stocking tops'. At the same time she made clear her sympathy for other manufacturers who had to compete without the advantage of government subsidies: 'I never want to take on another British Leyland, we shouldn't be in it at all, but now we're in it . . . we have to back Michael Edwardes' judgement'.[28] Thatcher's critics noted with grudging admiration her ability to get away with a decision which flagrantly contradicted her free market ideology. Prior, for example, noted the way in which she distanced herself from the consequences of the BL rescue: 'she was Boadicea, hammering away at those wicked people who were seeking to carry out policies alien to her own trusted beliefs and nature'.[29]

Cabinet conflicts and the 1981 budget

Thatcher's pragmatic approach to industrial relations was never likely to place her premiership in jeopardy. The most direct threat to her hold on power, in the first two years, was posed by a group of ministers who objected to what they regarded as the inflexibility of her wider economic strategy. The origin of the term 'wet' as a description of these Conservative dissenters remains obscure. It had a long pedigree as a public school term, meaning weakness or a lack of backbone. In the context of 1979–80 it was specifically applied by Thatcher and her supporters to those Tories who objected to the squeeze on public spending and the marked increase in unemployment. On the other hand those who supported the Prime Minister's approach, and maintained that there was no alternative to her austere policies, predictably became known as the 'dries'. The 'wets' did not resign from the government, choosing instead to wage a kind of guerrilla warfare against the Prime Minister's approach through coded speeches and leaks to the press. In time, as she grew in confidence, Thatcher moved to isolate and remove them. The first to go was Norman St John-Stevas, who was sacked in a minor Cabinet reshuffle in January 1981, but he was never a central figure. More important were Sir Ian Gilmour, Jim Prior and Peter Walker. Francis Pym, whom Thatcher moved from Defence to take the place of St John-Stevas as Leader of the Commons, was also in their camp.

What did the 'wets' stand for? Most of them came from the traditional, landed element of the Conservative Party, although the grammar school-educated Walker, who had made a fortune as a member of an asset-stripping city company, did not fit this mould. What they shared was a conviction that Thatcher's credo was inappropriate to the running of a sophisticated modern economy. In Prior's words, 'it was a very simplistic approach, a combination of her own instincts founded in the corner shop at Grantham, laid over by a veneer from Hayek and Friedman'.[30] Gilmour, who was much more overtly contemptuous of Thatcher, derided her for equating national economic policy with the week by week management of an individual household. 'For one thing,' he later wrote, 'a housewife knows what her income and expenses are.' He argued that unlike a housewife, if a government cuts its expenses, it also indirectly causes its income to fall. This results both in lower tax revenues and the necessity to spend more on unemployment benefit, with damaging consequences for economic well-being.[31] As the title of his book on the Thatcher era, *Dancing with Dogma* indicated, Gilmour and his fellow wets were suspicious of anything which smacked of ideological inflexibility. They saw themselves as pragmatic realists in a Cabinet where the tune was increasingly called by theorists who were fatally detached from the real world.

The wets viewed with deep misgiving the disappearance of old industrial Britain and the ensuing decisive shift towards the creation of a service-based economy. They regarded the Treasury's focus on lowering government borrowing as misguided, and argued the Keynesian case for continued public spending. Not only would it finance necessary modernisation of the country's infrastructure, it was also socially preferable to paying people to remain idle. This concern linked with a further strand in the wets' thinking: the so-called 'One Nation' tradition in Conservatism, inspired by the memory of nineteenth-century party leader, Benjamin Disraeli, which held that those in power had a paternalistic duty to look after the disadvantaged in society. Thus Gilmour insisted that support for the welfare state was essential to social harmony: 'those who wish to "conserve" the fabric of society and avoid the shocks of violent upheavals,' he wrote, 'must look to the contentment of all our fellow countrymen'. Thatcher and her followers, with their free market dogma and hunger for power, were the reverse of true Conservatives, trampling over the values the wets prized, 'like some unscrupulous property developer bulldozing listed buildings that stood in the way of a quick profit'.[32]

The March 1981 budget crystallised the wets' concerns over the policies of the Thatcher government. In their memoirs Thatcher and Howe disagreed over which of them was more committed to a further extension of economic radicalism. John Hoskyns' recollection was that both Prime Minister and Chancellor had to be stiffened against the institutional conservatism of the Treasury by the input of Thatcher's private advisers. The outcome was a budget whose key features went against the assumptions of mainstream economic thinking. Instead of allowing borrowing to increase – the standard Keynesian response to rising unemployment – it bore down still more on the level of the PSBR. With limits to the scope for cuts in expenditure, attention turned to the possibility of raising income tax rates. This was politically too difficult, so soon after the rates had been cut. Instead it was decided to achieve the same effect by sleight of hand, by omitting to raise tax allowances in line with inflation. The budget attracted immediate condemnation. No fewer than 364 economists, headed by two Cambridge professors and including a future Governor of the Bank of England, Mervyn King, wrote to *The Times* to restate Keynesian orthodoxy by protesting against the idea of cutting the deficit in the depth of a recession.

The economic effects of the budget remain controversial. Its supporters argued that it laid the foundations of the recovery, and it was certainly awkward for the 364 economists that growth slowly resumed from the time of their letter's appearance. The budget reduced government borrowing enough to make possible a cut in interest rates to 12 per cent, which its authors regarded as the key to the eventual revival of business activity. Above all, by decisively rejecting the option of a U-turn, Thatcher and Howe created an expectation that the government would repay its debt and that inflation would fall. In the short term, however, the signs were much less optimistic. A run on sterling in October obliged Howe to increase interest rates once again to 16 per cent. Unemployment did not begin to fall until 1986. Politically, however, the clear beneficiary was the Prime Minister. In their appalled response to the budget, the wets demonstrated their powerlessness. They had not expected that Thatcher and Howe would persist with their strategy, and they were taken by surprise when the details of the budget were revealed in Cabinet, shortly before it was announced in the Commons. Prior, Walker and Gilmour met to consider their response but decided that resignation would achieve nothing; the budget could not be derailed at this late stage. Although sympathetic to their position, it was clear that the heavyweight figures of Whitelaw and Pym would not put their heads above the parapet. In any case they were unable to offer a fully worked out alternative policy package. Walker later provided an additional reason for doing nothing, the possible adverse effect on sterling that three simultaneous resignations might have. The wets' failure to act demonstrated just how comprehensively they had been outmanoeuvred. They had missed their last opportunity to take a clear-cut stand. By unhappily staying on rather than departing on an issue of principle, they undermined their own cause.

The inner city riots and the eclipse of the wets

A month after the budget Thatcher's critics were handed what appeared to be a vindication of their warnings of social dislocation as a result of economic distress. In mid-April Brixton in south London was the scene of three days of rioting. Early in July there were similar disturbances in a number of other deprived urban areas, including Southall in west London, the Toxteth area of Liverpool and Moss Side, Manchester. These events heightened the fears of those who had warned of growing lawlessness during the previous decade. Yet on the whole, at least outside Northern Ireland, where sectarian conflict between Catholic nationalists and Protestant Unionists erupted in the late 1960s, post-war society had been largely peaceful and orderly. Attacks on the police, who lacked the equipment and training needed to deal with violence on this scale, and the racial dimension which featured in some of the disturbances, caused consternation in government circles. A Conservative Research Department paper sent to Number 10 called for a firmer response from the Home Office, alongside measures to reintegrate 'alienated young people into society'. Without a clear lead from the government, it warned, 'extremists of left and right will step into the vacuum and our own supporters will have another cause for alarm and disillusion'.[33] To many commentators the riots seemed to provide incontrovertible proof of their argument that an unemployment figure of 2.5 million was politically unsustainable, and that a change of direction was badly needed.

Both at the time and in her memoirs, Thatcher steadfastly refused to acknowledge any link between the violence and unemployment. She attributed the riots to the erosion of personal responsibility, and of a sense of pride in local communities, which she traced back to the more relaxed moral climate of the 1960s. At Prime Minister's Questions in mid-July she insisted that 'society must have rules if it is to continue to be civilised' and told a Labour spokesman that 'until law and order and public confidence have been restored, we cannot set about improving the economic or social conditions of this country'.[34] Thatcher did, however, agree to appoint a prominent judge, Lord Scarman, to enquire into the part played by poor relations between the police and local black youths in the outbreak of the Brixton riots. She also acceded to Michael Heseltine's request to lead a personal mission to Liverpool to look at ways of bringing together central and local government, business and voluntary groups in an attempt to regenerate the depressed inner city areas. Her lack of enthusiasm for any initiative which might involve increased expenditure – and might enhance the profile of a colleague whose ambitions she suspected – is, however, clear from the government files. In a meeting with the 'minister for Merseyside' shortly before his visit, she emphasised that 'very large sums of central Government money were already being spent in Liverpool and she believed that it was more a case of getting value for it than of additional resources'. She was prepared to sanction the award of only 'a very small amount of new money for the purpose [Heseltine] had described'.[35]

The riots provided the backdrop to perhaps the most fraught Cabinet meeting of the entire decade, on the eve of the summer recess. For Thatcher the most worrying aspect of the 23 July gathering was that when her habitual critics resisted Howe's plans for a renewed squeeze on public spending, they found support in unexpected quarters, notably from Nott and Biffen. With her tendency to view all political relationships through the lens of loyalty to her leadership, Thatcher recalled the opposition of the 'fair-weather monetarists',[36] which crystallised her growing conviction that a larger scale reconstruction of the Cabinet was now necessary. Other factors came into play to strengthen the premier's resolve. In August she received a hard-hitting memorandum, initiated by John Hoskyns but also bearing the signatures of her unofficial chief of staff, David Wolfson, and speechwriter Ronald Millar, attacking her whole approach to leadership. Although written from a supportive perspective, the harsh language of the document clearly stung Thatcher. It bluntly reprimanded her for bullying her colleagues, urged her to 'lead by encouragement, not by criticism', and predicted failure if she did not change the way she managed her government.[37] Thatcher did not engage with its authors, and she certainly did not heed its warnings about her personal style. But it may have helped push her into making other changes which she was already contemplating.

In August, Thatcher removed Peter Thorneycroft as party chairman, replacing him with the younger and more dynamic – as well as ideologically more solid – Cecil Parkinson. She remained on good terms with Thorneycroft, whose contribution to the 1979 victory had earned her gratitude, and at seventy-two he had no wish to manage another general election campaign. The timing of his resignation was, however, undoubtedly influenced by his public confession of what he whimsically called a feeling of 'rising damp', and his contradiction of claims by the Chancellor that the recession was at an end. Some Thatcher loyalists have suggested that behind this lay a more serious purpose on Thorneycroft's part, designed to promote Francis Pym and to remove the Prime Minister and her closest associates. Certainly Thorneycroft was prey to a scepticism which was fundamentally at odds with Thatcher's unswerving sense of purpose. He had startled a junior member of his team by saying, in reference to one of the policy commitments in the 1979 manifesto, 'Work, my dear boy? Of course it won't work. Nothing works. The thing to do is the best we can in the circumstances.'[38]

The appointment of a new chairman formed part of a wider reshuffle, which was carried out on 14 September. The removal of Gilmour and Soames from the Cabinet, and Prior's shift from Employment to Northern Ireland, constituted a serious blow to the wets. Prior was effectively neutralised, his loyalty bought by his acceptance of a department remote from the heart of Whitehall, rather than a discontented return to the backbenches. His retention of a seat on the Cabinet's economic policy committee, the E Committee, proved a meaningless concession as he found himself heavily outnumbered by its other members. He was to leave the government of his own volition in September 1984. In came two notably 'dry' ministers, the abrasive Norman Tebbit at Employment and Nigel Lawson at Energy. Joseph moved from Industry to replace Mark Carlisle, Thatcher's surprising choice as Education Secretary in 1979. He went quietly, in marked contrast to Gilmour, who dramatically described the government as 'steering full speed ahead for the rocks' as he left Downing Street. The changes certainly altered the balance of the Cabinet but there were still no more than ten 'true believers' in a Cabinet of twenty-two members. Pym and Walker remained untouched, and indeed the latter was to continue to serve in a succession of low-ranking Cabinet posts, almost until the end of the Thatcher administration, a token survivor of the era of consensus. Although the reshuffle definitely strengthened Thatcher's hold on power, and demonstrated afresh the direction in which she was determined to go, it did not mean that she was completely secure. There were limits to her ability to create a team wholly in her own image.

Towards a second term?

As 1981 drew to a close there were some optimistic signs for the government. Norman Tebbit, a more combative figure than his predecessor as Employment Secretary, was preparing a reform bill which would end the immunity of trade unions from claims for damages, and narrow the definition of a lawful dispute. Meanwhile, demoralised by its electoral defeat, the Labour Party descended into open civil war which worsened after Callaghan's retirement in November 1980. His successor, the sixty-seven year-old Michael Foot, was a romantic socialist, a fine writer and speaker, but completely unsuited to the task of holding together a deeply divided party. The spokesman of the hard left, Tony Benn, pushed Labour towards a programme based upon increased state control of the economy, unilateral nuclear disarmament, withdrawal from the European Community and a stronger voice for the rank and file in the choice of the party leader and the reselection of MPs. In March 1981 an open split occurred when the so-called 'gang of four' – a group of moderates who had served in recent Labour Cabinets – formed the breakaway Social Democrat Party in reaction to their old party's leftward shift. Roy Jenkins, David Owen, Shirley Williams and Bill Rodgers were substantive figures who saw an alliance with the Liberals as the way to 'break the mould' of British politics, offering a genuine alternative to two unappealing extremes.

These divisions on the centre-left were likely to work in Thatcher's favour. Yet there was still no guarantee that she would win a second term. With interest rates at 16 per cent, inflation at 12 per cent and unemployment about to peak at 3 million in January 1982, the key economic indicators provided little cause for comfort. Thatcher's approval rating in an October 1981 Gallup poll was a mere 28 per cent, the lowest for any premier since opinion polling began in the late 1930s. It remained at an average of only 36 per cent until spring 1982. Riding a remarkable tide of popularity, the SDP scored two impressive by-election victories, at Crosby in Lancashire in November 1981 and Hillhead in Glasgow the following March. The emergence of a viable third party raised the possibility of a hung parliament at the next general election. It was true that, by the spring of 1982, output was rising and both inflation and interest rates were beginning to fall. But it is not certain that Thatcher could have won a decisive victory without an unexpected development in overseas affairs. Argentina's invasion of the Falkland Islands in April 1982 tested Thatcher in a way that she had not hitherto experienced, yet the outcome of the crisis also imparted a startling momentum to her political fortunes.

Notes

1 Remarks on becoming Prime Minister (St Francis's Prayer), 4 May 1979, www.margaretthatcher.org/document/104078 (accessed 20 April 2014).
2 James Prior, *A Balance of Power* (London, Hamish Hamilton, 1986), p. 113.
3 Jonathan Aitken, *Margaret Thatcher: Power and Personality* (London, Bloomsbury, 2013), p. 247.
4 Margaret Thatcher, *The Downing Street Years* (London, Harper Collins, 1993), p. 19.
5 Interview for *Observer*, 12 January 1979, *Margaret Thatcher: Complete Public Statements 1945–1990 on CD-ROM* (Oxford, Oxford University Press, 1999), 79_007.
6 Thatcher, *Downing Street Years*, p. 104.
7 Thatcher, *Downing Street Years*, p. 26.
8 Alan Clark, *Diaries: Into Politics 1972–1982* (London, Phoenix, 2001), p. 139, entry for 27 November 1979.
9 Hansard, 14 June 1978, col. 1027, http://hansard.millbanksystems.com/commons/1978/jun/14/economic-situation (accessed 20 April 2014).
10 Ferdinand Mount, *Cold Cream: My Early Life and Other Mistakes* (London, Bloomsbury, 2008), p. 323.
11 Tim Bell, *Right or Wrong: The Memoirs of Lord Bell* (London, Bloomsbury, 2014), p. 64.
12 Michael Heseltine, *Life in the Jungle: My Autobiography* (London, Hodder and Stoughton, 2000), p. 232.
13 Geoffrey Howe, *Conflict of Loyalty* (London, Macmillan, 1994), p. 201.
14 John Hoskyns, *Just in Time: Inside the Thatcher Revolution* (London, Aurum Press, 2000), p. 262.
15 Quoted in Gillian Shephard, *The Real Iron Lady: Working with Margaret Thatcher* (London, Biteback, 2013), p. 205.
16 Peter Hennessy, *Cabinet* (Oxford, Basil Blackwell, 1986), p. 96.
17 John Ranelagh, *Thatcher's People: An Insider's Account of the Politics, the Power and the Personalities* (London, Harper Collins, 1991), pp. 18–19.
18 Ranelagh, *Thatcher's People*, p. 22.
19 Quoted in Shephard, *The Real Iron Lady*, p. 44.

20 Howe, *Conflict of Loyalty*, p. 173.
21 Margaret Thatcher, Remarks visiting the North West (defending economic policy), 31 August 1979, www.margaretthatcher.org/document/104136 (accessed 20 April 2014).
22 House of Commons PQs, 19 February 1980, www.margaretthatcher.org/document/104309 (accessed 20 April 2014).
23 Speech to Birmingham Chamber of Commerce, 21 April 1980, *Margaret Thatcher: Complete Public Statements*, 80_085.
24 Speech to Conservative Party conference ('The Reason Why'), 10 October 1980, *Margaret Thatcher: Complete Public Statements*, 80_220.
25 Quoted in Charles Moore, *Margaret Thatcher: The Authorized Biography: Volume One: Not for Turning* (London, Allen Lane, 2013), p. 539.
26 Thatcher, *Downing Street Years*, p. 141.
27 Michael Edwardes, *Back from the Brink: An Apocalyptic Experience* (London, Collins, 1983), p. 221.
28 TV interview for London Weekend Television *Weekend World*, 1 February 1981, *Margaret Thatcher: Complete Public Statements*, 81_023.
29 Prior, *A Balance of Power*, p. 128.
30 Prior, *A Balance of Power*, p. 119.
31 Ian Gilmour, *Dancing with Dogma: Britain under Thatcherism* (London, Simon & Schuster, 1992), p. 23.
32 Gilmour, *Dancing with Dogma*, pp. 278, 223.
33 'Riots: Shipley minute to Howarth (Riots in Liverpool and Southall)', 6 July 1981, www.margaretthatcher.org/document/121331 (accessed 20 April 2014).
34 HC PQ, 16 July 1981, *Margaret Thatcher: Complete Public Statements*, 81_211.
35 'Inner Cities – No. 10 record of conversation (MT-Whitelaw-Heseltine)', 14 July 1981, www.margaretthatcher.org/document/127049 (accessed 20 April 2014).
36 Thatcher, *Downing Street Years*, p. 149.
37 Hoskyns, *Just in Time*, p. 326.
38 Mark Garnett and Ian Aitken, *Splendid! Splendid! The Authorized Biography of Willie Whitelaw* (London, Jonathan Cape, 2002), p. 240. Reproduced by permission of The Random House Group Ltd.

4 Post-imperial fall-out – Rhodesia, the Falklands and Hong Kong: 1979–1984

Thatcher and the wider world

Overseas affairs were not uppermost in Margaret Thatcher's mind when she first took office. To some extent this can be explained by the magnitude of the task facing her, as she saw it, in tackling Britain's economic problems. Her lack of detailed knowledge, and perhaps of self-assurance, in foreign policy partly explain her appointment of the more experienced Lord Carrington as her first Foreign Secretary. She could not, however, entirely delegate responsibility in this area, even had she wished to do so. By the 1970s Britain's membership of a number of major international bodies, including the European Community, the Commonwealth and NATO, and the well-established round of summit meetings with other heads of government – reinforced by the media's focus on the activities of world leaders – placed insistent demands on the time and energy of the Prime Minister. In addition, even if she had not fully thought them through, Thatcher brought to the premiership a number of firm ideas and instincts about Britain's place in the world. She was fervently anti-communist, convinced of the centrality of the Atlantic alliance, and inclined to see 'Europe' as a forum in which she had to contend for British interests. Thatcher was also deeply suspicious of the mind-set of the Foreign Office mandarins, viewing their worldly-wise sophistication and their ingrained preference for compromise as masking a supine acceptance of national decline. In her memoirs she wrote of 'the habits which the Foreign Office seems to cultivate – a reluctance to subordinate diplomatic tactics to the national interest and an insatiable appetite for nuances and conditions which can blur the clearest vision'.[1] It was typical of Thatcher that, flying out to her first Commonwealth heads of government conference with Carrington in July 1979, she told him that she had never before heard of the phrase, 'a damage limitation exercise'.[2]

For their part defenders of the Whitehall establishment world-view derided what they saw as a simplistic, black and white approach: in the words of one senior diplomat, Thatcher exhibited 'a small town hostility to Europeans and a *Daily Express* under-standing of foreign affairs'.[3] Less acerbically, Sir Brian Cartledge, the overseas affairs private secretary whom she inherited from Callaghan when she arrived in Number 10, recalled that 'Margaret Thatcher's decisions were taken with reference to a few deeply, even passionately, held personal convictions and beliefs against which proposals or individuals were measured: if found wanting, the proposal or individual was discarded without further ado'.[4] Yet in spite of her suspicion of the Foreign Office as an institu-tion, Thatcher drew continually on the expertise of trained dip-lomats and built trusting relationships with a number of individuals, in spite of their different assumptions and back-grounds. They regarded her with a combination of admiration and frustration, frequently commenting on her tendency to see foreign policy in terms of a series of discrete problems to be solved and battles to be fought. Sir John Coles, who served as her private secretary in 1981–4, remembered her habit of asking, 'What's the next thing?' after a decision had been taken: 'not much reaching for an overall policy concept there'.[5] Similarly Sir Percy Cradock, who worked closely with the premier as her foreign policy adviser and chairman of the Joint Intelligence Committee from 1984, wrote that she viewed foreign policy 'not as a continuum . . . but rather as a series of disparate problems with attainable solutions or even as zero-sum games, which Britain had to win'.[6]

Several of the overseas issues to which Thatcher had to apply herself in the first half of her premiership were inherited from an era with which she might be thought to have been instinctively in sympathy, that of the British Empire. In the Falklands crisis of 1982, she was the last British leader to fight a war which in some respects resembled an old-style imperial conflict. Like many of her generation, she was touched by some residual nostalgia for empire. It is perhaps significant that her favourite, and frequently quoted poet, was Rudyard Kipling. This did not, however, translate into some anachronistic endeavour to recreate an overseas imperial role for Britain. No surviving member of the Conservative Party's old empire lobby in Parliament was given a prominent role in the Thatcher governments. All her Foreign Secretaries were pragmatists who sought to maximise Britain's influence overseas whilst recognising the limitations on the country's capacity for unilateral action. Thatcher herself, with the notable exception of the expedition to recover the Falkland Islands, demonstrated a surprising willingness to subordinate her own instincts when faced with the realities of Britain's diminished room for manoeuvre.

Rhodesia to Zimbabwe

The first major international problem awaiting Thatcher was the issue of Rhodesia, where an entrenched white minority government had been acting in defiance of Britain and the wider world for almost a decade and a half. Alone among Britain's African colonies, Rhodesia had not been granted independence in the wave of decolonisation which occurred in the early 1960s. The reason for this anomaly was the steadfast refusal of the settler government, headed by Rhodesia's intransigent premier, Ian Smith, to contemplate sharing political power with the black population. Faced with London's insistence on a transition to black majority rule, Smith had unilaterally declared independence in 1965, thus setting his country on a collision course with Britain and the wider international community.

Successive British governments had responded with an ineffective combination of economic sanctions and attempts at a negotiated solution. Military intervention had been ruled out, partly because of the practical difficulties of projecting power into a land-locked southern African state, and also because it was felt that the armed forces could not be called upon to act against a white community whom many British people viewed as their 'kith and kin'. The latter argument also resonated with a number of right-wing Conservative MPs, creating a problem of party management for a leadership which could not allow itself to be publicly associated with a racially discriminatory government engaged in an act of rebellion against the British Crown. The issue was highlighted in November 1978 when the Labour government brought forward a motion for the renewal of sanctions. In the largest parliamentary rebellion in Conservative post-war history, no fewer than 116 Conservative MPs rejected the official shadow cabinet recommendation to abstain.

Thatcher's own sympathies lay with the right-wing dissidents on her side. Writing to shadow defence spokesman Winston Churchill, the grandson of her wartime hero, whom she dismissed for defying her call for abstention, she softened the blow by acknowledging that 'I too feel strongly about events in Rhodesia – we all do'.[7] She mistrusted the 'Patriotic Front', the guerrilla movement headed by Robert Mugabe and Joshua Nkomo, which was fighting to topple the Rhodesian government with the support of neighbouring black states, viewing it as a Marxist movement inimical to Western values and interests. Her preference was for the 'internal settlement', reached by Smith with moderate black elements in March 1978, to prevail. She viewed with optimism the electoral success of a new government under the white leadership's favoured black collaborator, Bishop Abel Muzorewa, in April 1979. Speaking in the Commons shortly before travelling to the Zambian capital, Lusaka, to discuss the situation at a Commonwealth conference, she praised the election as 'an advance without parallel in the history of Rhodesia'. Of the Patriotic Front leaders, who had boycotted the contest on the grounds that the internal settlement entrenched white privileges, she declared that 'those who rely on force to achieve their ends must not have a veto over those who seek to advance their cause by democratic and constitutional means'.[8]

Others in her own party, notably Carrington, assessed the internal settlement in a much less positive light. The Foreign Secretary's analysis was that Britain's overriding interest in the region, the attainment of stability, could not be achieved without the inclusion of representatives of the guerrilla movement, who were continuing their campaign of violence. The shaky Muzorewa regime did not command the approval of the surrounding black states or of the United States, and continued British support for it might conceivably lead to an irretrievable rift in the Commonwealth. Any change which might hand power to communist-backed militants went against the grain for Thatcher. She was anxious about her reception at the Lusaka conference, telling Carrington that she planned to wear dark glasses in the belief that she would encounter acid-throwing protestors. In the event, in spite of some hostile comment in the Zambian press, she successfully established good relations with the country's president, Kenneth Kaunda, who wanted the Patriotic Front included in any settlement.

No less remarkably, Thatcher consented to a major policy shift, agreeing to the representation of all parties in the Rhodesian conflict in talks held at London's Lancaster House. The agreement reached in December paved the way for the temporary restoration of British colonial authority, with Lord Soames installed as governor specifically to superintend the holding of fresh elections the following April. The ensuing victory for Mugabe's Zanu PF party, and his elevation as first Prime Minister of the new state of Zimbabwe, was certainly not the outcome Thatcher had wanted, but it represented a recognition of the realities on the ground. At one level, the way in which this long-running problem had been resolved appealed to her. Britain had dealt with a difficult legacy from its own colonial past without the need for intervention by the United Nations or any other external actor. Less than a year into her premiership, she had presided over a solution which had eluded Wilson, Heath and Callaghan. Only Thatcher had been prepared to accept the risks entailed in assuming direct control of the situation in Rhodesia. As Foreign Office diplomat Robin Renwick recalled, 'what attracted the Prime Minister most about our plan was its boldness. She liked the idea of Britain acting as the decolonising power.'[9]

The subsequent transformation of Zimbabwe into a single-party dictatorship, and its descent into economic chaos after Mugabe's decision in 2000 to seize the land of white farmers, casts a negative light backwards on the Lancaster House agreement. It would be a harsh judgement, however, to hold Thatcher and Carrington responsible for events which occurred two decades later. At the time, faced with overwhelming pressure to end the Rhodesian civil war and find a workable settlement, they had little practical alternative. Most commentators have concurred that Thatcher deserves credit for setting aside her own prejudices and acting coolly to help bring the conflict to a close. In Carrington's words, 'it was one of those occasions . . . when her heart and basic instincts (which I don't think changed) were subordinated by her to what her intellect came to decide made political sense'.[10] She displayed her sure political sense, too, in keeping an unusually low profile once the Lancaster House talks had begun, leaving Carrington to chair the proceedings. By holding aloof she ensured that there was no chance of Smith's faction seeking to appeal to her against the decisions of her Foreign Secretary. Carrington himself later privately admitted that had the government's approach failed, 'she wouldn't have taken the can', and remarked on how she lent growing support as the process looked more likely to succeed.[11] Certainly it was the Foreign Secretary who bore the brunt of the Tory right's hostility at the 1979 party conference, where the pro-settler irreconcilables displayed banners reading 'Hang Carrington'. Although the agreement could not have been reached without her approval, she emerged with her reputation in the eyes of her core supporters intact.

The Falklands conflict: the gathering storm

Argentina's seizure of the Falkland Islands on 2 April 1982 was, for Thatcher, the most important, and also the least expected, post-imperial problem that she faced as premier. In directing the recovery of the islands by military means she became the first British Prime Minister to order troops into combat since the unhappy precedent set by Sir Anthony Eden in the Suez crisis of 1956. It was the only episode in her premiership of which she wrote an account whilst still in office, and when she came to incorporate it into her memoirs a decade later she was in no doubt of its significance. The future of the islanders, she wrote in Churchillian vein, was not the only issue at stake. Britain had to take action to defend its honour as a nation, and to uphold wider principles, namely that 'aggressors should never succeed and that international law should prevail over the use of force'. The ten week crisis made a deep impression on her personally: 'I do not think I have ever lived so tensely or intensely as during the whole of that time'.[12] It was a test of her nerve in an area of policy for which she was wholly unprepared. Failure to achieve the objectives she had set herself would almost certainly have brought about her fall from office.

The Falkland Islands had been in contention between Britain and Argentina for generations, with neither country possessing a clear-cut legal right to their possession. Argentina insisted that the islands – known in Spanish as the Malvinas – were part of their sovereign territory and had been illegally seized by Britain in 1833. The latter's claim was based on the fact of uninterrupted ownership for almost 150 years, and the strongly held wish of the islanders, almost all of whom were of British descent, to maintain their right to self-determination. In this they enjoyed the support of a well-organised Westminster lobby, which could be mobilised at the hint of any deal with Argentina being concluded over their heads. To a detached observer, however, the dispute seemed incomprehensible – in the words of Peruvian writer, Mario Vargas Llosa, it was like 'two bald men arguing over a comb'.[13] Were it not for the effective veto on change exercised by the population of the Falklands, the coolly rational officials of the Foreign Office would have been willing to negotiate away an unwanted commitment. The barren, wind-swept islands had only 1,800 inhabitants; they were 8,000 miles from Britain but only 250 miles from Argentina; and no vital national interests were at stake in the area. No British government – least of all the Thatcher administration in the early 1980s, with its overriding wish to bring down public spending – was willing to undertake the large-scale investment which would have been needed to make the islands defensible against a military expedition from Argentina. The preferred Foreign Office solution was known as 'leaseback', an arrangement whereby legal sovereignty would be transferred to Argentina, which would then allow Britain to administer the islands for a fixed period.

Thatcher's own position on the future of the islands on taking office was ambivalent. She was instinctively suspicious of 'leaseback' as a weak compromise which would cause an extensive Conservative backbench rebellion. In response to arguments put by the Foreign Office, however, she allowed the option to be explored. The minister responsible for approaching both the islanders and the Argentines was Nicholas Ridley, an economic Thatcherite, later to be a close Cabinet supporter of the Prime Minister, but at this stage occupying an uncongenial berth as a junior Foreign Office minister. His proposals for a ninety-nine year leaseback agreement met with strong opposition from the people of the Falklands and their parliamentary allies in London. What was not known at the time, however, was that when Ridley presented his proposals to the Commons in December 1980, backbench opposition had been orchestrated by Thatcher's loyal parliamentary private secretary, Ian Gow. As Jonathan Aitken, who witnessed the barracking that Ridley endured, later observed, 'it was not the first or the last example of how Margaret Thatcher sometimes undermined her ministers by surreptitiously getting her aides to brief against them'.[14]

Having contributed to the collapse of the only rational solution on offer, Thatcher failed to send a clear signal to Argentina that Britain would protect the islands. The defence cuts announced in 1981 were to fall most heavily on the Royal Navy to which, in the absence of an adequate air base, would fall the main responsibility for combating an assault on the islands. Not only were the two aircraft carriers *Hermes* and *Invincible* to go, but also the ice patrol ship, *Endurance*, was to be withdrawn. Thatcher regarded the under-armed vessel as militarily insignificant, but this was to miss the point. The main significance of its presence in the South Atlantic was as a visible symbol of Britain's continuing interest in the area. This was recognised by Lord Carrington, who appealed unsuccessfully three times to the Defence Secretary, John Nott, for a reprieve. News of the planned cuts may well have encouraged the Argentine regime to believe that it would not meet resistance.

The first sign of impending trouble came in the final days of 1981 when a group of Argentinian scrap-metal dealers made a brief unauthorised landing on South Georgia, an uninhabited dependency of the Falklands. On 3 March 1982 Thatcher responded to further suggestions of a hardening of the Argentine government's position by calling for contingency plans to be formulated. This was not, however, followed up. Two weeks later the scrap-metal dealers returned to South Georgia and raised the Argentine flag. Thatcher now approved the despatch to the area of HMS *Endurance*, which was still on station prior to its planned decommissioning. This had the unintended consequence of encouraging Argentina to accelerate its plans for military action. When it became clear, in the closing days of March, that an attack was imminent, Britain sent two nuclear-powered submarines to reinforce *Endurance*. They could not, however, reach the South Atlantic before the onset of an invasion which was now less than five days away.

British intelligence had worked on the assumption that there would be a gradual escalation of hostile pressure on the part of the Argentine government, which would give Britain time to respond. They were, however, dealing with a military regime in Buenos Aires, which had seized power in December 1981, whose intentions could not readily be gauged by any rational means. The junta was nominally headed by the army leader, General Leopoldo Galtieri, but it was internally divided and its decision-making processes lacked coherence. Conscious of the unpopularity of their repressive policies at home, and of the shaky condition of the Argentine economy, they viewed an expedition to recover the islands as a way of shoring up their fragile domestic position. Their intentions were unpredictable and not easy to read.

The committee set up after the war to enquire into its origins, chaired by veteran civil servant Lord Franks, concluded that the British government could not be charged with a failure to foresee or prevent the invasion. It is hard to argue with this specific finding. The only chance of effectively deterring a landing would have been to send a sizeable task force to the area in good time. However, it is unclear when the government should have taken such a decision. A maritime contingent of this kind would take three weeks to arrive. It is easier to assert with hindsight that the evidence available at the time was clearly pointing to an invasion in the near future. The despatch of such a force might have actually precipitated the Argentine action that it was intended to forestall. Moreover, had the junta not then ordered a landing on the islands, the task force could not have been maintained indefinitely in the South Atlantic. The case against Thatcher is a broader and more long-term one: that she allowed her government to give off inconsistent signals to a regime which was capable of desperate measures; she encouraged the rejection of the leaseback scheme without putting in place a viable alternative; and it was too late to make a difference by the time she gave the developing crisis her full attention.

The critical point came on 31 March when the British government received unambiguous information that the Argentine fleet had set sail for the Falklands. The hastily convened meeting which followed in Thatcher's room at the Commons was one of the most dramatic moments of her premiership, and one which clearly revealed her character. In the absence of Carrington on a foreign visit, the most senior minister present, apart from Thatcher herself, was the Defence Secretary. Nott's advice was that the islands could not be retaken once they had fallen. It seemed that the elaborate bluff which had so long sustained Britain's hold on the territory had at last been called. The argument was turned around, quite unexpectedly, by the arrival of the First Sea Lord, Admiral Sir Henry Leach. He was deputising for the Chief of the Defence Staff, Admiral of the Fleet Sir Terence Lewin, who was abroad. Without hesitation, Leach told the assembled ministers that a task force could be assembled ready to leave in forty-eight hours, headed by the aircraft carriers *Hermes* and *Invincible*. Given authority to act, the armed services could recover the islands. He had bitterly opposed the government's budgetary plans as short-sighted and now, with the cuts announced but not yet implemented, he had a chance to demonstrate the indispensability of the Royal Navy at a moment of crisis. He ended with a warning which went beyond his area of strict responsibility. If they did not take action, he warned, 'in another few months we shall be living in a different country whose word counts for little'.[15] Although not quoted in her memoirs, these words must have struck a chord with a Prime Minister who instinctively wanted to reverse the Argentine incursion, but until this point had not known how this might be possible.

A war leader emerges

Thatcher now moved from a position of hapless complicity in her government's neglect of the growing crisis, to one of direct responsibility for recovering the islands and restoring Britain's reputation. In an emergency session of Parliament, held the day after the invasion, she delivered a defiant speech which was wholly in tune with the mood of the Commons. On all sides MPs were clamouring for the expulsion of the aggressors. Even the Labour leader, Michael Foot, struck a bellicose note, his conviction strengthened by the fact that the enemy was a quasi-fascist regime which provided a natural target for the British left.

Nonetheless, the situation was charged with great danger. The distance involved presented severe logistical difficulties. At the end of an 8,000 mile journey, the task force would be asked to assault enemy forces who would have had a month in which to reinforce and entrench. There was no possibility of providing the fleet with adequate air cover from land bases. In addition the window for action was limited, with the storms of the South Atlantic winter likely to set in from June onwards. Older figures, such as Willie Whitelaw, who had served in the Second World War, were conscious of the practical difficulties of securing a bridgehead in such unfavourable physical circumstances, and with uncertain international support. The shadow of Suez hung over the deliberations of the military planners; in the words of John Nott, 'above all, what was in my mind in 1982 at the outset of the Falklands War was the memory of an operation twenty-six years earlier involving over 100,000 men being mounted for a war which lasted only a few days – and then being halted as it came within reach of achieving its objectives'.[16]

In addition there were considerable political difficulties. Cross-parliamentary support was likely to erode once the hard realities of conflict became clear. Although only one Cabinet minister, John Biffen, actually spoke against the sending of the task force when Thatcher asked her colleagues for their opinions, several other ministers' commitment to the expedition was less than secure. Robin Harris, a Thatcher loyalist working as a Treasury adviser at the time, recalled the laughter in the office when Geoffrey Howe remarked that Britain was at war but it would probably be 'over by tea time'.[17] Alan Clark, a backbench MP whose diaries are a rich source for House of Commons gossip, found Conservative MPs openly canvassing the prospect of a military humiliation paving the way for regime change at Westminster, with a 'lash-up coalition' replacing Thatcher in order to 'fudge things through for the last eighteen months of this Parliament'.[18]

In the short run, however, some rapid adjustments at the top of the government helped Thatcher to survive. Rank and file Tory anger at perceived government incompetence was appeased by the resignation of Carrington three days after the invasion. His departure was not entirely fair but he had been badly bruised by criticism that he and Nott received in a meeting with Conservative backbenchers, and he provided a convenient scapegoat. Thatcher was much less comfortable with the person she appointed to succeed him as Foreign Secretary, Francis Pym. She had little in common with this representative of old-style gentry Toryism, who was regarded in certain quarters as her likely successor if the expedition failed. Aloof and condescending rather than actually confrontational, he had survived the purge of the wets the previous autumn. As the crisis unfolded, Pym's preference for exhausting all possible diplomatic means of resolving the crisis was to drive a wedge between the Foreign Office and Number 10. His seniority in the party, however, made him the obvious choice to replace Carrington, and his promotion obviated the need for a wider reconstruction of the government at a time of great difficulty. Nott too offered his resignation. In spite of a notably poor parliamentary performance by the harassed Defence Secretary, however, his offer was refused. To have parted with the architect of the navy cuts, which had arguably opened the door to Argentina, would have called in question the position of the Prime Minister herself. After the initial shock of the invasion Nott recovered his poise, and at certain critical junctures he was to prove a useful ally.

The likelihood of military conflict made it necessary to streamline the decision-making process at the heart of government. Although she was careful to report back to the full Cabinet on a regular basis, true executive power for the duration of the crisis lay with a small War Cabinet, headed by the Prime Minister. Some of its other members selected themselves: Pym and Nott, the two most important relevant ministers, were joined by Whitelaw as the Prime Minister's unofficial deputy. Less predictably, the party chairman Cecil Parkinson was chosen for his ability to present the government's case and, no less importantly, because he could be counted on to side with Thatcher in the event of internal division. These ministers were supplemented by several senior military figures, of whom the most important was Sir Terence Lewin, and a number of officials. Sir Michael Havers, the Attorney-General, supplied advice on questions of international law. On the recommendation of Harold Macmillan, whom Thatcher privately consulted as the most senior living ex-premier, the Chancellor was excluded so that the War Cabinet would not be distracted by considerations of cost. Ministry of Defence personnel, who had been adjusting to the prospect of severe budget cuts, suddenly found themselves in a situation where money was no object. As one senior official later recalled, 'It made us rather lightheaded. We didn't ask the Treasury for anything. We just told them.'[19]

The Prime Minister knew that she had taken a huge gamble in sending the task force. Most commentators agree that no other post-war British leader, with the possible exception of Churchill, would have acted as she did. Having taken the initial decision, however, Thatcher was completely single-minded in seeing it through. From the outset she seems to have been clear that no compromise was really possible with the regime in Argentina. Too much was at stake for both sides. The military junta had whipped up public expectations at home and could not retreat. On her side, Thatcher was privately determined not to settle for anything less than the restoration of the status quo that existed before the invasion. The despatch of the task force demonstrated her commitment to reversing Argentina's occupation and ensuring that the wishes of the islanders – which she described on numerous occasions as being 'paramount' – would prevail. She insisted throughout that although British administration of the islands had been interrupted, the legal position had in no way been affected by the events of 2 April. As she told the Commons, 'I regard the Falkland Islands as being still British and us as still having sovereignty . . . an invasion, an unprovoked aggression, has not altered and does not alter the fact and the law of British sovereignty over those islands'.[20]

Diplomacy and war in the Falklands

Nevertheless Thatcher could not afford to ignore the wider international dimension. Whatever her own views might be, she had to be seen to pursue diplomatic alternatives to armed conflict.

Apart from the old Commonwealth countries of Australia, New Zealand and Canada, and the majority (though not all) of the European Community, most countries were either hostile or indifferent towards the British case. It was therefore important that Sir Anthony Parsons, Britain's ambassador at the United Nations, was able to use his diplomatic skill to secure a resolution calling on Argentina to withdraw its forces.

The country which in fact caused Thatcher the most difficulty was the one on which she had hoped to be able to rely most firmly. The most openly pro-American Prime Minister of the post-war era had developed a strong personal relationship with the new US President, Ronald Reagan, who had taken office in January 1981. Yet the USA did not automatically declare its support for Britain. Against the background of the Cold War, a significant body of opinion within the State Department, together with the US representative at the United Nations, Jeane Kirkpatrick, viewed Argentina as a critical ally against the spread of communism in Latin America. The administration was in fact internally divided on the issue, with the unequivocally pro-British Defence Secretary, Caspar Weinberger offering refuelling facilities, military equipment and access to American intelligence. The President, however, continued to equivocate, condemning Argentina's act of aggression but maintaining a neutral stance on the issue of sovereignty. Although respectful towards Thatcher's posture of dogged defiance, at heart the Americans did not believe that the fate of a collection of barren islands was worth the possibility of a prolonged state of hostilities between the two countries.

Thatcher was disappointed that the US Secretary of State, Alexander Haig, cast himself in the role of mediator, shuttling backwards and forwards between London and Buenos Aires. She faced a delicate diplomatic task. On the one hand she impressed on her American visitors that she meant business, with references to Neville Chamberlain's failed attempts to appease Nazi Germany combined with other unsubtle historical allusions. 'She gripped me by the elbow,' recalled Haig's aide, Admiral Vernon Walters, 'and showed me the portraits of Nelson and Wellington. I think I got the message.'[21] Haig pushed even-handedness to a pedantic extreme, not only attempting at one point to restrict the availability of facilities at the US base on the British-owned Ascension island, but also contemplating giving Argentina advance notice of the British attempt to recover South Georgia. The Prime Minister could not, however, afford to reject compromise solutions out of hand, unpalatable though they might be. Haig's final proposals, delivered to London on 23 April, were anathema to Thatcher. Both sides were to withdraw their forces from the area, paving the way for the installation of a joint US-British-Argentine transitional administration and followed by negotiations for a settlement with 'due regard' to the rights of the inhabitants. Here was a proposed basis for settlement which seemed reasonable, and would therefore be difficult to reject, but which fell short of what Thatcher wanted. With the islanders' wishes to be no longer 'paramount', to her this amounted to 'conditional surrender'.

The pressure on the premier was heightened by the fact that Pym favoured acceptance of the terms. We now know that, had the War Cabinet followed the path of conciliation at this stage, Thatcher would have resigned. It was Nott who proposed a viable solution: the proposals should be put to the junta first. Fortunately for Thatcher, the Argentines acted according to type, putting themselves firmly in the wrong by rejecting the plan as inadequate. This signalled the end of Haig's mission and was followed by a clear American 'tilt' in favour of Britain. Even as a British victory approached, however, Washington continued to appeal to Thatcher to find some way of helping the Argentine government to save face, so that Galtieri would not be replaced by a pro-Soviet alternative. Needless to say, this was of little concern to Thatcher in this, the greatest challenge of her premiership.

Less significant for the outcome of the conflict, but equally irritating to Thatcher, was the attitude of certain sections of the British media. She could rely on strong support from organs of the right-wing tabloid press, such as the *Sun*, whose brazen populism was captured in a spoof reader offer in *Private Eye*, referring to a popular family car of the time, 'Kill an Argie and win a Metro'. The BBC, on the other hand, caused anger in Number 10 with the painstaking neutrality of much of its reporting. Thatcher was particularly angered by its insistence on referring to 'the Argentines' facing 'the British', rather than 'our troops'. As one member of the War Cabinet recalled, 'I was absolutely disgusted with the BBC. Oh God, yes we all were – from Mrs T. down.'[22]

Perhaps the most graphic illustration of Thatcher's attitude towards the coverage of the war came on 25 April, when British forces achieved the first success of the campaign, the retaking of South Georgia. TV cameras captured the moment in Downing Street when the Defence Secretary, with Thatcher standing alongside, announced the news. As the assembled reporters excitedly asked questions about what was going to happen next, Thatcher sharply retorted, 'Just rejoice at that news and congratulate our forces and the Marines', pausing to deliver a further 'Rejoice!'[23] as she and Nott disappeared into Number 10. The exchange betrayed the Prime Minister's relief that the landing had not ended in disaster, and her impatience with a news media whose perspective she believed to be completely different from her own. The repetition of the word 'rejoice' was later to be interpreted, to Thatcher's chagrin, as evidence of an inappropriately celebratory attitude to the war itself.

The most controversial moment of the conflict was the decision, on 2 May, to sink the Argentine cruiser *Belgrano*. It was the task force commander, Rear-Admiral John 'Sandy' Woodward, who identified the vessel as a potential threat to the British fleet, in conjunction with an Argentine aircraft carrier which was also in the area. His request to order the submarine HMS *Conqueror* to attack was approved by the War Cabinet, with an ensuing loss of 321 Argentinian lives. The action led to widespread criticism because the *Belgrano* was outside the designated exclusion zone, an area around the Falklands within which Britain had declared its readiness to attack enemy ships. It was later alleged that Thatcher had ordered the sinking in order to sabotage a new peace initiative from the government of Peru. In a BBC *Nationwide* phone-in programme during the general election campaign a year later, Thatcher was harassed by an unknown member of the public, who returned time and again to the charge that the ship was sunk whilst sailing away from the islands. An audibly rattled premier insisted repeatedly that the ship was a danger to the task force, and had to be sunk. Her relentless questioner was not satisfied by her remark that 'one day, all of the facts, in about 30 years' time, will be published'.[24] This seems to have been a reference to intelligence material which could not be disclosed at the time. Revelations in a later publication by Major Thorp, a signals specialist who had investigated the sinking soon after the war, indicated that *Belgrano* had been ordered to go to a pre-arranged rendezvous point within the exclusion zone, rather than returning to port.[25]

The sinking made sense from a military point of view and had the effect of confining the Argentine surface fleet to base for the rest of the war. Nor is it true that there was a link to the Peruvian peace proposals, which were not made known to the War Cabinet until after *Belgrano* had been sunk. The action did, however, lose Britain a great deal of international goodwill. It marked an escalation of the conflict, which was underlined two days later when the first sinking of a British vessel, the destroyer HMS *Sheffield*, occurred. These two events increased the pressure on Britain to look seriously at the Peruvian proposals, which were very similar to the Haig plan of the previous month. On 5 May Thatcher felt obliged to consult the whole Cabinet, where there was a clear majority now in favour of a negotiated settlement. Even the Prime Minister herself was compelled to consider compromise. Once again, however, the Argentines' obdurate refusal to contemplate anything less than the recognition of full sovereignty rescued Thatcher. The United Nations Secretary-General, Javier Perez de Cuellar, made a final, abortive attempt to put together a peace deal but when this, too, was rejected by the junta, a full-scale armed clash could not be avoided.

Once the fighting had begun in earnest, with a British landing in San Carlos Bay on East Falkland on 21 May, Thatcher played a much less direct role in events. Recognising her own lack of specialist knowledge, for the most part she held back from intervening and relied on the judgement of the military leaders. She had a natural rapport with men whose trained professionalism and concentration on the practicalities mirrored her own sense of certainty. In return they respected her for the confidence that she placed in them, and were grateful for the knowledge that she would back them. 'From the military man's point of view,' Lewin recalled, 'she was an ideal Prime Minister. . . . One wanted a decision and she gave it.'[26] In spite of her growing image as a kind of iron Britannia, however, she was sensitive to the loss of life which inevitably followed: 255 British servicemen were killed in the campaign, along with 746 Argentines. Indeed she probably found this aspect of the crisis harder than did some of her male colleagues, who had experienced fighting at first hand in earlier conflicts. Several times Denis Thatcher, who had served in Italy in the Second World War, had to console and encourage her when news of casualties came through, or when she had to endure long periods of waiting for news from the battle zone. In Carol Thatcher's words, 'I remember her saying, "I wish I knew, I wish I knew," and Denis calmly replying, "This is how it is in a war."'[27] These were indeed anxious times and the eventual Argentine surrender, which took place on 15 June, could not be taken for granted. British landing craft were exposed to merciless attack by Argentinian aircraft. It was fortunate that a number of their bombs failed to go off, and that they failed to hit one of the two aircraft carriers. The sinking of the supply ship *Atlantic Conveyor* with its heavy equipment on 25 May left the British forces gravely short of the helicopters needed to ferry men across the difficult terrain. Argentine troops, securely dug into defensive positions, were not easily overcome. By the end of the campaign the British were running short of ammunition and, with weather conditions worsening, it was becoming harder to manage the ships of the task force. Victory was achieved by a perilously narrow margin and not a moment too soon.

The outcome of the war triumphantly vindicated Thatcher's stance and she gave full expression to her sense of triumph, clashing with Church of England clergy who wished to water down the element of celebration in the thanksgiving service at St Paul's Cathedral in July. In a speech at Cheltenham she asserted that Britain had 'ceased to be a nation in retreat', explicitly invoking the 'spirit of the South Atlantic' as a template for the vigorous confrontation of problems in other areas of national life.[28] The outcome of the conflict caused outsiders to view Britain with renewed respect, with even Soviet observers revising their assessment of a country which they had taken to be in irreversible decline. Some observers were to see the crisis as the point when Thatcher began to become dangerously assertive and self-reliant, and in a sense they were right. As her realistic approach to China over the future of Hong Kong would show, she had not ceased to recognise the continuing realities of Britain's world role. Unlike Eden at the time of the Suez crisis, she had not made the mistake of taking the Americans for granted. She had shown an ability to exercise caution whilst at the same time giving firm leadership.

Thatcher had indelibly associated herself with the future of the Falklands. The 'fortress Falklands' policy, in which her government and its predecessors had declined to invest, now became a reality. By the time Thatcher left office, the extension of the islands' runway and the installation of a permanent garrison, together with the immediate cost of the war itself, had brought the total cost to the Exchequer to approximately £3.5 billion. She made an emotional visit to the Falklands in January 1983 and in the spring of 2007, five years after her official retirement from public life, the eighty-one year old former premier attended a series of events in Britain to mark the twenty-fifth anniversary of the conflict. By her actions she had guaranteed the security of the islands for the foreseeable future, but the dispute with Argentina did not go away. The democratic government in Buenos Aires, which replaced the military junta soon after the war, has continued to assert its claim to the islands, in the expectation that one day a government in London will decide to divest itself of this most southerly vestige of empire.

The Hong Kong settlement

The military option which had resolved the Falklands crisis was wholly inapplicable in the case of the third post-imperial problem to confront Thatcher, the future of Hong Kong. Her negotiations with China over this quite different island group offer closer parallels with the Rhodesian settlement. Once again she was eventually obliged to set aside her personal preferences in a situation where she had limited room for manoeuvre. She had to compromise with people with whom she had nothing in common, and whom she instinctively mistrusted – in this case an entrenched communist regime in which the key figure, Deng Xiaoping, proved to be her equal in resourcefulness and obstinacy. The stakes for Britain, however, were much higher this time.

Rhodesia had been a burden and a distraction which Thatcher had been glad to lay down, a responsibility devoid of significant strategic or economic interest. By contrast, Hong Kong was

Britain's most important surviving colony in terms of its population size and wealth. In addition Britain's position was weak. It had administered the greater part of Hong Kong, known as the New Territories, on the basis of a ninety-nine year lease, negotiated with the now defunct Chinese Empire, which was due to expire in June 1997. It was of little use that Britain owned Hong Kong Island and Kowloon, which accounted for barely 10 per cent of the total land area of the colony, under the terms of a treaty signed in 1842. China could afford to ignore the British claim to this portion of the territory. Not only did the Beijing government possess overwhelming military force, it also had the advantage that Hong Kong was dependent on the mainland for water and other essential supplies. Britain's task, less than two decades from the expiry of the lease, was therefore to negotiate the most favourable terms for the colony from a position of relative disadvantage. It was vital to reach an agreement which would reassure the people of Hong Kong, thus ensuring that those who had driven its spectacular business success did not leave in the expectation of a harsh, anti-capitalist regime imposed by the Chinese leadership. The continued inward flow of investment depended on the maintenance of confidence in the future of the colony.

Thatcher met the Chinese leadership to discuss Hong Kong for the first time in September 1982. Journalist Hugo Young, who accompanied the British negotiating team, was surprised to see the 'iron lady' conform to the diplomatic conventions of the Far East, uncharacteristically 'entering with enthusiasm into the agonising small-talk which preceded the meetings, and lacing her public speeches with grace-notes from Chinese proverbs and the appropriate dabs of history'.[29] On the substance of the talks, however, she met with less success. Emboldened by the recovery of the Falkland Islands three months earlier, she initially overestimated her bargaining strength. It soon became clear that her preferred outcome, an arrangement which would concede sovereignty over Hong Kong Island and Kowloon in return for continued British administration after 1997, was not acceptable to her hard-headed hosts. Deng Xiaoping seemed unimpressed by her forecasts of a collapse of financial confidence if China used the power it undoubtedly possessed, simply to occupy the offshore territory. He also increased the pressure on Britain by making it clear that he would permit no more than two years for the negotiations to be completed.

Thatcher had encountered a nationalism every bit as stubborn as her own. Deng and his colleagues were determined to recover full sovereign control over an area which they viewed as an integral part of their country. In their opinion it had been conceded by an unequal treaty, forced on China when it had been culpably weak. The wheel of history had now decisively turned in their favour and they were determined not to give ground. Thatcher left the detail of the ensuing negotiations in the hands of Sir Geoffrey Howe, who succeeded Francis Pym as Foreign Secretary in June 1983, and returned to China in December 1984 to sign the agreement which he and his Chinese opposite numbers produced. It was Deng who provided the formula on which this was based. The concept of 'one country, two systems' meant that Hong Kong would be allowed a high degree of economic autonomy, and its capitalist identity would be protected for fifty years after its reversion to Chinese rule. The agreement provided no guarantees for democracy in Hong Kong.

Before Thatcher left Downing Street, the communist leadership showed its determination to retain its monopoly of power throughout China, by using military force to crush pro-democracy demonstrations in Beijing's Tiananmen Square. The June 1989 massacre shocked Western observers and influenced Thatcher's later, less than optimistic, assessment of prospects for the agreement she had signed. Interviewed on the eve of Hong Kong's transfer to Chinese rule, she regretted the regime's decision to replace the partly elected Hong Kong legislative council, established by Britain, with a nominated body. Reflecting on Deng's statement, in their September 1982 talks, that he would rather inherit a poverty-stricken colony than tolerate continued British administration, she considered that this 'shows you the communist mind – not concerned about the prosperity, about the well-being of the people'.[30] In spite of her regrets after the event, the Hong Kong agreement was a success for a Prime Minister with a very weak hand to play. It seems doubtful, given the balance of forces at the time, that she could have obtained better terms for the colony. As with Rhodesia, the episode demonstrated

Thatcher's innate realism and – notwithstanding her private feelings about the Foreign Office mentality – her reliance on traditional methods of diplomacy in pursuit of British interests. The iron lady had shown a capacity to bend when circumstances made it necessary.

Notes

1 Margaret Thatcher, *The Downing Street Years* (London, Harper Collins, 1993), p. 309.
2 Thatcher, *Downing Street Years*, p. 74.
3 Quoted in Paul Sharp, *Thatcher's Diplomacy: The Revival of British Foreign Policy* (London, Macmillan, 1999), p. 28.
4 Sir Bryan Cartledge, 'Margaret Thatcher: personality and foreign policy' in S. Pugliese (ed.), *The Political Legacy of Margaret Thatcher* (London, Politico's, 2003), p. 158.
5 Sir John Coles, *Making Foreign Policy: A Certain Idea of Britain* (London, John Murray, 2000), pp. 48–9.
6 Sir Percy Cradock, *In Pursuit of British Interests: Reflections on Foreign Policy under Margaret Thatcher and John Major* (London, John Murray, 1997), p. 22.
7 Letter to Winston Churchill (dismissal over Rhodesian sanctions), 9 November 1978, www.margaretthatcher.org/document/103498 (accessed 25 May 2014).
8 http://hansard.millbanksystems.com/commons/1979/jul/25/southern-africa (accessed 25 May 2014).
9 Robin Renwick, *A Journey with Margaret Thatcher: Foreign Policy under the Iron Lady* (London, Biteback, 2013), p. 31.
10 Lord Carrington, *Reflect on Things Past* (London, Collins, 1988), p. 292.
11 Interview with Lord Carrington, cited in Charles Moore, *Margaret Thatcher: The Authorized Biography: Volume One: Not for Turning* (London, Allen Lane, 2013), p. 502.
12 Thatcher, *Downing Street Years*, p. 173.
13 Quoted in Lawrence D. Freedman, 'The Special Relationship, Then and Now', *Foreign Affairs*, Vol. 85, No. 3 (May–June 2006), p. 64.
14 Jonathan Aitken, *Margaret Thatcher: Power and Personality* (London, Continuum, 2013), p. 324.
15 Lawrence Freedman, *The Official History of the Falklands Campaign, Volume One: The Origins of the Falklands War* (London, Routledge, 2005), p. 209.
16 John Nott, *Here Today, Gone Tomorrow: Recollections of an Errant Politician* (London, Politico's, 2002), p. 74.
17 Robin Harris, *Not for Turning: The Life of Margaret Thatcher* (London, Bantam Press, 2013), p. 207. Reproduced by permission of The Random House Group Ltd and Thomas Dunne Books. All rights reserved.

18 Alan Clark, *Diaries: Into Politics 1972–1982* (London, Phoenix, 2001), p. 317, entry for 7 April 1982.
19 Quoted in Max Hastings and Simon Jenkins, *The Battle for the Falklands* (London, Book Club Associates, 1983), p. 330.
20 House of Commons Intervention [Falkland Islands], 7 April 1982, www.margaretthatcher.org/document/104916 (accessed 25 May 2014).
21 Quoted in Renwick, *A Journey with Margaret Thatcher*, p. 54. `
22 Quoted in Michael Cockerell, *Live from Number 10: The Inside Story of Prime Ministers and Television* (London, Faber and Faber, 1988), p. 273.
23 Remarks on the recapture of South Georgia, 25 April 1982, *Margaret Thatcher: Complete Public Statements 1945–1990 on CD-ROM* (Oxford, Oxford University Press, 1999), 82_098.
24 TV Interview for BBC Nationwide (On the Spot), 24 May 1983, *Margaret Thatcher: Complete Public Statements*, 83_181.
25 D.J. Thorp, *The Silent Listener: British Electronic Surveillance: Falklands 1982* (Stroud, Spellmount, 2011), p. 170.
26 Quoted in John Campbell, *Margaret Thatcher: Volume Two: The Iron Lady* (London, Vintage, 2008), p. 139.
27 Carol Thatcher, *Below the Parapet: The Biography of Denis Thatcher* (London, Harper Collins, 1997), p. 198.
28 Margaret Thatcher, Speech to Conservative rally at Cheltenham, 3 July 1982, www.margaretthatcher.org/document/104989 (accessed 25 May 2014).
29 Hugo Young, *One of Us* (London, Pan, 1990), p. 291.
30 TV interview for CNN (Hong Kong reverts to China), 29 June 1997, www.margaretthatcher.org/document/109211 (accessed 25 May 2014).

5 Establishing supremacy: 1982–1985

Revival and the Falklands factor

The aftermath of Britain's victory in the Falklands witnessed a remarkable resurgence in Thatcher's political fortunes. The Gallup opinion poll recorded an increase in Conservative support from 31 to 46 per cent between March and July 1982, and an even more impressive rise in the Prime Minister's personal approval ratings from 34 to 52 per cent. The extent to which this was directly attributable to the recasting of Thatcher's image as a successful war leader remains open to question. As she did not seek a second term until June 1983, it is hard to be certain just how important the outcome of the conflict was in attracting electoral support. Twice in 1982 Thatcher referred to 'the spirit of the South Atlantic' as a template for the decisive handling of domestic problems – in a speech at Cheltenham in July, and again at the autumn's party conference. Thereafter, however, she made little explicit public mention of the military campaign. A rare exception was a televised guided tour of Number 10, shown in March 1983, in which she pointed out a portrait of the Duke of Wellington, whose example she claimed had inspired her during the Falklands, and a statuette of Royal Marines raising the Union Jack at Port Stanley. Even here, however, as the *Sunday Times* noted, these were fleeting references forming a minor part of 'a lengthy plug for Mrs Thatcher's ideas and values'.[1] The bulk of the interview was concerned with the functions and furnishings of the Prime Minister's residence, and with Thatcher's rise from modest origins to a position where she could implement her vision for the country. Her comments on the two art works centred on the human sadness and sacrifice of war, and there was no suggestion of overt martial celebration.

Perhaps the real significance of the so-called 'Falklands factor' was the way in which it confirmed the impression that, although Thatcher and her policies might be harsh and unattractive to many, at least she offered strong, decisive leadership. As Bernard Ingham, the Prime Minister's Press Secretary, informed her in a private briefing, 'you are respected and admired rather than liked' and in some quarters 'you are also heartily disliked and indeed hated, though still commanding respect'.[2] The war was broadly popular, with opinion polls recording levels of support for the sending of the task force in excess of 80 per cent, although it was clearly not the only factor influencing public opinion in the second half of 1982 and the opening months of 1983.

Military victory provided grounds for optimism at a time when other, more objective indicators of national well-being were not as clear-cut. Unemployment remained stubbornly high at more than 3 million until long after the election. The political impact of joblessness was, however, blunted by the fact that it disproportionately affected the old industrial areas of northern England, Scotland and south Wales, parts of the country which were never likely to be promising territory for the Conservatives. Inflation was down to 5 per cent by the end of 1982, and Howe's budget the following spring introduced some welcome adjustments to personal tax allowances, enabling a modest growth in consumer expenditure. For those in work, especially those in the less intensely unionised service sector, concentrated heavily in southern England and the Midlands, there were reasons to look forward to a better future. Those who were most likely to consider voting for Thatcher were small business people and the upwardly mobile working classes. Her strongest supporters were to be found among those who aspired to a higher material standard of living, who responded to her message of individualism and personal advancement, her rejection of the power of organised labour, and her robust brand of patriotism.

The sale of state-owned industries, with the opportunities they brought to participate in the growth of a 'share-owning democracy', had as yet only hesitantly begun. This was to be much more a feature of the second and third Thatcher governments. The purchase of council houses by their occupiers, however, was firmly established in the first term, with more than 370,000 homes acquired by the autumn of 1982. By giving tenants the chance to own their properties, the government simultaneously encouraged them to transfer their political allegiances. As a rueful Tony Benn told a miners' gathering after the 1983 election, in which he lost his Bristol seat, 'the saddest thing for me was to go along some council housing estates and find the familiar sign of a new front door and a brass knocker – and a Tory sign in the window'.[3] The policy was genuinely popular with people who would not normally have been considered as potential Conservative voters. With her gift for identifying a populist position, Thatcher hailed the right to buy as promoting 'an irreversible shift of power to the people'. Labour might 'huff and puff' at the removal of local authority control over tenants but 'they do not dare pledge themselves to take those houses back because they know we are right, because they know it is what people want'.[4]

The Labour Party was out of step with a significant swathe of public opinion across a range of policy areas. Here again the Falklands conflict threw into relief the problems of a political opposition which appeared weak on matters of national defence. Labour was now committed to a policy of unilateral nuclear disarmament, which aroused the enthusiasm of rank and file activists but failed to reassure ordinary voters at a time when Cold War tensions remained high. Although Michael Foot as party leader articulated broad support for resistance to aggression following Argentina's occupation of the Falklands, a motion opposing the despatch of the task force was only narrowly defeated in the party's National Executive Committee. Future Labour Cabinet minister Jack Straw, at the time a backbench MP, later recalled the damaging effect of internal party divisions over the war, which denied them the 'chance of bathing in any reflected sense of patriotism and national pride. Collectively we looked like vacillating apologists for the Argentinean regime'.[5] After the war some prominent Labour figures, including deputy leader Denis Healey and the future leader, Neil Kinnock, were poorly received when they publicly accused Thatcher of callously seizing political advantage whilst servicemen lost their lives. More thoughtful commentators on the left, such as Eric Hobsbawm, a prominent Marxist historian, recognised the success of Thatcher in tapping into an unexpected but genuine vein of populist patriotism, which many had mistakenly supposed to be wholly obsolete by the 1980s: 'we have won a little war involving few casualties, fought far away against foreigners whom we can no longer even beat at football, and this has cheered people up, as if we had won a World Cup with guns'.[6]

If the war threw caused division in the ranks of the official opposition, it did no favours to the newly formed Social Democrats, whose series of dramatic by-election victories stalled in spring 1982. The SDP's parliamentary gains had been achieved mainly at the expense of Labour, attracting twenty-eight of its MPs in 1981–2 but only one Conservative MP, the little-known Christopher Brocklebank-Fowler. Few 'wet' inclined Conservatives were tempted to join an organisation with an uncertain future; and at local level, a combination of financial pressures, social and family ties kept the majority within the Tory fold. Whatever their feelings about the current direction of the party, most of them felt, as Ian Gilmour protested in a private conversation, 'it is not Margaret Thatcher's party, it is as much ours as hers'.[7] After the Falklands, defection would have seemed positively treasonable to anyone tempted to jump ship. As support for the SDP and their Liberal allies slipped from nearly 40 per cent to less than 25 per cent, it looked as though the prospect of a centrist realignment of British politics was rapidly receding.

The SDP–Liberal Alliance in any case suffered from more fundamental problems, which became fully apparent as the general election approached. The dual leadership of Roy Jenkins for the SDP and David Steel for the Liberals was intended to provide a winning combination of experience and freshness. Instead, it never seemed convincing and Jenkins, a highly cerebral, executive figure occupying an unaccustomed position on the opposition benches, never appeared at ease in the combative atmosphere of the Commons in the early 1980s. In addition, the attempt to offer a studiously moderate, rational alternative to the two old parties – in the much used phrase of the time, policies which were 'tough but tender' – never really gained a purchase on the imagination of the electorate. It was easy to portray their advocacy of a return to consensus politics, embodied in the concept of the 'social market', as a doomed attempt to recreate 'a better yesterday'. Organisationally the SDP never evolved into a genuinely popular grassroots movement. It was too much a party of the *Guardian* reading intelligentsia, without Labour's links to the trade unions. The SDP suffered from a fatal inability to work out exactly how it would 'break the mould' of British politics. On the one hand it appealed to the previously uncommitted, with limited political experience, who wanted to reach out to progressive-minded people of goodwill across the spectrum. At the parliamentary level, meanwhile, it tended to be dominated by ex-Labour politicians, who saw the SDP as little more than an opportunity to recreate the Labour Party of the Attlee-Wilson era, purged of its hard left elements. There were also differences on how the new party should relate to its Liberal allies. Many SDP members regarded a merger as the logical outcome from an early stage, whilst others – notably David Owen, who succeeded Jenkins as party leader after the 1983 general election – were much less enthusiastic.

Thatcher herself was scathing about the Social Democrats, ruthlessly denying them the space in which to carve out a plausible identity. When she referred to them at all, it was to criticise them for not staying in their old party to defend their viewpoint. In an interview with the BBC's political correspondent, for example, she stated that 'the Labour Party will never die' and that 'those people who came out should have had the idealism and the guts to stay within and fight'. By implication, only the Conservatives could provide strong leadership: 'if you're in government . . . you've got to *make* decisions, you've got to uphold decisions and stick to them, and that miscellaneous mishmash in the middle won't achieve anything'.[8] Fundamentally Thatcher regarded the SDP as virtually indistinguishable in policy terms from the failed Labour governments of the 1970s, in which its leaders had served. Of the 'Gang of Four' she developed the greatest regard for Owen, possibly because he took a stronger stance on defence issues than his colleagues. After the bulk of the SDP amalgamated with the Liberals in 1988, leaving Owen isolated as an independent MP, for a time she harboured vain hopes of attracting him to join the Conservative Party.

Re-election

In spite of her clear advantage over both opposition parties, Thatcher did not regard the outcome of the 1983 general election as a foregone conclusion. She agonised over the date, finding excuses to postpone taking a decision in the final strategy meeting with her closest colleagues. Once she had taken the plunge, however, with 9 June the declared date, she threw herself into the campaign with characteristic vigour. In truth, of all post-war general elections up to that point, it was the one whose outcome was the least uncertain. The Conservatives began with a fifteen point lead in the opinion polls and nothing occurred during the campaign to prejudice their chances of winning. Demographic trends made it harder for Labour to win seats, as Britain's old industrial base shrank and the Tory-inclined suburbs became more populous. Foot's party further reduced their chances, however, with the production of a manifesto which spoke only to the agenda of its hard-core left-wing supporters. Pledges of unilateral nuclear disarmament and withdrawal from the European Community – seen at this time by Labour as a capitalist club with little to offer working people – were accompanied by proposals for compulsory planning agreements with private business, more government controls and massive tax increases.

Although the Labour leader remained an energetic and often an outstanding public speaker, he lacked almost all the other skills needed in a modern political leader. A MORI poll commissioned by the party three weeks before polling showed that a worrying 39 per cent of respondents considered Foot to be performing 'not at all well'. Too old at seventy to change his ways, he mistrusted the stratagems of political image-makers, coming across to the electorate as the wholly sincere but slightly eccentric and frequently shambolic intellectual that he was. Few had forgotten the embarrassment of his unconventional appearance on Remembrance Sunday in 1981, when he wore what the press described as a 'donkey jacket' at the solemn Cenotaph service. The decade's leading satirical magazine, *Private Eye*, focused cruelly on his age and the difficulties he faced in holding together a deeply divided party. A typical front cover from March 1983, under the headline 'Labour Leadership New Shock', showed a nurse bending over a white-haired, bespectacled figure in a wheel-chair, who bore an uncanny resemblance to Foot, asking, 'If you want to stay on, nod your head'.[9]

The Conservative campaign did not run entirely smoothly; there was an absurd moment at Stoneleigh Abbey, Warwickshire, when the Prime Minister and her entourage were pulled across a field in a farm trailer, away from the crowd assembled to greet them. Such glitches, however, were minor compared with the series of accidents that dogged the Labour campaign. At the very beginning Foot failed in an attempt to project a sense of optimistic dynamism, when he hurried down the steps of his party's Walworth Road headquarters, in full view of the TV cameras, only to find his car waiting but the driver nowhere to be seen. On another occasion, as he rose to his feet at a meeting to endorse a Labour candidate, the table in front of him collapsed. These indignities were less serious than the party's failure to connect with the wider electorate, or even to present a united front on key policy areas. Most difficult to negotiate was the issue of defence, on which in the course of twenty-four hours Foot, his deputy Denis Healey, and the shadow spokesman, John Silkin, managed to give three different interpretations.

It was not difficult for Thatcher and her colleagues to portray Labour as both extreme and divided. With Cecil Parkinson as party chairman and Lord McAlpine, another trusted Thatcher intimate, as treasurer, Conservative Central Office fought an effective campaign. One bold stroke was the decision to purchase a thousand copies of the Labour manifesto, which were sent out to major Conservative supporters in order to remind them of the opposition agenda they were seeking to defeat. Saatchi and Saatchi, the advertising agency which the Conservatives had engaged for the 1979 election, scored some telling hits on the opposition. One poster showed extracts from the Labour and Communist manifestos alongside each other, to underline how similar many of their policies were. Nor did the Alliance succeed in mounting an effective challenge to Tory dominance. Their announcement of Roy Jenkins as their 'Prime Minister Designate', was never convincing. It was undermined by the SDP leader's rather wooden television appearances, which led to an awkwardly managed decision, midway through the campaign, to make David Steel the public face of the Alliance.

Thatcher herself was the indisputable star of the Conservative campaign, followed by the media as she criss-crossed the country by helicopter, bus and car, from Padstow to Inverness. Just as in 1979, she submitted to a range of photo-opportunities arranged by her campaign team, never betraying anything short of total absorption in whichever activity she was engaged: serving fish and chips, driving a dumper truck, trying out an early mobile phone. In a Bristol machine tool factory, Carol Thatcher, who accompanied her mother and later published a diary of the campaign, noted that she 'whipped round, totally and enthusiastically immersed, questioning their operators about what they did, how quickly, what happened to the end product and please could she have a go at the machine'. Also in evidence was her abiding fascination for the power of technology to project her image more effectively. At a Scottish television studio, Carol recorded her mother asking the interviewer how long the transmission would be, when would it go on air and how much of her was in shot.[10] She had already mastered the autocue, then a novel device for public speaking, after first seeing President Reagan use it on his state visit to Britain the previous summer. Near the close of the campaign, Thatcher appeared at a youth rally at Wembley Stadium, at which comedian Kenny Everett roused the audience with cries of 'Let's bomb Russia!' and 'Let's kick Michael Foot's stick away!' Although never personally guilty of such inanities, Thatcher's own campaign was relentlessly negative, focusing on the dangers posed by socialism to Britain's economic health and national security more than on her government's plans for the future. Her personal guidelines for Conservative candidates, issued at the beginning of the campaign, emphasised that Labour's 'lurch to the left' threatened 'total disruption at home and abroad' and, if implemented, 'would reverse and destroy everything we have accomplished in the past four years'. They were also urged to give strenuous opposition to the Alliance for, 'if the electorate were sufficiently beguiled by it, the result could be to let Labour in – as the Liberals have done more than once in the political past'.[11]

The Conservative manifesto was a remarkably moderate and unexciting document. Apart from promises of local government reform in London and measures of privatisation, it contained little to counter the charge that it merely offered 'more of the same'. Thatcher was later to criticise the manifesto for its inability to 'inspire the Government with the sort of crusading spirit which would have got us off to a good start in the new Parliament'[12] – a curious observation from the person who carried ultimate responsibility for the tone and content of the document. At the time, however, it mattered little. One opinion poll during the campaign suggested that 46 per cent of prospective Conservative voters were influenced by her leadership but only 31 per cent by the party's policies.

The election was unquestionably a triumph for Thatcher, who emerged with a majority of 144 seats – a gain of more than a hundred compared with 1979. It was a disaster for Labour, driven back to its declining industrial heartlands, with just under 28 per cent of the vote and a total of 205 seats, only three of which were to be found in the south outside London. Only the erratic effect of Britain's first past the post electoral system, which left the Alliance with only 23 seats on 25 per cent of the vote, minimised the scale of the disaster for Labour. Most worrying of all from the opposition's viewpoint was an 8 per cent swing to the Conservatives among trade union members. The result immeasurably strengthened Thatcher's position, vindicating her populist appeal to non-traditional sources of support for the Conservative Party, and paving the way for her dominance of the political scene in the mid-1980s.

In planning to reshape her Cabinet after the election, Thatcher had made up her mind to remove Francis Pym from the Foreign Office. Already uncongenial to her for his 'wet' leanings and failure to take a robust line in the Falklands War, he had sealed his fate by an incautious public remark during the election campaign, to the effect that landslide victories rarely produce successful governments. Even now, however, she did not have things all her own way. She was frustrated in her wish to promote Cecil Parkinson, the victorious party chairman whom she had come to see as a possible successor when the time came. On election night he confessed to her that he had been having an affair with his secretary, who was pregnant with his child. Although Thatcher was personally tolerant of others' sexual indiscretions, here was a potential scandal which made it politically unwise for her to appoint him, as she had intended, to succeed Pym. Instead she moved Geoffrey Howe to the Foreign Office, in part a justified reward for his unstinting dedication to the government's economic strategy as Chancellor. Parkinson was moved to the lower-profile position of Trade and Industry, from which he was forced to resign when the affair became public during the October party conference. Whitelaw left the Commons to become Leader of the Lords, a role to which his skills as an emollient elder statesman were well suited. His replacement as Home Secretary, Leon Brittan, had been an effective Chief Secretary to the Treasury, but turned out to lack the toughness and seniority needed for success in a more high-profile role. The other significant appointment was that of Nigel Lawson, a committed free marketer who had served his apprenticeship as a junior Treasury minister and then Energy Secretary, to replace Howe at the Exchequer. He was to oversee a period of remarkable prosperity in the mid-1980s, before the return of inflationary pressures heralded the onset of fresh economic problems, and of differences within the Tory high command, as the decade drew to a close. Although it was to be some time before serious difficulties arose, Thatcher had unwittingly elevated two individuals whose later disenchantment with the Prime Minister would have a devastating effect on her political fortunes. At the Foreign Office, Howe began to exhibit a quiet but dedicated pro-Europeanism, which was to open up a serious rift with Thatcher by the end of the decade. The intellectually self-confident Lawson – one of the few ministers who was prepared to challenge Thatcher in argument – would also prove to have a mind of his own, and to be difficult to handle as a senior colleague. In 1983, these personal issues lay in the distant future. The immediate challenges that Thatcher faced, as her second term began, were of a very different kind.

Taking on the unions

In her first term Thatcher had been persuaded to follow a step by step approach to trade union reform. Norman Tebbit's 1982 Employment Act removed unions' immunity from civil actions arising from industrial disputes, a legal privilege which they had possessed since 1906. It also tightened up restrictions on the closed shop, and made government funds available to finance union ballots. Yet it was not until 1984, with a third Employment Act passed by Tebbit's successor, Tom King, that unions were compelled to hold pre-strike ballots, and required to consult their members every ten years on the payment of the political levy to the Labour Party. The closed shop was not formally outlawed until 1990. The government was setting out a clear direction of travel, whilst pursuing its union reform agenda with a marked degree of caution.

A significant exception, in January 1984, was Thatcher's decision to ban trade union membership at GCHQ, the government's secret information collecting agency at Cheltenham. The background to this move was a series of strikes by workers at the centre, which Thatcher regarded as an unacceptable threat both to national security and to Britain's credibility in the eyes of the USA, with whom it shared intelligence material. The decision was to some extent understandable, in that a total of 10,000 working days at the establishment had been lost in the space of three years, and MI5 and MI6, the best-known branches of the security services, were not unionised. Nevertheless to deprive employees of the right to belong to a union seemed to many to be an unacceptable denial of popular rights, which was on a different plane from the legal reduction of trade union powers and privileges. The move was announced by Sir Geoffrey Howe as political head of the Foreign Office, the government department with responsibility for GCHQ, but it was driven by Thatcher herself. She turned down a compromise offered by the Cabinet Secretary, Sir Robert Armstrong, whereby union membership might have been retained in exchange for guarantees of no further industrial disruption at GCHQ. Armstrong's proposal attracted Howe, a natural moderate who was later to see Thatcher's insistence on an outright ban as an early indication of her inability to accept that a sense of patriotism could be compatible with other loyalties: 'a citizen, she seemed to feel, could never safely be allowed to carry more than one card in his or her pocket, and at GCHQ that could only be Her Majesty's card'.[13]

The episode illustrated a number of other prime ministerial character traits. It showed Thatcher's capacity to throw aside her natural caution in pursuit of an objective on which she had resolved. Little did it matter to her that the ban involved the government in a long-running series of legal challenges from the minority of GCHQ employees who refused to comply. Nor was she bothered by the accusations of tyranny levelled at her by political opponents, with Shadow Foreign Secretary, Denis Healey, vividly describing her as 'the great she-elephant, she who must be obeyed, the Catherine the Great of Finchley'.[14] Indeed she may well have rejected the Armstrong compromise after her Press Secretary, Bernard Ingham, warned that it would look like a U-turn.

The affair also takes its place in a series of government-inspired actions which suggested an obsessive concern with security on Thatcher's part. In March 1984, a junior Ministry of Defence clerk, Sarah Tisdall, was imprisoned for passing information to the *Guardian* newspaper regarding the arrival of US Cruise missiles at the Greenham Common air base in Berkshire. The following year the government prosecuted a more senior civil servant, Clive Ponting, who had leaked evidence to Labour MP Tam Dalyell that Defence Secretary Michael Heseltine had misled the Commons about the sinking of the *Belgrano*. The jury accepted his claim to have been acting in the public interest and acquitted him. Following on the heels of the GCHQ ban, these incidents hinted at a growing authoritarianism on the part of the government. It was an aspect of Thatcherism to which its author was unwilling to draw attention, when she came to recall the events of the 1980s. In *The Downing Street Years* the GCHQ affair receives only a passing mention in a footnote.

The miners' strike

Much more significant, and treated at appropriate length in Thatcher's memoirs, was her handling of the year-long miners' strike of 1984–5. In terms of Thatcher's survival as Prime Minister, and her ability to carry out her agenda in government, it was as important as the Falklands had been in her first term. The main events of the strike were captured on television, vividly illustrating the polarisation of politics in the mid-1980s. Confrontations between striking miners and those who wished to continue working, and the conflict between pickets and the unprecedented numbers of police who were drafted in to maintain order in the coalfields, engendered a long-lasting sense of division and grievance. Almost three decades later it ensured that Thatcher's death would be greeted with an astonishing glee in many former coal-producing parts of northern England. The general secretary of the Durham Miners' Association, for example, who turned seventy on the day of her passing, described it as 'one of the best birthdays I have ever had' and declared that 'there's no sympathy from me for what she did to our community. It's a great day for all the miners.'[15]

The issue which triggered the dispute was the National Coal Board's announcement, in March 1984, of its intention to close twenty uneconomic pits, with a loss of 20,000 jobs. This was widely believed to be the preliminary to a more ambitious rationalisation of the industry, under the hand of Thatcher's new appointee as chairman of the Board, Ian MacGregor. He was a Scots-born businessman who had made a fortune, and a reputation for strike-breaking, in America. He had already impressed the Prime Minister as head of British Steel, where he had restored profitability by shedding manpower. In the course of the coal strike she was to develop reservations about his handling of public relations, and she even feared that he might allow himself to be outmanoeuvred in negotiations with the miners' leader, Arthur Scargill. Initially, however, according to Jim Prior, who had recommended MacGregor as the man to overhaul the steel industry, 'she once went so far as to say that he was the only man she knew who was her equal'.[16]

There could not have been a greater contrast than that between MacGregor's robust free market philosophy and the Marxist ideology of his principal antagonist in the mining industry. Arthur Scargill had become President of the National Union of Mineworkers in April 1982 on the retirement of the more moderate Joe Gormley. A hard-nosed negotiator, with a gift for both platform oratory and media relations, Scargill was not prepared to accept the closure of a single pit on grounds of economic necessity. His ideal was the mass deployment of pickets to change government policy. Scargill looked back with pride on his role in closing down the Saltley coking plant in the West Midlands, twelve years earlier, an action which had inflicted a signal humiliation on the Heath government. Beyond the rescue of threatened mining communities, however, he had a wider political agenda – to mobilise working people in pursuit of a socialist remaking of society. During the strike he declared that 'We want to save our jobs. But more – we want to prepare the way for a transformation, rolling back the years of Thatcherism'.[17] In calling the action he made two vital mistakes. He declined to call a national ballot on strike action, instead relying on pickets from the more militant regions, such as his native Yorkshire, to bring their weight to bear on other areas. In this way he surrendered a key moral advantage to his opponents. Second, he gravely mistimed the strike by calling the miners out in the spring, so that they would have to maintain their solidarity for nine months, in face of growing material hardship, before the onset of winter imposed an increased demand for coal.

The miners' leader was also unfortunate in that Thatcher's government was much better prepared for industrial action than it had been at the time of the threatened strike in February 1981. A secret Cabinet committee, codenamed MISC57 and chaired by a trusted official, Peter Gregson, was set up to oversee government planning. Stockpiles of coal were built up at the power stations in the years that followed. Road hauliers were ready to move coal in case railwaymen came out on strike in support of the miners – a fear which in fact proved groundless. Thatcher possessed several other advantages. Conservatives of all hues were united in a wish not to be beaten by the union which had toppled the Heath government a decade earlier. Thatcher's Energy Secretary, Peter Walker, the only prominent Cabinet 'wet' still in office after the 1983 election, was just as determined as the Prime Minister to defeat Scargill. Walker was particularly struck by the fact that the NUM leader was opposed to employees' involvement in the management of industry, on the grounds that 'if it succeeded the workers would become happy participants in a capitalist system and difficult to detach from it. The whole objective of Marxist philosophy is to overcome and destroy capitalism.'[18]

Scargill further damaged his cause by his refusal to condemn the intimidation of working miners which occurred in many pit villages. Although there were undoubted questions surrounding the drafting of large numbers of police across county boundaries to contain the strike, televised scenes of violence on picket lines damaged the strikers' cause far more. The episode which created the strongest impression was the so-called 'Battle of Orgreave'. This was a coking plant in South Yorkshire to which Scargill directed thousands of flying pickets in May–June 1984, in a bid to deny fuel to Scunthorpe steel works, resulting in sustained clashes between miners and mounted police. Opinion polls suggested that the number of people who disapproved of the methods employed by the striking miners never fell below 79 per cent.

Divisions within the labour movement also helped the government. The TUC leadership could not disown the miners, but it had no real sympathy with Scargill's all or nothing strategy. For various reasons the miners were themselves far from united. In the less militant Nottinghamshire and South Derbyshire coalfields, a majority defied the NUM leadership. This fissure within the movement led eventually to the formation of a breakaway organisation, the Union of Democratic Mineworkers. Edwina Currie, one of a small number of Conservative MPs elected for mining constituencies, recalled a miner asking her with incredulity, 'What's this about rolling back the tides of Thatcherism, Edwina? We voted for the tides of Thatcherism. That's why you're here.'[19] Of course it is unlikely that more than a minority of miners had been converted to the philosophy of the Conservative government. The Midlands was less affected by pit closures, and the miners there simply wanted to carry on working. They also resented the tactics of mass picketing, and objected to Scargill's failure to hold a ballot.

The strike presented Neil Kinnock, who had succeeded Michael Foot as Labour Party leader in October 1983, with his first major challenge, and it was one to which, by common consent, he failed to rise. Seventeen years Thatcher's junior, and with no experience of government, he was already struggling to assert himself against his recently victorious antagonist. In their clashes on the floor of the House of Commons, Thatcher used her mastery of detail and her authoritarian personality to patronise him. Her dismissive replies to Kinnock's challenges at the despatch box were legion: 'the Right Hon. Gentleman doesn't have a clue about the way in which these matters work'; 'if the Right Hon. Gentleman had listened a bit more carefully he might have learnt a little more'.[20] The miners' strike, however, tested Kinnock at a more fundamental level. Although by background and inclination a member of Labour's soft left tradition, he pragmatically recognised the need to move the party towards the political centre, from which it might hope to secure electoral success. He faced a formidable challenge in seeking to distance his party from the activities of far left groups such as Militant Tendency, who had gained control of Liverpool City Council, and from prominent individuals such as Tony Benn, returned to the Commons in the March 1984 Chesterfield by-election, and Ken Livingstone, the leader of the Greater London Council.

From a Welsh mining background himself, Kinnock's emotional sympathies were with the strikers battling to save their livelihoods. Political calculation, however, combined with distaste for Scargill's cavalier attitude towards formal democratic procedures, prevented him from fully aligning himself with the strikers. Kinnock fell between two stools, trying to square the circle in his first conference speech as party leader by even-handedly condemning the violence of 'the stone-throwers' on the picket lines and 'the cavalry charges' of the police, along with 'the violence of despair' and of long-term unemployment.[21] Two decades later, he admitted that 'I still curse myself for not taking the chance and saying to a miners' meeting . . . you will not get sympathetic action without a ballot'.[22] In truth, however, such a move could have precipitated a serious split in the Labour movement. Thatcher ruthlessly exploited Kinnock's difficulties. In an exchange in the Commons in July 1984, for example, she quoted a branch colliery president who had described Kinnock as the 'puppet' of 'the people who believe in extra-parliamentary tactics'. Labour, she alleged, was 'a party which has allied itself to the wreckers against the workers'.[23]

Victory at a price

On the whole, Thatcher handled the crisis effectively from the government's point of view. At the beginning of the strike she reined in MacGregor, who expressed a desire for aggressive,

American-style law enforcement tactics. In his account of the strike he recalled telling her that in the USA, the authorities would have called out the National Guard. 'She reminded me rather sharply that it wasn't America and such a move would be political dynamite.'[24] Nonetheless, Thatcher insisted that there should be much stronger police protection for those who wished to carry on working. She told MacGregor and Walker that it was 'essential to stiffen the resolve of Chief Constables to ensure that they fulfilled their duty to uphold the law'.[25] She also intervened more than once to demand that the courts speed up the processing of criminal cases involving pickets. In her public pronouncements she constantly emphasised the importance of upholding the right of working miners to go about their business unmolested. Speaking to an audience of farmers at Banbury, Oxfordshire, for example, she declared with unusual vehemence, 'I must tell you that what we have got is an attempt to substitute the rule of the mob for the rule of law, and it will not succeed'.[26] Behind the scenes, however, she was less certain of ultimate victory than her defiant public stance might have suggested. In July, a major crisis loomed with the onset of industrial action by the dock workers. Cabinet papers reveal that at this stage the Prime Minister and her closest colleagues were considering the use of troops to maintain the flow of essential supplies, and the declaration of a state of emergency. In the event, the crumbling of the dock strike after twelve days lifted the immediate pressure from the government. She thus avoided the political damage suffered by Edward Heath, whose calling of no fewer than five states of emergency in his three and a half year premiership exacerbated the sense of an uncontrollable national crisis in the early 1970s.

In public the government maintained the official position that the dispute was being handled by the National Coal Board. This was true to the extent that ministers did not negotiate directly with the miners' leaders. Indeed, Thatcher never met Scargill in person, and she held talks with the TUC leaders only once, towards the end of the strike. Again, she learned from the example of Heath, who had met with union leaders as Prime Minister without success. She did, however, maintain contact with working miners' groups, and used the services of David Hart, an eccentric right-wing businessman with access to Downing Street, as a source of information and as a link to anti-Scargill elements in the Nottinghamshire coalfield. This detached posture gave the government a degree of flexibility which it would have lost through direct engagement in the dispute, and ensured that Scargill's rhetoric was directed more against MacGregor than against the government. Nor did the government use its own employment laws to make the NUM liable for its actions in the civil courts. On this point Thatcher had to be persuaded by her Energy Secretary that it was better to rely instead on the existing provisions of traditional common law to support police action against pickets. Walker feared that if the government made use of the legislation, there was a danger of the miners reuniting, and of the strike winning more sympathy from the wider trade union movement. It was a group of working miners, supported behind the scenes by David Hart, who took the NUM to court for its failure to call a ballot. Their action resulted in a court order for the sequestration of union funds and the dramatic presentation of a legal writ to Scargill in the midst of the September 1984 TUC conference. This helped to deter other unions from taking any action which might incur the seizure of their own financial resources.

Thatcher was directly involved in another development in the autumn of 1984 which, had the Coal Board been left to handle it without ministerial intervention, might have saved Scargill from defeat. This was the threat of strike action by a separate union, the National Association of Colliery Overmen, Deputies and Shotfirers, known as NACODS, who were responsible for maintaining the safety of the mines. Had the so-called 'pit deputies' withdrawn their labour, the working mines in Nottinghamshire would have been forced to close and the slow return of miners to work would have been derailed. To the alarm of Thatcher and Walker, MacGregor did not seem to have appreciated the importance of NACODS to the dispute as a whole, and he was prepared to risk their taking industrial action. It was only on the insistence of the Prime Minister and the Energy Secretary that he reached a deal with them which guaranteed the continuing isolation of the NUM. Thatcher personally telephoned the Coal Board chairman in October 1984 to ensure that he did everything possible to reach a settlement with NACODS, abandoning his plan to replace the pit deputies with private staff who would not have been able to perform their functions.

Two more prime ministerial interventions behind the scenes played a part in bringing final victory for the government. In December she used her newly established contact with Mikhail Gorbachev, who was soon to be appointed leader of the USSR, to stop in its tracks Scargill's bid to secure financial support from the Soviet trade unions. In February 1985, alerted by a vigilant Walker, she overruled MacGregor when he came close to agreeing a settlement with the TUC by which no pit could be closed unless it was 'deemed exhausted' – a formula which, had it found its way to the miners' leaders, would have effectively represented a climb-down by the Coal Board. By this stage the drift of miners back to work was eroding the last vestiges of union solidarity. Scargill's credibility had been seriously damaged by revelations that he had sought funding from the despotic regime of Colonel Gaddafi, leader of Libya. More importantly, as the economic pressures on striking miners and their families mounted during the winter, the NUM leader's predictions of imminent victory sounded increasingly hollow. On 3 March 1985, almost a year after it had started, the strike came to an end.

The outcome of the strike was the Conservative Party's delayed revenge for the humiliation inflicted on the Heath government a decade earlier. It established beyond doubt the right of the Coal Board to manage the industry, and inflicted a severe setback to militant trade unionism. To admirers of Thatcher such as her adviser and biographer, Robin Harris, it had shown that 'no union or group of unions could ever again make the country ungovernable' and had made the success of the modern British economy possible.[27] Scargill's defeat boosted Thatcher's image as a strong leader, just as the Falklands had done in the sphere of foreign policy. Kinnock later asserted that, by diverting the Labour Party from the much-needed process of internal reform, the strike prevented it from making the gains it needed in the 1987 general election, which in the long run would deny him the chance of victory in the 1992 contest.

The government's victory had, however, been achieved at a considerable price. The immediate cost of the strike has been estimated at £2.75 billion, with the police operation alone carrying a price tag of £200 million. If the overall effect on national output is included, the total figure was probably more than £5 billion. For Thatcher, her success came at a personal price which did not perhaps concern her, but which was still significant. Although most voters deplored Scargill's tactics, and welcomed his defeat, there was a sense of unease at Thatcher's lack of sympathy with the decimated pit communities at the centre of the dispute. John Monks, a moderate TUC official who met Thatcher towards the end of the strike, recalled her total lack of interest in finding a face-saving formula for the NUM: 'there was no generosity, no quarter, no echo of Churchill's "in victory, magnanimity"'.[28] Her public rhetoric, too, suggested an inability to move beyond a straightforward desire to crush her opponents. Newspaper reporting of an address she gave to the 1922 Committee of Conservative MPs in July 1984 left an indelible impression of harshness. In the speech she explicitly compared the strike to the struggle against Argentina two years earlier, declaring that 'at the time of the [Falklands] conflict they had to fight the enemy without; but the enemy within, much more difficult to fight, was just as dangerous to liberty'. The phrase stood out, overshadowing a more conciliatory later remark that 'once the disputes were resolved, the Government should seek a good working relationship with the trade unions'. Referring to this final phrase, *The Times* noted that 'she did not enlarge on this and her meaning was not plain'.[29] 'The enemy within' would resound across the years, creating an impression of a leader who was unable to distinguish between foreign foes and British citizens who were at odds with the government.

We now know that Thatcher had intended to return to the same theme in her speech to the October 1984 party conference in Brighton. She was obliged to change the text at short notice, as a result of a shocking event completely unrelated to the mining dispute. On the night before she was due to deliver the speech, IRA terrorists detonated a bomb in the hotel in which she was staying, causing five deaths and serious injury to others. In the original version of the speech, Thatcher had planned to warn of an organised threat to liberty involving not just the striking miners but large sections of the Labour movement. She was going to refer to 'the shadow which has fallen across freedom since last we met' and to link the violence of the pickets with the growth of a new wave of political extremism, which had taken over the main opposition party. 'What has the modern Labour Party come to when its leader has to set aside a large part of his [conference] speech to try and persuade his members that the law should be obeyed; that the way to gain power is through the ballot box, not by insurrection.'[30] The terrorist attack meant that such stark political partisanship would have been inappropriate. The sentiments expressed in the draft speech did, however, clearly reflect her own sense of the Conservative Party as the embattled defender of values threatened by the rise of left-wing militancy on the coalfields and elsewhere.

Thatcher contemplated, but did not carry out, the privatisation of the coal industry; that step was to be taken by John Major's government after her fall from office. She did, however, make further pit closures likely by her privatisation of electricity generation, which meant that the power industry no longer had to buy its fuel in the protected market which was British coal. Privately she was critical of the scale of the shutdown – thirty-one of the remaining fifty mines – announced by her successor's government in October 1992. She had developed a personal regard for the working Nottinghamshire miners, who now felt betrayed by the revelation that they would not be spared from the projected rationalisation. In her memoirs Thatcher wrote of her sense of obligation to those who had defied the militants. 'Where would we be if we had closed the pits at which moderate miners would have gone on working, and kept more profitable but more left-wing pits open?'[31] Nonetheless, there can be little doubt that her defeat of the 1984–5 strike was the decisive event in the long-term contraction of the mining industry. The humbling of the country's most formidable union made possible the steady reduction of Britain's dependence on coal in subsequent decades. Thatcher's victory both reshaped the economic landscape and consolidated her hold on power.

Notes

1 Quoted in Michael Cockerell, *Live from Number 10: The Inside Story of Prime Ministers and Television* (London, Faber and Faber, 1988), p. 278.

2 Media: Ingham Minute to MT ('Media relations – stocktaking and look ahead'), 3 August 1982, www.margaretthatcher.org/document/122990 (accessed 12 June 2014).

3 Quoted in Brian Harrison, *Finding a Role: The United Kingdom 1970–1990* (Oxford, Oxford University Press, 2010), p. 147.

4 Margaret Thatcher, Speech to Conservative Party Conference, 8 October 1982, www.margaretthatcher.org/document/105032 (accessed 12 June 2014).

5 Jack Straw, *Last Man Standing: Memoirs of a Political Survivor* (London, Pan Books, 2013), p. 147.

6 Eric Hobsbawm, 'Falklands fallout' in Stuart Hall and Martin Jacques (eds), *The Politics of Thatcherism* (London, Lawrence and Wishart in association with *Marxism Today,* 1983), p. 269.

7 Quoted in Ivor Crewe and Anthony King, *SDP: The Birth, Life and Death of the Social Democrat Party* (Oxford, Oxford University Press, 1995), p. 114.

8 TV interview for BBC (SDP failure to 'fight from within', 'The Labour Party will never die'), 3 June 1983, *Margaret Thatcher: Complete Public Statements 1945–1990 on CD-ROM* (Oxford, Oxford University Press, 1999), 83_233.

9 *Private Eye*, No. 554, 11 March 1983.

10 Carol Thatcher, *Diary of an Election: With Margaret Thatcher on the Campaign Trail* (London, Sidgwick and Jackson, 1983), pp. 40 and 83.

11 General Election: MT letter to all Conservative Candidates (1983 General Election), 18 May 1983, www.margaretthatcher.org/document/131420 (accessed 22 June 2014).

12 Margaret Thatcher, *The Downing Street Years* (London, Harper Collins, 1993), p. 305.

13 Sir Geoffrey Howe, *Conflict of Loyalty* (London, Macmillan, 1994), p. 348.

14 Quoted in Hugo Young, *One of Us: A biography of Margaret Thatcher* (London, Pan, 1990), p. 357.

15 David Hopper, quoted in *The Daily Telegraph*, 9 April 2013, p. 23.

16 James Prior, *A Balance of Power* (London, Hamish Hamilton, 1986), p. 130.

17 *Sunday Times*, 28 October 1984, quoted in Michael Crick, *Scargill and the Miners* (London, Penguin, 1985), p. 140.

18 Peter Walker, *Staying Power: An Autobiography* (London, Bloomsbury, 1991), p. 167.

19 Quoted in Iain Dale (ed.), *Margaret Thatcher: A Tribute in Words and Pictures* (London, Weidenfeld & Nicolson, 2005), p. 170.

20 Quoted in Martin Westlake, *Kinnock: The Biography* (London, Little, Brown, 2001), p. 259.

21 Leader's speech, Blackpool 1984, Neil Kinnock (Labour), quoted in http://www.britishpoliticalspeech.org/speech-archive.htm?speech=190 (accessed 2 July 2014).

22 Quoted in Francis Beckett and David Hencke, *Marching to the Fault Line: The Miners' Strike and the Battle for Industrial Britain* (London, Constable, 2009), p. 76.

23 Government policy (Hansard, 31 July 1984), http://hansard.millbank systems.com/commons/1984/jul/31/government-policy (accessed 2 July 2014).

24 Ian MacGregor, *The Enemies Within: The Story of the Miners' Strike, 1984–5* (London, Collins, 1986), p. 193.

25 Coal, No. 10 record of conversation (MT-MacGregor-Walker), 14 March 1984, www.margaretthatcher.org/document/133144 (accessed 5 July 2014).

26 Remarks on Orgreave picketing, 30 May 1984, www.margaretthatcher. org/document/105691 (accessed 5 July 2014).

27 Robin Harris, *Not for Turning: The Life of Margaret Thatcher* (London, Bantam Press, 2013), pp. 234–5. Reproduced by permission of The Random House Group Ltd and Thomas Dunne Books. All rights reserved.

28 Quoted in Gillian Shephard, *The Real Iron Lady: Working with Margaret Thatcher* (London, Biteback, 2013), p. 79.

29 *The Times*, 20 July 1984, quoted in Speech to 1922 Committee ('the enemy within'), www.margaretthatcher.org/document/105563 (accessed 5 July 2014).

30 Conservatism: Draft MT speech (on arrival at Brighton), 8 October 1984, www.margaretthatcher.org/document/136222 (accessed 4 October 2014).

31 Thatcher, *Downing Street Years*, p. 686.

6 Pinnacle of power: 1985–1988

An uncertain ascendancy

The three years which followed the collapse of the miners' strike saw Thatcher at the high point of her power and influence. On 11 June 1987, she consolidated her position with a third general election success. Although her majority slipped a little, from 144 to 102 seats, this was still an impressive achievement. It was true that her party had won the 1951, 1955 and 1959 contests, but this had been under three different leaders. The last individual to equal this record was Lord Liverpool, Tory premier in the early nineteenth century, whose consecutive victories in 1812, 1818 and 1826 had been gained in a wholly different, pre-democratic political context. On 3 January 1988, Thatcher overtook H.H. Asquith as the twentieth century's longest-serving Prime Minister. Long before this milestone it had become impossible to dismiss Thatcher as a temporary phenomenon. By the middle of the decade, it was acknowledged across the political spectrum that, for good or ill, she had already made an indelible mark on her country, and that she possessed an unprecedented opportunity to continue shaping its future. She attracted remarkable loyalty from her grassroots supporters, including young Conservatives whom SDP co-founder Shirley Williams was to describe as 'boy warriors in twill trousers and striped shirts who would gladly have given their lives for her'.[1] Meanwhile her enemies, both within the Conservative Party and in the ranks of the official opposition, had to accommodate themselves to her ascendancy. An internal Labour Party report in 1985 into the political attitudes of the generation who had started to think about politics in the mid-1970s, identified a significant section of the electorate as 'Thatcher's Children'. The attitudes of this group were typified by a liking for the values of toughness, individualism and aspiration, which they associated with the Prime Minister: 'they admired Thatcher even if they loathed her, liked aggression, and hated Militant and other left-wing groups, whom they believed were trying to pull the country back and stop growth and efficiency'.[2]

In the world of culture and academia, with some exceptions, Thatcher was almost universally detested. Resentment at her hostility to subsidies for the arts was combined with scorn for her self-righteousness and her supposedly narrow-minded tastes. Theatre director Jonathan Miller, for example, expressed disgust for her 'odious suburban gentility and sentimental, saccharine patriotism, catering to the worst elements in commuter idiocy'.[3] Meanwhile a new genre of 'alternative' comedians and popular musicians, many of whom came from depressed northern cities, reacted to Thatcher in even more vitriolic terms. Manchester-born Morrissey, lead singer with The Smiths, was interviewed by Special Branch in 1988 as a possible security threat over the lyrics of the song, 'Margaret on the guillotine'. Elvis Costello escaped similar attention for another composition openly anticipating Thatcher's death, 'Tramp the dirt down'. It seemed that in some circles, the only response to Thatcher's political success was to escape into fantasies about her physical demise. More innocent was the satire of *Private Eye*, in which the Prime Minister was portrayed in two long-running cartoon strips. In 'Battle for Britain', based on a genre of Second World War story comics popular with boys, she was the sinister 'Herr Thatchler', whose fascist regime was opposed by the Labour Party in the form of plucky but incompetent British soldiers. After the 1987 election it was replaced by a spoof on the post-war science fiction comic strip series 'Dan Dare', with Thatcher as the evil Maggon, 'Supreme Ruler of the Universe'.

By this stage Thatcher had become an instantly recognisable figure, even among sections of society who did not follow public affairs with rapt attention. In an increasingly visual political culture, of course, she stood out as the only woman both on the government front bench and at Conservative conferences, flanked by male politicians in identical grey suits, many sporting the large framed glasses that were in vogue in the second half of the decade. Numerous observers commented on how well the premier coped with the relentless pressure of the job and, as she entered her sixties in October 1985, how little the passage of time had affected her physical appearance. Her adoption of 'power dressing', the late 1980s fashion for less feminine business suits with padded shoulders, enhanced her aura of personal dominance. A study by two leading psychiatrists in December 1985 found that even sufferers from advanced dementia, who could not remember other everyday information, were able to give 'Maggie Thatcher' or 'Mrs Thatcher' as the name of the current Prime Minister. 'Neither Mr Macmillan nor Mr Wilson in their fifth year of office,' they concluded, 'was recalled as often by the demented population as Mrs Thatcher.'[4]

What seemed to outsiders an unchallengeable supremacy did not, however, entirely correspond with reality. Between the spring of 1985 and the autumn of 1986, the Conservatives registered less than 35 per cent approval ratings in a succession of opinion polls. The economic recovery which made it possible for Thatcher to win a third term proved to be short-lived, with difficulties surfacing once again by the end of the decade. The mid-1980s also witnessed new concerns about Thatcher's style of leadership. Long-standing concerns regarding her autocratic handling of professional relationships intensified in this period. Behind the scenes she was increasingly reliant on the support of her two most important Downing Street advisers – her Press Secretary, Bernard Ingham, and her influential Foreign Affairs Private Secretary from 1984 onwards, Charles Powell. Cabinet reshuffles became more frequent and, in some of these, the Prime Minister seemed to be reacting to, rather than controlling events. In private, and sometimes in public, tensions with senior ministers were a potentially destabilising force for the government. Thatcher remained a force to be reckoned with almost until the end of her premiership, with a remarkable capacity to drive forward her own agenda. Nonetheless the seeds of her eventual downfall were being sown in the years of her apparently unassailable ascendancy.

The Westland affair

It was a dispute over the future of a little-known helicopter manufacturing firm which threw into relief the dangers of Thatcher's methods of government. On the face of it, the issues involved in the Westland affair of December 1985 to January 1986 seemed relatively unimportant. Yet they raised questions of constitutional principle and political practice which at one point seemed to threaten the survival of the government.

The crisis had its origins in the problems of the Somerset-based Westland Helicopter Company, which faced the prospect of bankruptcy in the autumn of 1985. The firm's directors favoured a rescue package organised by the American company, Sikorsky. This was challenged by Michael Heseltine, Defence Secretary since January 1983, who argued that it was strategically important to ensure that Britain's only helicopter manufacturing firm was saved by a European-based consortium. This brought him into direct conflict with Thatcher and Leon Brittan, Trade and Industry Secretary since his demotion from the Home Office in September. Their position was that the government should leave the decision to Westland's board. Heseltine challenged this view by lobbying a number of European arms procurement directors, with a view to their refusing to buy non-European helicopters. The clash between Heseltine and Thatcher intensified after he claimed, following a meeting of the Cabinet's economic committee on 9 December, that she had cancelled a further planned session at which he intended to develop his case. She insisted that no such meeting had been scheduled, and the relevant Number 10 files provide no evidence of a cancellation. When Heseltine tried to raise Westland in full Cabinet on 12 December, she refused to allow a discussion. He was further angered when it turned out that his protest at this move was not recorded, as he had requested, in the Cabinet minutes. Government files released at the end of December 2014 indicate that Thatcher must have been aware of Heseltine's determination to fight his corner. A minute from her parliamentary private secretary dated 23 December 1985 recorded a discussion between the Defence Secretary and Lord Fanshawe, a former Tory MP and a director of Westland, in which Heseltine 'had given him the impression (but perhaps had not actually said) that he would resign if the company did not adopt the European option', and had spoken about his 'humiliation' in Cabinet.[5]

Over Christmas Heseltine continued to make the case for a European bid, even though Westland's directors had by now announced their acceptance of the Sikorsky package. In so doing he set himself against the collective will of the Cabinet, since he had no allies among his colleagues. The narrow issue of Westland's fate had, in fact, developed by now into a battle of wills between Thatcher and one of the few ministers who was prepared to stand up to her. Behind the arguments lay a deep-seated clash of personalities. Undoubtedly Thatcher appreciated Heseltine's political skills, and had appointed him Defence Secretary in the justified expectation that he would take on the anti-nuclear protest movement in a suitably robust manner. At the same time, however, she was mistrustful of his gift for self-promotion, usually absenting herself from his conference speeches, which perhaps went down too well for her liking with the Tory faithful. Her dislike of him was evident in her memoirs where, after acknowledging that they shared certain characteristics – 'we are ambitious, single-minded and believe in efficiency and results' – she went on to say that 'whereas with me it is certain political principles that provide a reference point and inner strength, for Michael such things are unnecessary'.[6] Although he was never bracketed with the Cabinet 'wets' – indeed on issues such as privatisation and the sale of council houses, his position was undeniably 'Thatcherite' – he favoured an interventionist approach to industry which did not fit easily with the premier's free market instincts. The dispute also highlighted Thatcher's evident preference for an American rather than a European solution. Indirectly Westland raised the issue of differing attitudes towards closer European integration at the highest levels of government, an issue which would prove a damaging fault-line in Thatcher's final years as Conservative Party leader.

The war of words between Prime Minister and Defence Secretary reached a new level early in January 1986, when the latter stated his view that the Sikorsky plan would prove damaging to European contracts. With a clear intention of weakening Heseltine's argument, Thatcher referred his claim to Sir Patrick Mayhew who, as Solicitor-General, acted as one of the government's law officers. An excerpt from Mayhew's subsequent letter to Heseltine, referring to 'material inaccuracies' in his case, was then made public. The episode presented a direct challenge to Thatcher's authority as Prime Minister and some of her colleagues wondered why she had not dismissed the rebellious minister before Christmas; indeed, Brittan privately urged this course of action on her. In an interview after the crisis was over, she stated that had she done so, 'the press would have said, "There you are: Old Bossy Boots at it again and she is being anti-European!"'[7] Thatcher loyalist, Nicholas Ridley, who told her at the time that he resented Heseltine's refusal to accept the doctrine of collective responsibility, found her too wary of what he might do if sacked: 'it was her familiar fear of the dangers of having powerful figures loose on the backbenches'.[8] At Cabinet on 9 January, however, she reasserted herself by declaring that all statements on Westland would have to be cleared with the Cabinet office. Heseltine regarded this as unacceptable and, to the astonishment of his colleagues, walked out of the Cabinet to announce his resignation to the waiting media. Thatcher moved quickly to regroup, promptly announcing Heseltine's replacement by the Scottish Secretary, Sir George Younger. Both at the time and in her memoirs, she insisted that Heseltine had found himself in a minority of one. For his part, he claimed that she had denied him the hearing he deserved, misusing the doctrine of collective Cabinet responsibility to prevent him from making his case.

This was not the end of the crisis. For Thatcher, potentially the most damaging aspect of the affair was the question of who had authorised the leaking of the Solicitor-General's letter which, by strict constitutional convention, should have remained confidential. In a Commons debate on 23 January she denied knowledge of the leak. In the febrile atmosphere of the time, however, a scapegoat was required and this was to be Leon Brittan, who resigned the following day after admitting that he had authorised the release of Mayhew's letter. Several years later he claimed that he had received 'express permission' from Bernard Ingham and Charles Powell to do so – an admission which, had it been made at the time, might conceivably have brought about Thatcher's downfall. In his own later account of the episode, Ingham refused to go beyond an acknowledgement that he should have explicitly warned Brittan's press officer, Colette Bowe, not to release the letter, rather than merely declining to seek Thatcher's approval of it. If he was guilty of anything, he argued, it was of 'tacit acceptance in the sense that I did not actively object to a ministerial decision to disclose' the letter.[9]

The episode raised serious concerns, not just about Thatcher's conduct of relations with her colleagues, but also about her integrity. Even if she had not personally been behind the leaking of Mayhew's letter, she made clear in a Commons statement on 23 January that she had wanted the substance of his opinion made public. 'It was a matter of duty that it should be made known publicly that there were thought to be material inaccuracies which needed to be corrected in the letter of my right Hon. Friend the Member for Henley [Mr Heseltine]'. She protected herself by saying that, 'had I been consulted, I should have said that a different way must be found of making the relevant facts known'. However, she insisted that 'the Department of Trade and Industry acted in good faith in the knowledge that it had the authority of its Secretary of State and cover from my office for proceeding'.[10] At the time Thatcher was deeply anxious about her own future, telling a group of advisers before a further Commons debate on 27 January that 'I may not be Prime Minister by six o'clock tonight'.[11] Some Conservatives speculated privately on her political mortality. Chris Patten, for example, confided to journalist Hugo Young his belief that 'we are at the end of an era. Into the tomb the great queen crashes.'[12] A leading backbench MP, Nicholas Soames, reported that many of his colleagues 'were very unhappy and barely willing if at all to support her . . . for the first time there is semi-serious talk of her having to go'.[13] Once again, however, the luck which had attended her did not desert the beleaguered premier. Neil Kinnock's inability to press home the attack enabled Thatcher to survive the debate. Instead of asking precise, damaging questions, he delivered a generalised onslaught which failed to divert her from her prepared line of argument. She had taken care to neutralise Brittan, who might have made damaging revelations, by extending to him the possibility of an eventual return to office – in fact this was the end of his Westminster career, although he was to receive the consolation prize of appointment as a European commissioner three years later. Also critical to Thatcher's survival was the fact that Heseltine had already struck a deal with the party's whips, that he would not exacerbate the dispute, provided that she publicly took some responsibility for what had gone wrong. This is why, unusually for her, she expressed regret for the way in which the leak had been effected, and even acknowledged that other aspects of the affair could have been handled better.

Westland was not a scandal of Watergate proportions. It did not prevent Thatcher and her party from winning a further general election less than eighteen months later. In the longer term, however, the crisis pointed out some worrying lessons about her style of government. Geoffrey Howe, who sympathised with Heseltine's pro-Europeanism, but felt that he pushed his case too far, was also concerned by the ruthlessness with which Leon Brittan was cast aside: 'the Cabinet was beginning to look more like a Catherine wheel than a council of colleagues,' he wrote in his memoirs.[14] Howe was one of several commentators to note the way in which the affair highlighted the power, and the lack of accountability, of the unelected advisers on whom Thatcher increasingly depended. Ingham and Powell were shielded from criticism for their role in the leaking of the letter, and they continued to serve at the heart of Number 10 until Thatcher's fall, almost five years later. Thatcher had appeared weak in the early stages of the crisis, when she might have closed down discussion and forced Heseltine's resignation before further damage had been done. As the crisis progressed, she had shown herself to be something less than the conviction politician of her popular image, much more as a street-fighter who would go to extraordinary lengths to ensure her own survival. One of her ideological admirers, free market theorist Lord Harris, later admitted that 'it was an episode when she behaved like other politicians. She brought into question that which has marked her out from other politicians, namely that she does not dissemble and that she makes it clear where she stands.'[15]

More importantly for her future, the affair left Thatcher for the first time with a credible eventual challenger for the leadership, free to cultivate support on the backbenches and to bide his time. Heseltine had to be careful not to seem openly disloyal to her, and when questioned about his intentions, he would habitually insist that he 'could not foresee the circumstances' when he would run against her. He was, however, a much more dangerous potential antagonist than any of the 'wets' who had been sacked or resigned, and if circumstances changed, he might one day be a serious focus for discontent.

The 'loony left' in local government

The spring of 1986 witnessed the culmination of another defining battle of Thatcher's second term, her conflict with a group of left-wing Labour councils, of which the most prominent was the unitary authority for the capital city, the Greater London Council. As with the Westland affair, the issue was not well handled and its outcome could be described as a pyrrhic victory for the government.

Local government was a persistent concern for Thatcher. At the heart of the issue was the question of funding. Local authorities drew their funding from two main sources, grants allocated by central government and the rates, a local tax based on property values. At Heath's behest in the October 1974 election, Thatcher had fronted Shadow Cabinet proposals for the abolition of the rates. She disliked the rates for the way that they bore down disproportionately on the small property owners whom she thought of as 'our people', but was determined not to raise the issue again before an alternative form of financing had been worked out. A review of the rating system in 1981 had failed to produce a viable plan and so for the time being Thatcher had shelved thoughts of far-reaching reform. Instead she engaged in protracted guerrilla warfare with the Labour-controlled authorities, which she regarded as irredeemably committed to wasteful expenditure. As Environment Secretary in the first Thatcher term, Heseltine reduced the central grants paid to the highest spending councils, but this resulted in their raising the rates to meet the shortfall. In response the government took powers to 'cap' the rates levied by the worst offenders. The 1983 Conservative manifesto also pledged the party to abolish the Greater London Council together with six other metropolitan authorities (Greater Manchester, Merseyside, South Yorkshire, West Yorkshire, Tyne and Wear and West Midlands).

It was the fate of the GLC that proved the most controversial of all. To a great extent this was because of the character of the man who was its leader from May 1981. Ken Livingstone was a charismatic and resourceful politician. A dedicated activist who lived modestly in a bedsit and espoused a range of left-wing causes, from gay and lesbian rights to the withdrawal of British troops from Northern Ireland, he was the antithesis of Thatcher. He adopted a deliberately provocative stance towards the government, displaying a banner on the roof of his Thames side head-quarters, showing the rising number of unemployed people in London, so that it was visible from the Houses of Parliament on the opposite bank. In addition, although the funding of pressure groups like Babies against the Bomb and the English Collective of Prostitutes actually constituted a small percentage of the GLC's overall expenditure, Livingstone's association with so-called 'loony left' policies inevitably drew the ire of the Tory press and politicians. In his memoirs he flippantly attributed her hostility to the fact that 'we were the sort of people her parents warned her not to talk to when she was a little girl'. More seriously, he went on, 'apart from her desire to crush all opposition she was tapping into an old Tory fear of radical politics erupting out of London's heaving slums'.[16]

There was a long tradition of Conservative scepticism about the concept of a unitary authority for London, and party spokes-men argued that the functions of the GLC could be more eco-nomically delegated to borough and district councils. Abolition was a personal priority for Thatcher herself, who saw it as a trial of strength with an institution which embodied socialism, almost on Number 10's doorstep. The decision to abolish the council, however, led the government into a prolonged struggle, not only with Labour but also with sections of Conservative and non-party opinion. Livingstone's talent for publicity enabled him to present the issue as a conflict between an overbearing central government and the virtuous forces of local democracy. After setting 31 March 1986 as the date for the council's abolition, the government played into its opponents' hands with the decision to cancel the final GLC elections, scheduled for May 1985. The move, which required the passing of a separate 'paving bill' through Parlia-ment, proved to be a major own goal, and the government faced not only a large-scale rebellion in the normally quiescent House of Lords but also criticism in the Conservative press. The *Daily Express* warned the government, 'Be very careful about tampering with the democratic process', whilst the *Mail on Sunday* described the paving bill as 'an appalling precedent' for the future.[17]

With the Conservatives' huge Commons majority, of course, eventual abolition was never in doubt, but the political price Thatcher paid was high. In September 1985 she removed the hapless Environment Secretary, Patrick Jenkin, under whom the process had started, and replaced him with a junior minister, Kenneth Baker, whose presentational skills were regarded as superior. During its final year the doomed GLC continued to spend heavily on its favoured projects. More fundamentally, abolition left London, unusually among world capitals in the developed world, without a body which could take a strategic overview of issues such as transport, where major investment in infrastructure was needed by the 1990s. Few commentators have considered that the plethora of lower level councils and unelected quangos, among whom the functions of the GLC were divided, adequately filled the gap that had been left. After 1997, Tony Blair's Labour government made the creation of a new London-wide body, the Greater London Authority, and of an elected mayor, one of its priorities. In one of the heavier ironies of modern British history the first London mayor, running as an independent in the 2000 contest because of his differences with New Labour, but later readmitted to the party, was none other than Ken Livingstone.

Revival and renewal

In the short run, the bruising battles over Westland and local government did not inflict serious political damage on Thatcher. By the autumn of 1986, there were clear signs of economic resurgence. Inflation continued to decline and would reach 3.6 per cent on the eve of the 1987 general election, whilst unemployment had at last begun to fall from a peak of 3.2 million. In what was to be the last party conference before her third general election campaign as Conservative leader, Thatcher took the opportunity to highlight the onset of recovery. She also publicly celebrated the success of a policy with which she had by then

become indissolubly connected, the privatisation of major industries and services. She depicted her government's transfer of state
assets to the private sector, and the ensuing sale of shares in these
enterprises, as a template for countries across the globe:

> from France to the Philippines, from Jamaica to Japan, from
> Malaysia to Mexico, from Sri Lanka to Singapore, privatisa-
> tion is on the move. . . . Popular capitalism is nothing less
> than a crusade to enfranchise the many in the economic life
> of the nation. We Conservatives are returning power to the
> people.[18]

The triumphalist tone of Thatcher's conference speech concealed the slow start of privatisation in Britain. She was initially
cautious about the policy, fearing that it would prove politically
unfeasible, and requiring to be persuaded by more radical colleagues and advisers such as John Redwood, a committed free
market thinker who headed the Downing Street Policy Unit in
1983–5. In Thatcher's first term, relatively few well-known state
enterprises were sold off. The government was inhibited in part,
at least until Conservative prospects markedly improved in 1982,
by the danger that Labour might win the next election and carry
out renationalisation on terms disadvantageous to shareholders.
By winning in 1983, Thatcher significantly reduced the risk of
this happening and it became possible to extend the programme.
A key turning point was the flotation of British Telecom on the
stock market in November 1984, which proved a commercial
success. When Thatcher addressed the October 1986 conference,
the sale of British Gas was about to be launched, with the support of an advertising campaign using the slogan 'Tell Sid', in a
clear attempt to interest ordinary people who would not normally
have considered buying shares. In subsequent years it would be
followed by the sale of other big names including British Airways,
British Petroleum and British Steel. The water and electricity
companies were privatised in Thatcher's final year of office.

Privatisation was an immensely controversial policy. Powerful
voices in the City of London expressed scepticism in the early
days about the feasibility of attempting such an ambitious overhaul of the status quo. From a more principled position, Labour

Party leaders, trade union representatives and others criticised the government for selling off assets which should, they argued, continue to be managed on behalf of the whole community. Even the former Conservative Prime Minister, Harold Macmillan, belatedly ennobled as Lord Stockton at the age of ninety in February 1984, raised concerns in a widely publicised speech, likening the government to an impoverished country house owner who meets current expenditure by selling off the 'family silver'. There was widespread suspicion of a policy which threatened to transform public monopolies into private ones, without any accountability to the consumer. Nor should one exaggerate the popularity of privatisation with the general public. Although the number of shareholders increased from 3 million to 11 million between 1979 and 1990, relatively few individuals built up investment portfolios. It was much more common for people to buy shares in a single company and then to sell them in order to make a quick profit. The ownership of British companies by institutions actually increased from 72 to 79 per cent during the Thatcher decade.

In political terms, however, privatisation proved a success. In tandem with the continued sale of council houses, it enabled Thatcher to generate a populist appeal based on the concept of a 'capital-owning democracy'. The general public had little regard for nationalised industries, which by the 1980s were viewed as inefficient and a drain on the taxpayer's resources. Time and again, in the run up to the 1987 election, Thatcher and her colleagues portrayed privatisation as a policy which was eliminating old distinctions between employers and workers, giving people a real sense of ownership. Addressing a Manchester business meeting shortly after the sale of British Gas, for example, she hailed the birth of 'a world where ordinary folk with ordinary incomes can become property owners and share owners', enabling them to 'have their own independence, build their own security, build their own future'.[19] Or, as Oliver Letwin, a member of the Prime Minister's Policy Unit, put it more prosaically in a review of the policy published in 1988, 'overwhelmingly the most important element in making privatisation a positive political success has been the fundamental step of creating a great interest group in its favour'.[20]

Privatisation was part of a wider movement towards the removal of state regulation and direction, and the development of an 'enterprise culture', which typified Britain in the mid-1980s. The so-called 'Big Bang' reform of the City of London, the deregulation of the financial markets which took place in October 1986, was an important part of this process. The Thatcher government reasoned that the London Stock Exchange had fallen behind New York as a financial centre because of a hide-bound, restrictive culture dominated by an exclusive 'old boy network'. A series of changes, including the removal of traditional rules governing the sale of stocks and shares and the adoption of electronic, screen-based trading, opened up the financial sector. Combined with Nigel Lawson's steady reduction of direct taxation, these changes created new opportunities for personal enrichment. There emerged in popular culture the figure of the 'yuppie' – an archetypal young City trader, making unimaginable amounts of money and leading a life of conspicuous consumption. Meanwhile at a more everyday level, ordinary people enjoyed an improving standard of living, taking on mortgages and funding purchases through credit cards, which became widely available for the first time.

Thatcher had little directly to do with much of this, although her government created the conditions within which the new service sector industries could develop. She consistently denied the charge frequently made by her critics, that the country was becoming increasingly divided between a booming South and a depressed, post-industrial North. 'You cannot stop change; you cannot stop technological change', she insisted when challenged by an interviewer during the 1987 election campaign. New industries, she maintained, were replacing the old, declining ones. Although she admitted to qualms about the size of many salaries paid to workers in the financial services sector, this was inevitable if the most talented wealth-creators were to be attracted:

> the City has to compete with salaries with other people who take them away. I think part of it was the transition the City went through – Big Bang – when I think there was a lot of the so-called competition for getting the best people.[21]

At a personal level Thatcher felt little empathy for the 'whizz-kid' culture over which she presided. Still marked by her puritanical upbringing, she continued to live quite frugally, shunning debt and refusing to use a credit card. She did nothing, however, to restrain the growth of an environment in which material success seemed to have become the most important value. Thatcher despised the guilt of middle-class liberals who felt that paying higher levels of tax was socially desirable, and was completely untouched by the satire of comedians such as the young Harry Enfield, whose vulgar, banknote flourishing character, 'Loadsamoney', became an emblem of the second half of the 1980s. She had been instrumental in opening a Pandora's Box from which emerged the spirit of greed and selfishness, borne on the bracing winds of competition and meritocracy.

Winning a third term

Burgeoning economic growth helped prepare the ground for Thatcher's bid for a third, historic term of office. She was also assisted by Lawson's popular March 1987 budget, which further reduced income tax, and by her decision to make a highly publicised visit to the USSR – the first by a serving Prime Minister in almost three decades – which burnished her image as a world figure.[22] At the start of the campaign, in mid-May, the Conservatives appeared to have exorcised their earlier problems with a clear lead over their opponents in the opinion polls. They enjoyed a 43 per cent approval rating, with Labour on 29 per cent and the SDP–Liberal Alliance on 26 per cent. Indeed these figures hardly changed in the course of the next four weeks. Yet in spite of this, the campaign was a much less happy experience for Thatcher and her colleagues than the two previous ones had been, and at one point there was near-panic within the Tory high command at what was perceived to be the prospect of defeat.

To be certain, Thatcher's opponents were able to put up a much better fight than they had done four years earlier. Under Neil Kinnock, Labour had begun to distance itself from the policies and public image of the hard left. His denunciation of the Militant Tendency-run Liverpool city council at the 1985 Labour conference, and the subsequent expulsion of extremists from the party, signalled a new mood of discipline and realism. Labour had also vastly improved its presentation, with the employment of talented advertising experts, including a young Director of Communications, Peter Mandelson, who were much more attuned to the need to win over uncommitted, middle of the road voters. The Alliance had also scored two impressive by-election victories, at Greenwich in February and Truro in March, once again raising speculation of a breakthrough in the centre ground of politics.

In addition, behind the scenes the Conservative leadership was much less united than it had been in 1983. One of the most surprising features of the campaign was Thatcher's growing private unease with her party chairman, Norman Tebbit. Although the two had long been ideological soul mates, with Tebbit widely regarded as an uncompromising standard bearer of Thatcherism, by 1987 relations between the two were strained. In his memoirs Tebbit complained that the campaign had been much harder to fight effectively because of Thatcher's refusal to appoint either a director of communications or an official at Conservative Central Office to take responsibility for routine management and expenditure, so that too much descended on his own shoulders.[23] For her part the premier had begun to suspect that Tebbit nurtured independent ambitions of his own. He did not seem to give the same priority that Cecil Parkinson had done to utilising the leader as the party's principal electoral asset. There was in fact little justification for these suspicions – near the end of the campaign Tebbit told her of his intention to retire from front-line politics to care for his wife, who had been left paralysed by the IRA bomb at the 1984 party conference, an episode in which he too had sustained serious injuries. At the time, however, Thatcher was sufficiently anxious to appoint another ministerial colleague, Lord Young, to act as her own agent within the campaign team. David Young was a successful businessman who had been appointed to the Cabinet as a member of the House of Lords. Thatcher trusted and valued him – 'other people bring me problems,' she once supposedly said, 'but David brings me solutions.'[24] Unfortunately, as a technocrat who lacked a conventional party political background, he was never fully accepted by those who had risen through membership of the Commons. One week before polling day, on what became known as 'Wobbly Thursday', 4 June, Young confronted Tebbit to tell him that they were going to lose the election, and to insist on the employment of a rival advertising firm and the spending of an additional £2 million in order to save the party from defeat.

Most informed commentators consider that this analysis was hopelessly mistaken and that the eventual outcome of the election was never really in doubt. The clash between Young and Tebbit was prompted by a single opinion poll, out of step with most other indicators of public opinion, which suggested that the gap with Labour had narrowed to only 4 per cent. For all his party's success in fighting a much more professional campaign, doubts remained about Kinnock as a potential Prime Minister. Although capable of articulating his values in a compelling way in set-piece speeches, he could be trapped into indiscretions when his policies were placed under the spotlight. Most damaging was his incautious suggestion, when challenged by an interviewer about his continuing commitment to a non-nuclear defence policy, that action by British citizens could make a Soviet occupation of the British homeland 'untenable'. With an end to the Cold War not yet in sight, the remark reopened concerns about Labour's readiness to be entrusted with national defence, by conjuring up visions of guerrilla resistance to the Red Army. Headlines in the Tory press ridiculed 'Dad's Army Kinnock' and 'The Man with the White Flag'. Thatcher herself seized on the interview to remind voters of the weakness of Labour's credentials as a serious party of government: 'People can't trust a party which would give up nuclear weapons unilaterally and substitute some kind of guerrilla band for them. You can't have guerrillas unless you've been occupied. That's what it seems to me they were talking about.'[25] Defence also played badly for the Alliance, with a clear difference between the robustly pro-NATO stance of SDP leader David Owen and the unilateralist leanings of the Liberal Party rank and file. On domestic policy, the Alliance's attempt to present a balanced set of policies – 'tough but tender' – failed to gain traction with the electorate. The tensions of its dual leadership were cruelly captured by the satirical TV puppet show *Spitting Image*, which was at the height of its popularity at this time. The Liberal leader David Steel was invariably depicted as a tiny, squeaky figure poking out of the much larger Owen's pocket. In truth the opposition to Thatcher was never likely to upset her chances of re-election.

The election was a decisive victory for Thatcher. Once again the vagaries of the first past the post voting system enhanced the winner's lead over the other parties; with 43.4 per cent of the vote, a slight increase on 1983, the Conservatives won 376 seats, whilst Labour's total was 229 and the Alliance emerged with a paltry 22 seats. Although not as good as the 1983 result, a majority of 102 was still impressive. In important respects the outcome confirmed trends which had been evident in the previous contest. The North–South divide was marked, with the Conservatives losing almost half of their twenty-one Scottish constituencies and failing to make an impression in many parts of the industrial north. The coalition of upwardly mobile working and lower middle-class voters, who had delivered victory for Thatcher four years earlier, had remained loyal. She had retained the support of those sections of the community, concentrated mainly in the South and the Midlands, who had bought into her government's home and share ownership revolution. Analyses of the election indicate that people who were in secure employment, but were less likely to belong to trade unions, were most inclined to vote Conservative. It was hardly surprising that Thatcher viewed it as an unqualified endorsement of her leadership, entitling her to drive forward her policies into new areas. Few can have predicted, at the time, that she would be out of Downing Street in little more than three years.

New people, policies and problems

Thatcher made relatively few changes to the Cabinet in the wake of her victory. The only significant departure, apart from Norman Tebbit, was that of John Biffen, the Leader of the Commons, who had been marked down for dismissal as he had become increasingly disillusioned or, in the words of a press item supposedly inspired by Number 10, a 'semi-detached' member of the government. Thatcher retained Peter Walker, the only surviving Cabinet 'wet', out of respect for his ability, although his move from Energy to Wales was, if anything, a demotion. Lord Young moved to the Department of Trade and Industry as a reward for his role in the election campaign. Cecil Parkinson returned, having spent almost the whole of the previous Parliament in the wilderness after the scandal which had interrupted his career in the midst of the 1983 conference. This was a rare example of Thatcher giving a second chance to a minister who had fallen by the wayside, although the possibility of his succeeding his patron had long ago evaporated. He served in two successive middle-ranking posts, at Energy and Transport, and was to retire from the Cabinet on the fall of Thatcher in November 1990.

The question of an eventual successor was one which played intermittently on the premier's mind, although of course in public she swatted away any attempt to open a discussion which might touch on her political mortality. She had once admitted to a confidant, the crossbench peer and fervent Thatcher admirer, Woodrow Wyatt, that 'I sometimes think I can't go because who on earth is there to succeed me'. A year after the 1987 victory, she told him that she had to 'wait for a younger generation who are going to do the things I believe in'.[26] No doubt Thatcher was indulging in a degree of self-deception; she was not the first dominant leader to find excuses for staying on. These remarks do, however, indicate the sense of isolation that she felt within the Cabinet. Politically it was difficult to move any of the most senior ministers, Lawson, Howe or Douglas Hurd, who had taken over the Home Office in September 1985, although for various reasons she did not want to contemplate any of them as her successor. Instead, speculation focused in turn on the long-term prospects of two younger figures who received promotion in June 1987, whom she believed to share her own political philosophy. John Moore, who was moved to run the Department of Health and Social Security, failed to cope with the demands of office, even after his large department was split in two in July 1988. Dogged by poor health, he left the government a year later. It was in fact another Thatcher protégé, the forty-four year old John Major, who was eventually to succeed her. Entering the Cabinet now for the first time as Chief Secretary to the Treasury, with responsibility for scrutinising ministerial colleagues' departmental budget bids, he rapidly gained the respect of his peer group but at this stage he was barely known outside Westminster.

The first year of the new term saw the departure of Thatcher's long-standing deputy, Willie Whitelaw. He resigned in January

1988 after being taken ill the previous month at a Westminster carol service. His unique combination of common sense, experience, good humour and loyalty would be sorely missed. He had been a universally trusted, all-purpose trouble-shooter, a senior figure with no ambition to take over the top job. No one else in British politics offered quite the same mix of characteristics. Yet with her enduring capacity to use people and to continue moving on, Thatcher failed to consult him unofficially in his retirement, even though he had made clear his willingness to offer assistance if asked.

In the aftermath of the election victory Thatcher certainly showed no sign of a willingness to slow down the pace of change. On the contrary, she now proposed to tackle areas of government, such as education and health, in which thus far surprisingly few major initiatives had been taken. Kenneth Baker, who had succeeded Keith Joseph as Education Secretary in May 1986, later recorded his impressions of the Prime Minister as a leader driven by a restless reforming zeal: 'Margaret felt she had to keep the Thatcherite revolution going forward, if only in the belief that if she stopped pedalling then everybody would fall off the bicycle'.[27] Ministers found that in the second half of her premiership, she was more inclined to micro-manage their departments and to take initiatives independently of her colleagues, often with the aid of inexperienced Downing Street advisers. Norman Fowler, who headed the DHSS until the 1987 election, found that he had to threaten resignation in order to deter her from appointing Roy Griffiths, deputy managing director of Sainsburys, who had carried out a management review of the NHS, as the 'prime minister's adviser on the health service'. Looking back, Fowler identified the growing importance of advisers, who were answerable only to the premier, as 'the beginning of a new form of political governance', in which lay 'the seeds of destruction of the Thatcher government'.[28]

Thatcher frequently sought to impose her own ideas on policy matters, although it was still possible for a determined and well-informed minister to get his own way. A good example is her intervention in the creation of the 1988 Education Bill, which introduced a number of changes, including the establishment of a national curriculum, the opportunity for secondary schools to opt out of local authority control, and the creation of specialist city technology colleges, which would be funded directly by central government. In important respects the bill embodied ideas close to Thatcher's heart. In interviews prior to the election, she had spelt out her vision of a return to traditional teaching of the basics, with clear measurement of pupils' attainment:

> I think we have a bounden duty to see that in eleven years of compulsory education we do our level best to see that children come out of school with the fundamentals, the numeracy, at least the arithmetic, the basic language – that is reading and writing and being able to express yourself orally and being able to write clearly.[29]

Her grudging acceptance of non-selective secondary education was clear when asked if she felt that comprehensive schools were 'here to stay'. 'Some comprehensives work well,' she conceded, 'but what one simply must have is a variety of schools . . . and with city technological colleges again we have a chance of an alternative out of the grip of the local education authority.'[30] On both issues Thatcher clashed with the responsible minister. Baker successfully, if exhaustingly, resisted her insistence on restricting the national curriculum to three core subjects, which would have taken up 70 per cent of teaching time, eventually producing a much more varied academic diet, against the Prime Minister's express wishes. Thatcher was also much more radical, and less realistic, than her Education Secretary in her desire to push forward the policy of opting out from local authority control. Whereas she expressed an expectation that most schools would take advantage of this new freedom, in fact only 1,100 out of a total of 24,000 had adopted so-called 'grant-maintained' status by 1997, when the incoming Labour government ended the practice.

On reform of the NHS, Thatcher was equally interventionist, if less consistent. By instinct she wanted to cut rising costs, and to increase the sphere of private medical care, yet her innate political caution restrained her from pursuing policies which might be interpreted as undermining a service on which the great majority of the population depended. As DHSS Secretary, John Moore lost the confidence of the Prime Minister through his inability to push through a reform programme which would meet these competing priorities. His more robust successor as Health Secretary, Kenneth Clarke, succeeded in introducing a system which improved the efficiency of NHS management without breaching the principle of free core provision. This was the 'internal market', under which district health authorities and doctors with responsibility for managing a budget, known as GP fund-holders, became purchasers of health care from NHS trust hospitals. In this case it was Thatcher who was more cautious than the departmental minister concerned, almost cancelling the plans at one point in fear that the reforms would be presented as privatisation of the NHS. When she agreed to let Clarke proceed, she told him, 'It is *you* I'm holding responsible if *my* NHS reforms don't work.'[31]

The disagreements over education and health, however, were potentially much less damaging than the conflict which was developing between the premier and her long-serving Chancellor. Undoubtedly she respected Lawson's ability, and in her memoirs she generously insisted that, in spite of their differences, 'if it comes to drawing up a list of Conservative – even Thatcherite – revolutionaries I would never deny Nigel a leading place'.[32] In practice, however, Thatcher found him secretive in his working methods, and too much inclined to make policy without consulting her. By 1987, a major source of division between the two had opened up over policy towards the European Exchange Rate Mechanism (ERM), a system whereby member states sought to achieve exchange rate stability by keeping their currencies in parity with each other. Lawson's determination to join the mechanism, which he regarded as an indispensable tool in ensuring monetary stability, brought him into conflict with his neighbour in Number 10.

This was not, however, the only cause of tension between these two strong-willed individuals. In March 1988, Lawson produced his most spectacular budget, in which he reduced the basic rate of income tax from 27 to 25 per cent and the higher rate from 60 to 40 per cent. Although this was consistent with the broad thrust of Conservative fiscal policy, and it was warmly welcomed by the party's backbenchers, the premier feared that Lawson's overall strategy was likely to lead to a revival of inflation. By the summer her anxieties were being borne out as inflation reached 6.6 per cent, obliging the Chancellor to raise interest rates from 7.5 per cent in May to a punitively high 12 per cent by August. Barely a year after her third electoral triumph, the durability of the Thatcherite economic miracle was being called into question. No less worryingly, her conduct of relations with one of her most senior colleagues had allowed a serious rift to open up at the highest level of government. Genuine differences over policy were exacerbated by sharp clashes of personality. At the peak of her power, there were signs that Thatcher's underlying position was highly insecure.

Notes

1 Shirley Williams, *Climbing the Bookshelves: The Autobiography* (London, Virago, 2009), p. 160.
2 Philip Gould, *The Unfinished Revolution: How the Modernisers Saved the Labour Party* (London, Little, Brown and Company, 1998), pp. 53–4.
3 Quoted in John Campbell, *Margaret Thatcher: Volume Two: The Iron Lady* (London, Jonathan Cape, 2003), p. 477.
4 Dr Ian Deary and Dr Simon Wessely, 'Dementia and Mrs Thatcher' in Philip Marsden-Smedley (ed.), *Britain in the Eighties: The Spectator's View of the Thatcher Decade* (London, Paladin, 1991), p. 137.
5 Westland: Wicks minute for MT ('Westland'), 23 December 1985, www.margaretthatcher.org/document/136773 (accessed 1 January 2015).
6 Margaret Thatcher, *The Downing Street Years* (London, Harper Collins, 1993), p. 423.
7 TV interview for Channel 4, 'Face the Press', 25 January 1986, *Margaret Thatcher: Complete Public Statements 1945–1990 on CD-ROM* (Oxford, Oxford University Press, 1999), 86_030.
8 Nicholas Ridley, *'My Style of Government': The Thatcher Years* (London, Hutchinson, 1991), p. 49. Reproduced by permission of The Random House Group Ltd. and Peters Fraser & Dunlop (www.petersfraserdunlop.com) on behalf of the Estate of Nicholas Ridley.
9 Bernard Ingham, *Kill the Messenger* (London, Fontana, 1991), p. 335.
10 House of Commons Statement [Westland plc], 23 January 1986, www.margaretthatcher.org/document/106314 (accessed 28 July 2014).
11 Geoffrey Howe, *Conflict of Loyalty* (London, Macmillan, 1994), p. 471.
12 'Chris Patten: Phone, 26 January 1986', quoted in Ion Trewin (ed.), *The Hugo Young Papers: Thirty Years of British Politics – Off the Record* (London, Allen Lane, 2008), p. 224.
13 Sarah Curtis (ed.), *The Journals of Woodrow Wyatt*, Volume 1 (London, Macmillan, 1998), p. 74, entry for 26 January 1986.

14 Howe, *Conflict of Loyalty*, p. 472.

15 Lord Harris, interviewed 21 May 1990, quoted in John Ranelagh, *Thatcher's People: An Insider's Account of the Politics, the Power and the Personalities* (London, Harper Collins, 1991), pp. 249–50.

16 Ken Livingstone, *You Can't Say That: Memoirs* (London, Faber and Faber, 2011), p. 232.

17 Quoted in Livingstone, *You Can't Say That*, p. 243.

18 Speech to Conservative Party Conference, 10 October 1986, www.margaretthatcher.org/document/106498 (accessed 28 July 2014).

19 Speech at Manchester Chamber of Commerce dinner, 11 December 1986, www.margaretthatcher.org/document/106537 (accessed 28 July 2014).

20 Quoted in Hugo Young, *One of Us: A biography of Margaret Thatcher* (London, Pan, 1990), p. 502.

21 TV interview for BBC Panorama, 8 June 1987, www.margaretthatcher.org/document/106647 (accessed 28 July 2014).

22 See pp. 182–3 for discussion of this visit.

23 Norman Tebbit, *Upwardly Mobile* (London, Futura, 1989), p. 326.

24 Quoted in Young, *One of Us*, p. 516.

25 Speech at East Midlands airport, 25 May 1987, *Thatcher CD-ROM*, 87_159.

26 Curtis, *Wyatt Journals* Volume 1, p. 124, entry for 20 April 1986 and p. 548, entry for 8 May 1988.

27 Kenneth Baker, *The Turbulent Years: My Life in Politics* (London, Faber and Faber, 1993), p. 270.

28 Norman Fowler, *A Political Suicide: The Conservatives' Voyage into the Wilderness* (London, Politico's, 2008), pp. 21 and 22.

29 Interview for *Daily Express*, 22 April 1987, *Thatcher CD-ROM*, 87_135.

30 Interview for *Daily Mail*, 11 May 1987, *Thatcher CD-ROM*, 87_163.

31 Quoted in Nicholas Timmins, *The Five Giants: A Biography of the Welfare State* (London, Harper Collins, 1995), p. 472.

32 Thatcher, *Downing Street Years*, p. 308.

7 The troubled Union – Northern Ireland: 1979–1990

Thatcher and the Troubles

Margaret Thatcher became Prime Minister in 1979 during an acute phase of one of the most intractable problems faced by post-war British governments. A decade earlier, Harold Wilson's Labour government had been obliged to intervene in Northern Ireland following the outbreak of conflict between the two rival communities who inhabited the province. The so-called 'Troubles' would scar the history of Northern Ireland until the brokering of a settlement under Tony Blair's government in 1998. The cause of the disturbances which erupted in 1968–9 was the Catholic minority's unsatisfied demand for equal rights with their Protestant neighbours. Catholics had experienced decades of discrimination, whilst Protestant Unionists had enjoyed unbroken political dominance in the devolved system of government that had been created at Stormont, a suburb of Belfast, when Ireland was partitioned in 1922. The situation became increasingly fraught in the early 1970s with the revival of the IRA, the self-styled military wing of the republican party, Sinn Fein, and by the countervailing emergence of paramilitary groups claiming to represent the Protestant population. Whereas the self-styled loyalists insisted on the maintenance of the Union with Britain, Catholic nationalists identified with the government of the Irish Republic, which saw itself as the guardian of their interests and looked for the eventual unification of the whole island. Unionist fears that they might be abandoned at some point by London, and transferred to the authority of the Dublin government, were a further complicating factor.

The Northern Ireland question was a major preoccupation for the Heath government. In March 1972, after it had become clear that the Unionist administration at Stormont had no prospect of reconciling the nationalist community, Heath restored direct rule from London. As Education Secretary, Thatcher played little or no role in this momentous decision. Nor was she involved in the abortive Sunningdale agreement, concluded shortly before Heath's fall, an attempt to introduce a form of power-sharing devolved executive, bringing together moderate representatives of the Unionist and nationalist viewpoints. As Leader of the Opposition she acquired a reputation as a determined upholder of the Union but it would be more correct to say that she was primarily motivated by hostility to the IRA, and to terrorism in general. She left the detailed policy-making to her Shadow Northern Ireland Secretary, Airey Neave. The latter, a committed Unionist, favoured what was known as an integrationist approach, under which Northern Ireland would be treated in the same way as other parts of the United Kingdom. His influence led to the inclusion in the 1979 Conservative manifesto of a proposal to create elected regional councils, with powers over local services. At the start of the election campaign, however, he was assassinated by a bomb planted by the Irish National Liberation Army, a break-away movement from the IRA, in the House of Commons car park.

Neave's murder had two important effects on Thatcher. At a personal level she was deeply shocked by the loss of a close colleague, who had masterminded her election as Conservative leader four years earlier. Had he lived, he would undoubtedly have played an important role in her first government. Politically, his death removed the leading advocate of a policy position to which, in reality, only a handful of hard-line Conservative Unionists were truly dedicated. The most influential senior Conservatives with influence in this area of policy, including Thatcher's first Northern Ireland Secretary, Humphrey Atkins (1979–81), were more flexible in their thinking. Although there was certainly no question in their minds of promoting the concept of a united Ireland, they sought better relations, both between the two communities in Northern Ireland, and between Britain and the Irish Republic. This approach, which bore fruit in a White Paper published in the autumn of 1979, pointed towards an attempt to revive devolution in the province, with safeguards for the representation of the Catholic minority.

Thatcher's own views were deeply ambivalent and the evidence for what she really felt is contradictory. Although she read quite widely about the subject, she had little understanding of, or feeling for, Irish nationalist culture, identifying it in a rather simplistic way with terrorism. As Charles Powell, her foreign affairs private secretary, recalled: 'for her, many of the justifications for nationalism were little more than mythology or folklore, to use two words she frequently used'.[1] According to James Prior, who served as Northern Ireland Secretary in 1981–4, she made little distinction between the militant republicanism of Sinn Fein and the non-violent approach of the moderate nationalist Social Democratic and Labour Party (SDLP). When warned that Sinn Fein might replace the SDLP as the majority Catholic party, she retorted, 'Oh, but they're not a Unionist Party.'[2] On the other hand there are indications of her sense of frustration with the official representatives of Ulster Unionism, whom she found difficult to work with. Richard Needham, the longest serving junior Northern Ireland Office minister, described her attitude as 'one of exaggerated despair. She would have liked somehow to get rid of the problem. She did not like or trust the unionists.'[3]

Deep down, Thatcher was impatient with a situation which did not easily lend itself to a rational solution. More than once she suggested in private to her advisers that Northern Ireland could be made more readily defensible by redrawing the border line so that irredeemably nationalist populations could be relocated within the Republic, leaving a more coherently Unionist North. She found it hard to appreciate that, in the words of her third Northern Ireland Secretary, Douglas Hurd (1984–5), 'there was no tidy dividing line. The intertwining of the communities was hopelessly complex.'[4] The cost of the heavy police and military presence in Northern Ireland was another concern for the head of a government committed to curbing the growth of public expenditure. A sum of £400 million was expended on counter-terrorism in 1979–80, and this was set to rise as a reorganisation carried out by the IRA made it harder for the security services to infiltrate their structures, and the terrorists acquired more sophisticated weaponry. Thatcher was also obliged to allow a higher level of state intervention in Northern Ireland than in mainland Britain, partly because of the higher levels of unemployment and deprivation there, but mainly in order to help bind the province to the Union. It has been estimated that 90 per cent of industrial jobs in Northern Ireland were supported by government subsidies in the 1980s, and about 40 per cent of all employment there was in the public sector. In Prior's words, 'we are all Keynesians here'.[5]

Thatcher's instincts were undoubtedly Unionist. She asserted this aspect of her identity in her memoirs, where she described the patriotism of the Unionist community as 'real and fervent, even if too narrow', and declared that 'any Conservative should in his bones be a Unionist too'.[6] Northern Ireland was, however, never her foremost concern, and she found it hard to empathise with those whose lives were lived in the midst of the conflict there. Her attitude to the appointment of Cabinet ministers with responsibility for the province suggested that other political imperatives often took precedence over the interests of Northern Ireland. Prior was clearly moved to Belfast in September 1981 in order to side-line a prominent 'wet' opponent of Thatcher's economic policies. When she needed to carry out another reshuffle in September 1985, she did not hesitate to move Douglas Hurd from Northern Ireland to the Home Office, even though he had been in post for only a year. His successor, Tom King, was required to take up the reins with little prior knowledge, even though negotiations for the Anglo-Irish agreement were only six weeks away from completion. It was hardly surprising that both sides in the Northern Irish conflict felt a degree of cynicism about where the province stood. In the words of John Hume, leader of the SDLP, 'it would appear that the office of the Secretary of State for Northern Ireland has been a purgatory for those on their way up and a limbo for those on their way down'.[7]

To Thatcher Northern Ireland was a responsibility which required her attention, rather than a cause with which she was emotionally engaged. The most important thread in her thinking was her concern with the security dimension. BBC political correspondent John Cole, himself a moderate Ulster Protestant, quoted an unnamed associate of the Prime Minister, who once told him that 'her principal interest in the province was the safety of English soldiers serving there; "English" rather than "British", he said'.[8] This was clearly demonstrated on 27 August 1979, when the Queen's cousin, Lord Mountbatten, was assassinated by the IRA and, in a separate incident, eighteen soldiers were killed in an ambush close to the border with the Irish Republic. Thatcher flew to the province and, in a symbolic gesture of solidarity with the security forces, donned the camouflage jacket of one of their members. She did, however, recognise that more was needed than effective policing. Her willingness to make progress on constitutional change reflected, in part, the importance in her mind of Britain's relationship with the USA. Although Washington never aggressively pushed the cause of Irish nationalism, and at the highest levels there was an appreciation of the threat posed to Britain by IRA terrorism, the fact remained that the Irish-American community was an influential lobby group in American politics. In his eight years as President (1981–9), Ronald Reagan spoke fifteen times on the situation in Northern Ireland, and he used his close political relationship with Thatcher behind the scenes to push for political progress on a number of occasions. For the sake of good transatlantic relations, Thatcher had to show a willingness to build bridges to the nationalist community and the government in Dublin. Her relations with the two Prime Ministers of the Irish Republic, Charles Haughey (1979–81, 1982 and 1987–92) and Garret FitzGerald (1981–2 and 1982–7) were wary and business-like rather than cordial. Nonetheless Thatcher recognised the importance of working constructively with them, even though any such initiatives unavoidably raised the suspicions of Northern Irish Unionists.

The hunger strikes

Northern Ireland presented Thatcher with her first major challenge in 1980–1, when groups of republican prisoners in the Maze prison complex in County Antrim went on hunger strike. This was the culmination of a long-running campaign of resistance to the British authorities, sparked by the Callaghan government's decision in 1976 to end what was known as 'special category' status in Northern Ireland's prisons. Essentially the inmates were demanding the restoration of the right – briefly conceded to them by the Heath government – to be identified as political prisoners rather than as ordinary convicts. As part of this struggle, they demanded the right to wear their own clothes rather than prison uniform, to associate freely with each other within the jail, and to be excused from the obligation to undertake work. The Thatcher government faced an initial set of hunger strikes in the autumn of 1980, which were called off after two months, and then a more serious protest which ran from March to October 1981. The most prominent hunger striker was Bobby Sands, who acquired additional publicity for the republican cause by being elected as MP for Fermanagh and South Tyrone, in a by-election held whilst the drama in the Maze was being played out. Sands and nine other inmates died in what became a protracted trial of strength with the government. IRA supporters depicted them as martyrs, whilst violence against the security forces intensified.

The crisis demonstrated Thatcher's willingness to confront the IRA at seemingly any cost, and made her an enduring hate figure to the republican movement. By resisting all proposals for compromise, offered by figures as varied as Michael Foot and the leading Catholic bishop, Cardinal Thomas O'Fiaich, she confirmed her reputation as the 'iron lady'. She took the view that, although the deaths were to be regretted as entirely avoidable individual tragedies, the issue at stake was clear-cut. As she told the Commons after Sands' death in May 1981,

> what hunger strikers are asking for – the one who died last was in fact a murderer; let us not mince our words – is political status by easy stages. They cannot have it. They are murderers and people who use force and violence to achieve their ends.[9]

In taking this stance Thatcher had the support of the greater part of British public opinion. Few were quite as blunt as John Junor, editor of the *Sunday Express*, who hoped that 'every other IRA terrorist' would join Sands on hunger strike and 'stay on it until they are all in wooden suits'. Nonetheless the consensus position of the British press was that the hunger strikers were despicable criminals who deserved to lose. The *Sun* declared that 'blackmail has failed', whilst the *Daily Mail* described Sands' elaborate IRA funeral as a 'macabre propaganda circus' and 'a gangster parody'.[10]

Yet although the strike was called off, following pressure from the Catholic Church and the survivors' families, it was by no means clear that the British government had won. The main consequence of the strikes was to raise the profile of hard-line republicanism among working-class Catholics. Sands' image was used repeatedly in murals across Northern Ireland to recruit support for the cause for which he had died. Sinn Fein won 13 per cent of the vote in the 1983 general election, rivalling the SDLP on 18 per cent. Among the MPs elected was the Sinn Fein president, Gerry Adams, although in accordance with republican practice he refused to acknowledge the British Crown's authority by taking up his seat. Moderate nationalists in Northern Ireland, and their allies in the South, were dismayed by the boost given to extremism. Sean Donlon, the Irish Republic's ambassador to the USA, later recalled the episode as a setback to efforts to move Irish–American opinion away from support for the IRA, which were gradually yielding success: 'we were just about there, but with the hunger strike the stone began to roll back down the hill again'.[11]

What was not known at the time was that, behind the intransigent public face that she presented, in July 1981 Thatcher authorised tentative contacts with the IRA in an attempt to find a solution to the crisis. Cabinet documents released thirty years later show that MI6 was operating a secret channel, using a Northern Irish businessman, Brendan Duddy, as the link with the republicans. The government files contain a list of possible concessions, including permission for prisoners to wear their own clothes, which might be granted if the strike were to be called off. Although she never admitted her own involvement, the letter appears to have been annotated in Thatcher's own hand. Moreover a memorandum from Humphrey Atkins, sent to the Prime Minister the following day, mentions that she had approved the sending of the message. In the event the approach came to nothing, possibly because the IRA decided to hold out longer in the hope of a clear victory, or alternatively because those republicans immediately involved feared accusations of double-dealing from their peers. But there can be no doubt that, albeit at a distance, the 'lady behind the veil',[12] as a junior Northern Ireland Office minister called her, was privately prepared to contradict her public assurances that there could be no negotiations with terrorists. Given the extreme sensitivity of the situation at the time, with the danger of further loss of life, such flexibility behind the scenes may well have been the wisest course to take.

The Brighton bomb

Thatcher remained uncertain about the best way to approach the Northern Ireland problem after the hunger strikes had ended. She allowed the new Northern Ireland Secretary, James Prior, to develop plans for what was known as 'rolling devolution' in 1981–2, a scheme to establish an assembly in Belfast which might evolve into a model of genuine power-sharing between Unionists and nationalists. The project failed to win the support of either the Ulster Unionist Party or the SDLP. More remarkably, Thatcher reluctantly allowed the legislation to go forward, but made her opposition clear to her colleagues, privately describing it as 'a rotten Bill'.[13] Not for the first time, she distanced herself from a measure which might compromise her reputation with the Conservative right, allowing her fervently pro-Unionist parliamentary private secretary, Ian Gow, to orchestrate backbench opposition to it. Political progress was also hampered by the freezing of relations with Irish premier Charles Haughey, when he opposed Britain's actions in the Falklands conflict after the sinking of the *Belgrano* in May 1982.

Although it conflicted with her own instincts, Thatcher recognised that better relations with Dublin were an essential piece of the Northern Ireland jigsaw. The election of the more cerebral, but also more straightforward, Garret FitzGerald as the Republic's premier in December 1982 made possible a new diplomatic initiative. There was, on the face of it, limited compatibility between the two sides. Although he was prepared to give up the formal claim to the reunification of Ireland, which was embodied in the Republic's constitution, FitzGerald was keen to devise a political solution which would overcome the Northern Irish nationalist community's sense of alienation from British

institutions. Thatcher was not prepared to concede joint authority, which was FitzGerald's preferred outcome, and even banned
use of the word 'alienation' on the grounds that it was a 'Marxist'
term. Her overriding concern was to find some way of commit-
ting the Republic to more effective measures against the IRA.
Although the Dublin government had no sympathy with the men
of violence, it clearly needed a much more positive result than
this. Thatcher's notion of a joint security zone covering the
border area was wholly unacceptable since it raised the possibility of British troops pursuing terrorists into Southern territory.
Nonetheless, talks continued in secret. It was indicative of Thatcher's grudging willingness to show some degree of flexibility,
almost in spite of herself, that the key players were not the
personnel of the Northern Ireland Office, which was judged to
be too unimaginatively pro-Unionist. Instead the critical relationship was between Cabinet Secretary Robert Armstrong, who
privately sympathised with nationalist aspirations behind a mask
of professional civil service neutrality, and his opposite number
in Dublin, Dermot Nally. A strong bond was established between
the two mandarins and their respective officials, who included
Armstrong's deputy, David Goodall, a thoughtful, highly intelligent individual who was also a Catholic.

On 12 October 1984, an event occurred which would test the
Prime Minister's commitment to diplomacy to the limit. Weeks
earlier, IRA operatives had installed a bomb in the Grand Hotel,
Brighton, where Thatcher and many of her closest associates were
due to stay during the annual Conservative Party conference. In
the early hours the device was detonated, killing five people and
injuring thirty-one, including Trade and Industry Secretary Norman Tebbit and his wife, who would be confined to a wheelchair
for the rest of her life. The terrorists' principal target miraculously
escaped a similar fate, largely because, as she was characteristically still working on her papers, she was in a part of her hotel
suite which was not seriously affected by the blast. In spite of
the misgivings of some of her staff, Thatcher decided to demonstrate her resilience, and that of the British political system, by
refusing to abandon the conference. Later that morning, according
to plan, she delivered her speech to the delegates, now appropri-
ately modified to proclaim her defiance of the IRA: 'the fact that

we are gathered here now, shocked but composed and determined, is a sign not only that this attack has failed, but that all attempts to destroy democracy by terrorism will fail'.[14] The severe tone in which the final phrase was delivered reinforced the premier's image as an unbending, indomitable leader.

Privately, of course, Thatcher was deeply affected emotionally, both by her visits to the recovering survivors in hospital and by reflection on how close she had come to death or serious injury. The atrocity obliged her to accept a much more stringent personal security regime, although the steel gates which now control access to Downing Street were not installed until 1989. On visits to Northern Ireland, she was flown in convoys of three helicopters, one of them a 'decoy' in order to make the terrorists' task more difficult. They followed a swaying course to minimise the chances of being hit by one of the advanced missiles supplied to the IRA by the anti-Western Libyan leader, Colonel Gaddafi. For the rest of her life Thatcher lived with the possibility of another attempt on her life, sometimes mentioning to close associates her aware-ness of her vulnerability.

The Anglo-Irish agreement

In the short term, the bomb attack slowed down the progress of talks with Dublin, as Thatcher was anxious not to give the impression of being coerced into making concessions to the Republic. It did not, however, derail the negotiations, although the process stalled in November 1984 when, after talks with FitzGerald at Chequers, Thatcher abruptly rejected three options proposed by an official Dublin-sponsored think tank, the New Ireland Forum: unification, a federal union of North and South, and joint Anglo-Irish administration of the province. The negotia-tions revealed Thatcher's fundamental incomprehension of nation-alist demands. At one point she contrasted them with other European minorities, such as the Macedonians, Croats and Serbs, who had no special rights in Yugoslavia – an analogy which FitzGerald refused to accept. She also expressed anxiety that concessions in Northern Ireland might encourage unrest among disaffected Asian communities in mainland Britain's inner cities. Almost exactly a year later, however, Thatcher and FitzGerald met at Hillsborough Castle in Northern Ireland to sign an agreement which Unionist opinion condemned as an outright betrayal of their interests. Although the document made clear that the status of Northern Ireland could only be changed with the consent of a majority of its population, and it did not grant executive powers in the province to the Republic, this was not enough to reassure them. The key point was that the Anglo-Irish agreement, for the first time, gave the Dublin government a right to be consulted on Northern Irish affairs. To this end it established a new pair of institutions: an Anglo-Irish intergovernmental conference in Belfast, to be jointly chaired by the Northern Ireland Secretary and the Irish Foreign Minister, and a joint secretariat to provide support for it.

The agreement was negotiated in conditions of great secrecy. According to Nigel Lawson, this was because Thatcher had reason to fear the leaking of sensitive information if too many people were involved. Most Cabinet ministers, including the Chancellor himself, knew nothing until the agreement was presented for their approval, 'almost as a *fait accompli*'.[15] The key figure was Robert Armstrong, who was supported by Sir Geoffrey Howe as Foreign Secretary, Tom King as Northern Ireland Secretary and his immediate predecessor, Douglas Hurd. If Michael Heseltine was also privy, as Lawson speculated, this is not reflected in the former Defence Secretary's memoirs. Thatcher herself seems to have signed the agreement without much enthusiasm, being persuaded by Armstrong that Britain could expect improved security co-operation from the Republic as a benefit. She seems to have felt that there was no alternative, given the need to do something to reduce nationalist support for Sinn Fein-IRA. She acknowledged another factor in an aside to one of her confidants, Conservative Party Treasurer Alistair McAlpine: 'it was the pressure from the Americans that made me sign that Agreement'.[16] In his memoirs Howe supplied a typically more measured assessment of the part played by Washington. As he explained it, the Thatcher government was 'continually aware of a very resistant strand in American opinion of deep misunderstanding of Britain's role in Ireland'. The agreement had to be placed in the context of the need constantly 'to establish, indeed re-establish, the legitimacy of the presence of British troops' and of British institutions in the province, by taking account of the 'Irish dimension'. It was also intended to undermine fund-raising for terrorism by Irish-American groups, and to encourage the US authorities to extradite suspects wanted for trial in the United Kingdom.[17]

Thatcher was taken aback by the virulence of Unionist hostility to the agreement. Opinion polls registered levels of opposition among Northern Irish Protestants between 75 and 80 per cent. All fifteen Unionist MPs resigned their seats to fight by-elections on the issue, held on the same day in January 1986, and all except one were returned. They were angry not only with the content of the agreement but also because they had not been consulted about the process leading up to the signing. Thatcher was fortunate that diehard support for the Union, once part of mainstream Conservatism, now attracted limited support within her own party. Only twenty-one Conservative MPs voted against the agreement, although it was wounding that the only member of the government to resign over the issue was Ian Gow, now a junior Treasury minister, to whom she had remained personally close.

The limited nature of Conservative opposition reflected a long-term ideological shift, accelerated by the termination of official links with the Ulster Unionists following Heath's suspension of the Stormont assembly, and completed under Thatcher. The typical Conservative of the 1980s was defined far more by attitudes towards economic policy, welfare and defence than by any theoretical attachment to the nation state. Enoch Powell, who still professed an almost mystical reverence for the concept of British nationhood, had left the Conservative Party a decade earlier to join the Ulster Unionist Party. Thus he found little sympathy in the ranks of his old party when he denounced Thatcher in the Commons for allowing what he regarded as a foreign power to exercise influence over Northern Ireland: 'Does the right Hon. Lady understand – if she does not yet understand she soon will – that the penalty for treachery is to fall into public contempt?'[18]

The second half of the decade witnessed an intensification of the violence in Northern Ireland, as Protestant paramilitaries built links with mainstream Unionist politicians, whilst the IRA redoubled its attacks on symbols of British authority and tradition.

Perhaps the most shocking incident was the bombing of a Remembrance Day service at Enniskillen in County Fermanagh in November 1987, in which eleven people died. When the service was defiantly held again two weeks later, Thatcher showed her solidarity with the bereaved community by attending in person. Charles Powell identified this as the moment when 'the iron really entered her soul; she thought that the time and political capital that she had invested in the Anglo-Irish negotiations was negated by the continuance of terrorism'.[19] Thatcher's presence at Enniskillen was typical of the uncompromising defence of the Union which was to the fore in her final years as Prime Minister.

Four months later, Thatcher was embroiled in fresh controversy when members of the SAS shot dead three terrorist suspects on Gibraltar before they could plant a bomb, prompting a bitter dispute between the government and Thames Television over a documentary which questioned the official version of events. Shortly afterwards, the government prohibited the broadcasting of statements by Sinn Fein representatives, in an attempt to deny them what Thatcher termed the 'oxygen of publicity', only to see the television companies circumvent the ban by having actors read their words. In July 1990, she suffered another personal blow at the hands of the terrorists when Ian Gow was murdered by an IRA car bomb on his own drive in Eastbourne. Republican terrorists were planning another attempt on Thatcher's life later that year. As she left office before the attack could be carried out, the IRA instead transferred their attentions to her successor, firing mortar bombs from Whitehall as John Major presided over a meeting in the Cabinet room in February 1991.

Thatcher and the peace process

Judged by the criterion Thatcher prized most highly, the improvement of security in Northern Ireland, the Anglo-Irish agreement could scarcely be rated a success. In the three years to the end of 1985 there were 195 deaths as a result of political violence; in the three years from 1 January 1986, the corresponding figure was 247. It is understandable that in her memoirs Thatcher expressed disappointment at the results of the agreement, arguing that the concessions to Irish nationalist feeling had angered the

Unionists without delivering the level of security co-operation for which she had hoped. She also suggested that 'in the light of this experience it is surely time to consider an alternative approach'.[20] She did not specify what she had in mind, although it can be assumed that her words implied a reversion to a straightforward policy of law enforcement.

Yet it may be that Thatcher was too hard on her own record in Northern Ireland. *The Downing Street Years* was published in 1993, a year before the IRA declared the first of two ceasefires which made it possible for first John Major and then Tony Blair to develop what became known as the peace process. She lacked her successors' willingness to focus consistently on the Northern Ireland problem, and perhaps she lacked the temperament for such engagement. Senior diplomatic adviser, Robin Renwick, considered that she would not have 'been able to muster the infinite patience and care which John Major and later, Tony Blair devoted to managing Irish sensitivities and helping to overcome the innumerable obstacles to an agreement'.[21] Nonetheless, without actively willing it, Thatcher had prepared the ground for an initiative which culminated in the Good Friday agreement of 1998 and the creation of power-sharing institutions in Northern Ireland. Although she did not defeat the IRA, her tough policies in the late 1980s contained the republican threat, without succumbing to the temptation to introduce still more repressive measures, which might have irretrievably alienated mainstream nationalist opinion. Weeks before she left office her last Secretary of State, Peter Brooke, declared that Britain 'has no selfish strategic or economic interest in Northern Ireland', and made clear that it could in the future accept unification by consent. [22] The statement served the purposes of the SDLP leadership, who had been trying to persuade Sinn Fein that Britain should no longer be regarded as a colonial power, and that it was possible for nationalists of different kinds to engage in constructive dialogue with the government in London.

Thatcher's own role in this, as in other attempts at reconciliation in Northern Ireland, was permissive and indirect rather than pro-active. Concessions to the nationalist viewpoint did not come naturally to her. Some of the most hostile comments after her death came from representatives of that tradition. John Hume, for example, described her as an 'extremely divisive figure', whilst Gerry Adams went further in claiming that her 'espousal of old draconian militaristic policies prolonged the war and caused great suffering'.[23] On the Unionist side there was, belatedly, partial forgiveness for the Anglo-Irish agreement from politicians who, almost three decades later, had learned to share power with old nationalist enemies. The Reverend Ian Paisley, who as leader of the hard-line Democratic Unionist Party had led protests against her policies in November 1985, said that 'I condemned some of her actions but . . . she listened to the views of the Unionist people and respected them. In every phase of her life she was great.'[24] Thatcher would not have been surprised by such widely diverging assessments. In office she had held the line against what she saw as the forces of anarchy. It was not a role which was ever likely to make her a popular figure. At the same time, unwittingly, she had helped to make possible a fragile yet still valuable peace in the United Kingdom's most divided region.

Notes

1 Quoted in Eamonn Mallie and David McKittrick, *Endgame in Ireland* (London, Hodder and Stoughton, 2001), p. 49.
2 James Prior, *A Balance of Power* (London, Hamish Hamilton, 1986), p. 197.
3 Quoted in Paul Arthur, *Special Relationships: Britain, Ireland and the Northern Ireland Problem* (Belfast, Blackstaff Press, 2000), p. 212.
4 Douglas Hurd, *Memoirs* (London, Abacus, 2003), p. 302.
5 Quoted in Michael Cunningham, *British Government Policy in Northern Ireland 1969–2000* (Manchester, Manchester University Press, 2001), p. 68.
6 Margaret Thatcher, *The Downing Street Years* (London, Harper Collins, 1993), p. 385.
7 Quoted in David Bloomfield and Maeve Lankford, 'From whitewash to mayhem: the state of the secretary in Northern Ireland' in Peter Catterall and Sean McDougall (eds), *The Northern Ireland Question in British Politics* (London, Macmillan, 1996), p. 152.
8 John Cole, *As It Seemed To Me: Political Memoirs* (London, Phoenix, 1996), p. 291.
9 Margaret Thatcher, House of Commons PQs, 14 May 1981, http://www.margaretthatcher.org/document/104649 (accessed 10 August 2014).
10 Quoted in Roy Greenslade, 'The IRA hunger strike and Fleet Street's graveyard of truth', *Guardian*, 17 June 2011.

11 Quoted in Mallie and McKittrick, *Endgame in Ireland*, p. 38.
12 Michael Alison, quoted in Charles Moore, *Margaret Thatcher: The Authorized Biography: Volume One: Not for Turning* (London, Allen Lane, 2013), p. 611.
13 Prior, *Balance of Power*, p. 199.
14 Thatcher, *Downing Street Years*, p. 382.
15 Nigel Lawson, *The View from No. 11: Memoirs of a Tory Radical* (London, Bantam, 1992), p. 669.
16 Alistair McAlpine, *Once a Jolly Bagman: Memoirs* (London, Weidenfeld & Nicolson, 1997), p. 272.
17 Geoffrey Howe, *Conflict of Loyalty* (London, Macmillan, 1994), p. 422.
18 House of Commons Debates, 14 November 1985, vol. 86, col. 682, http://hansard.millbanksystems.com/commons/1985/nov/14/engagements (accessed 10 August 2014).
19 Quoted in Mallie and McKittrick, *Endgame in Ireland*, p. 64.
20 Thatcher, *Downing Street Years*, p. 415.
21 Robin Renwick, *A Journey With Margaret Thatcher: Foreign Policy Under the Iron Lady* (London, Biteback, 2013), p. 120.
22 Quoted in Cunningham, *British Government Policy in Northern Ireland*, p. 79.
23 Quoted in *The Times*, 9 April 2013, p. 17.
24 Quoted in *The Independent*, 9 April 2013, p. 9.

8 Between the superpowers: 1979–1990

Margaret Thatcher, Cold Warrior

Margaret Thatcher was the last British Prime Minister to face the unique set of challenges posed by the Cold War. She came to power at a time when East–West relations were in an uneasy state of equilibrium, as the superpowers had apparently learned to live alongside each other in the era of *détente*. Within months of her election, however, US-Soviet tensions increased once again following the USSR's invasion of Afghanistan on Christmas Day 1979. This was followed by a series of confrontations in different parts of the globe, leading to an increasingly hostile international atmosphere in the opening years of the new decade. Poland provided a flashpoint in December 1981, when its communist regime outraged the West by imposing martial law on its civilian population. This draconian action was a direct response to pressure from Moscow, which had lost patience with the Warsaw government's tolerance of an independent trade union, Solidarity. Then, in the autumn of 1983, following the Soviet Union's introduction of SS20 intermediate range nuclear missiles into its eastern European satellite states, Thatcher demonstrated her determination to confront it from a position of strength, with the installation of US Cruise missiles at the Greenham Common air base in Berkshire. From 1985, however, with the appointment of a new and more conciliatory Soviet leader, Mikhail Gorbachev, tensions gradually began to relax until, by the end of the decade, the two sides had started to dismantle their nuclear armouries, whilst communist control of Eastern Europe was disintegrating with unexpected speed. Thatcher's last major public act as Prime Minister, in

November 1990, was to attend an international conference in Paris, at which heads of government officially marked the end of the forty-five year confrontation between East and West.

Thatcher's conduct of policy in the final decade of the Cold War is one of the most controversial aspects of her period of office. As the USA's principal European ally, Britain participated in these events, even if its relative economic and military weakness meant that its role was always a supporting rather than a leading one. Particularly after the election as US President of Ronald Reagan, with whom she formed a strong political and personal bond, she was widely viewed as willing to subordinate British interests to those of her stronger transatlantic partner. In her early years in Number 10, Thatcher became a hate figure to the anti-nuclear protest movement, and to large sections of the British left. It was easy to caricature her and Reagan as dogmatic anti-communists, who were prepared to take risks with global peace; they were described by miners' leader, Arthur Scargill, for example, as the 'most dangerous duo, President Ray-Gun and the plutonium blonde, Margaret Thatcher'.[1] *Socialist Worker* magazine produced a spoof cinema poster, with Reagan and Thatcher posing in the style of Clark Gable and Vivien Leigh in the romantic epic, *Gone with the Wind*, against a background of a nuclear explosion. Underneath was the slogan, 'She promised to follow him to the end of the earth. He promised to organise it!' Yet it was not only the political left who felt that Thatcher was too unequivocally pro-American. In his memoirs, Sir Geoffrey Howe drew attention to his attempts as Foreign Secretary in 1983–9 to offer some kind of counterbalance to the premier's enthusiastic Atlanticism, referring pointedly to 'Margaret's technique of influencing American thinking by starting from a premise of loudly proclaimed loyalty'.[2] This chapter examines the realities of Thatcher's relationship with the Washington administration. It goes on to consider the nature of her contribution to the development and eventual ending of the Cold War.

America's puppet?

Margaret Thatcher was at one with her recent predecessors as Prime Minister – with the exception of Edward Heath, who had emphasised Britain's European identity to an unusual degree – in attaching central importance to the American alliance. Since 1945 successive British governments had recognised the importance of an association based upon shared values and culture, as well as upon the hard-headed advantages of collaboration in defence and the sharing of intelligence material. Thatcher's 1979 agreement to purchase submarine-based Trident nuclear missiles from the US confirmed the centrality of the relationship. She did, however, stand out for the depth of her emotional empathy with American values, and for her willingness to support US policy positions overseas. With Jimmy Carter, who had been US President for more than two years before her arrival in Downing Street, she developed a cordial and mutually respectful relationship without any great personal warmth. Nonetheless, Thatcher took every opportunity to assure him of British solidarity in the face of what she perceived as a global communist challenge. Following the arrival of Soviet troops in Cuba, an area of special sensitivity to the US, but of limited direct importance to Britain, she told Carter that she was 'especially encouraged by your statement that you are accelerating efforts to increase the capability of the United States to use its military forces worldwide', and emphasised the 'imperative need to demonstrate to the Russians that the West will not tolerate further action of this kind'.[3]

The most important phase of Thatcher's relationship with the USA, however, began when Ronald Reagan succeeded Carter as President in January 1981. In contrast to his Democratic Party predecessor, the Republican Reagan was an instinctive conservative with whom Thatcher felt very much at ease. They had first met in 1975 when the sixty-four year old Reagan, at that time a former governor of California, was visiting London. Although he was not then regarded in British political circles as a particularly important figure, he struck up an immediate rapport with the newly elected Conservative Party leader. Once he had been installed in the White House, he and Thatcher revived and strengthened the link which they had originally established.

Whereas it had taken the invasion of Afghanistan to cause Carter to harden his approach to the Eastern bloc, Thatcher and Reagan had always regarded the Soviet Union as the spearhead of a hostile ideology, whose advance the West must resist at all costs. 'Communism,' Thatcher declared in a speech delivered in her first month in office, 'never sleeps, never changes its objectives, nor must we.'[4] The two leaders were both, in different ways, outsiders to their respective political establishments. Thatcher's mission to end the long years of British decline was paralleled by Reagan's desire to restore American greatness after the successive reverses it had suffered in the 1970s, with the country's defeat in the Vietnam War, President Nixon's disgrace in the Watergate scandal and the humiliating occupation of the US embassy in Iran by Islamic militants, in the final year of Carter's presidency.

Shared political values were reinforced by a strong personal chemistry, even though in many ways they were quite different personalities. Reagan was relaxed, good-humoured and much better at communicating the 'big picture' than at focusing on the detail. He had an instinctive grasp of political issues which, unlike Thatcher's, was not backed up by assiduous background work. 'In my experience,' one White House adviser said of Reagan, 'he fails the essay questions but gets the multiple choices.'[5] It is impossible to imagine Thatcher saying, or even being amused by, his flippant reflection that 'they say hard work never killed anyone, but I figure, why take a chance?'[6] Yet there developed between the two leaders a mutual admiration and affection. François Mitterrand wryly remarked that 'Mrs Thatcher, who can be so tough when she talks to her European partners, is like a little girl of eight years old when she talks to the President of the United States.'[7] Although the French President's observation was clearly exaggerated, undoubtedly Thatcher warmed to Reagan much more than she did to any other world leader. She also used her feminine charm to influence him in the direction of support for British interests, and he was tolerant of her occasional outbursts, clearly appreciating her strength of character.

Within the overall context of broad agreement on most policy areas, however, it should be noted that Thatcher did not slavishly follow Washington's line at all times. Where British interests were jeopardised by aspects of American policy, she was prepared to stand up to her ally. This was demonstrated long before Reagan's installation in the White House, when his predecessor looked to her to form a united front in opposition to the Soviet occupation of Afghanistan. At the level of rhetoric Thatcher was quick to match Jimmy Carter's sharp response, recognising the Soviet action as a direct challenge to the global balance of power. Her government used the diplomatic weapons at its disposal to make clear its disapproval of Russian aggression, helping to secure United Nations condemnation and trying – with limited success – to persuade British athletes not to attend the 1980 Moscow Olympics. At the same time, however, conscious of the importance of not damaging British commercial interests, Thatcher ensured that Britain participated in only the most limited economic sanctions. The decision not to renew the 1975 Anglo-Soviet credit agreement, for example, was a largely symbolic act which was unlikely to inflict significant disruption on trade between the two countries. The need to protect the fragile British economy took precedence over giving full support to the American government's planned trade boycott.

Even during the Reagan presidency, Thatcher was prepared to assert herself when circumstances demanded. Richard Perle, his Assistant Defence Secretary, recalled that 'she never approached the conversations she had . . . with American officials and with the president from a position of supplication or inferiority. Quite the contrary.'[8] She clashed with Reagan in 1981–2 when he tried to punish the Soviet Union for its role in the declaration of Polish martial law by including technology for a gas pipeline linking Siberia and Western Europe in a package of sanctions. With major British investment committed to the project, Thatcher was not prepared to go along with US policy. Not only was the company involved, John Brown Engineering, a significant employer, there was also an issue of legal principle in that contracts had already been signed. She fought her corner in protracted and eventually successful negotiations, even showing a willingness to offend Washington by highlighting its inconsistency in calling for sanctions which would affect European firms, whilst pacifying the powerful American farm lobby by allowing continued grain exports to the Soviet Union.

Two further episodes in 1982–3 underlined the reality that Thatcher could not rely automatically on US support, or even on prior consultation where the superpower's own vital interests were at stake. As we have seen in Chapter 4, she was disturbed by Reagan's slowness to come down unequivocally on her side in the Falklands crisis, and his administration's persistence in pursuit of a compromise solution to the Anglo-Argentinian conflict. Equilibrium was restored to the relationship by an official visit made by Reagan to Britain towards the end of the fighting, in the course of which, in an address to parliamentarians at Westminster, he commended the efforts of British forces to liberate the islands:

> those young men aren't fighting for mere real estate. They fight for a cause, for the belief that armed aggression must not be allowed to succeed and that people must participate in the decisions of government under the rule of law.[9]

It is perhaps significant, however, that this passage does not appear in Thatcher's memoirs; indeed the whole visit, so carefully prepared at the time, is covered in only half a page. Even if not seriously enough to undermine the basis of their relationship, Thatcher's confidence in Reagan had been shaken.

In October 1983 that confidence was to be tested again. A coup in the small Caribbean island of Grenada led to the replacement of one Marxist regime by another, more violent one. Concerned for the safety of its own citizens on the island, and more broadly for the stability of a region so close to the United States, Reagan responded to a request for support from neighbouring governments by sending in the Marines to overthrow the coup plotters and to restore order. The incident was significant because the President kept Thatcher in the dark until the invasion was underway, even though Grenada was a Commonwealth country whose nominal head of state was Queen Elizabeth II. The action caused Thatcher considerable embarrassment because, shortly before, Geoffrey Howe had assured the Commons that there was no reason to anticipate an invasion. In transatlantic discussions by telephone, it was clear that Thatcher had been deeply angered by her ally's unilateralism. Unusually, she also reprimanded her leading ally in public, grounding her argument in considerations of international law. In a BBC World Service phone-in she rejected the idea that the Western democracies should use force 'to walk into other people's countries, independent sovereign territories', and stated that 'there are many, many peoples in countries in the world who would love to be free of [communism] . . . that doesn't mean to say that we can just walk into them and say now you are free, I'm afraid'.[10] This argument may have weighed with Thatcher, although it seems unlikely that it was uppermost in her mind. After all, six years later she would congratulate Reagan's successor, George Bush Senior, on his intervention in Panama to remove its leader, General Noriega.

The Grenada episode hurt Thatcher because of her exclusion from the Washington decision-making process. Reagan's explanation, that he had feared a leak within his own administration, had he involved Britain, carried little conviction. It seems much more likely that he did not inform his counterpart until the operation was a *fait accompli* because he sensed that she would object. The Grenada intervention opened Thatcher to ridicule from her parliamentary opponents, who were quick to point out how it punctured her claims to exercise special influence in Washington. Shadow Foreign Secretary, Denis Healey, for example, described her in the Commons as 'an obedient poodle to the American President' and accused her of 'an unforgivable dereliction of duty' in failing to avert the invasion.[11]

The intervention also increased the political pressure on Thatcher at the time that Cruise missiles were being installed in Britain. This was being carried out in spite of misgivings on the part of a significant section of public opinion, which feared that the USA would not consult London before taking a decision on use of these weapons. It rubbed salt in the wound that the Americans, triumphant after a militarily successful operation, were slow to understand the reasons for Thatcher's embarrassment. Indeed, some members of the Washington administration were disappointed at what they saw as Britain's ingratitude for the material help received during the Falklands conflict. Secretary of State George Shultz recalled his annoyance in his memoirs, writing that 'whatever the reasons for Prime Minister Thatcher's opposition, she did not exhibit any particular concern for "the special relationship" between Britain and America'.[12]

Grenada was, however, an isolated case of direct confrontation between the two leaders. Thatcher recognised that, in general, Britain's interests were best served by seeking to minimise differences between the two countries and by offering the President support, even when she had private doubts about the wisdom of US policy. A good example is Reagan's support for the right-wing 'Contra' faction, which was mining the waters of Nicaragua in defiance of the International Court of Justice at The Hague. Recognising the strength of Reagan's hostility to the leftist regime in power in this Central American state, she overruled her Foreign Secretary and declined to endorse a United Nations resolution in support of the Court's ruling.

For Thatcher, the benefits that she was likely to garner as a result of America's gratitude outweighed any reservations she might have about the behaviour of her transatlantic ally. In April 1986 she braved considerable domestic unpopularity when she gave permission for US warplanes to take off from British bases for an attack on Colonel Gaddafi's Libya, a 'rogue state' which the Americans blamed for a number of terrorist attacks. Even her ultra-loyal deputy, Whitelaw, privately regarded the American leader as 'a madman'[13] for initiating such action. Thatcher herself had serious doubts, cross-questioning Reagan in advance on which targets were to be hit, and on how the attack was to be justified in public. Yet in spite of her very real concerns, she believed that the US should not be opposed, once its mind was made up. An important gain for Britain, which Reagan linked specifically to Thatcher's support over Libya, was his support for legislation to enable the extradition of IRA members from the USA, which was pushed through Congress in defiance of the influential Irish-American lobby.

Thatcher and Gorbachev

For all the furore that they aroused at the time, Grenada and Libya were essentially side-shows, with little bearing on the most important thread in international relations in the 1980s: the changing relationship between East and West. Thatcher's most important achievement in foreign affairs was to be found in this area. Without abandoning her deep-rooted opposition to communism, or her wariness towards Soviet intentions, in the mid-1980s she played an important role in developing dialogue with the Russian leadership. No less significantly, she helped to encourage Reagan – the President who in March 1983 described the

USSR as an 'evil empire' – to believe that a more constructive relationship with Moscow was possible.

Crucially, a new phase in the Cold War began at the point in her premiership when Thatcher stood at the peak of her power and self-confidence. In her first term, overseas affairs had often taken second place to other, more immediately pressing policy matters, and the premier had been willing to take advice from her much more experienced Foreign Secretary, Lord Carrington. None of his successors – Geoffrey Howe, John Major and Douglas Hurd – would come close to equalling his prestige, or would enjoy a relationship of near-equality with the Prime Minister. Moreover, they had to work with a premier emboldened by the outcome of the Falklands conflict, and strengthened politically by her re-election in June 1983. By then Thatcher was also the most senior of the major West European leaders, having taken office two years before François Mitterrand in France and three years before the election of the new West German Chancellor, Helmut Kohl. In carrying out her ideas she was buttressed, from early 1984, by the appointment as foreign affairs private secretary of Charles Powell, an able official on long-term secondment from the Foreign Office. Although by background and training a civil servant, Powell instinctively shared many of the Prime Minister's attitudes on international relations. By staying at Number 10 until after the end of her premiership, he came to exercise a formidable influence behind the scenes. The closeness of their working relationship led one veteran mandarin, Sir Percy Cradock, to observe that 'it was sometimes . . . difficult to establish where Mrs Thatcher ended and Charles Powell began'.[14] For the remaining six years of her premiership, Thatcher was to be in a stronger position to develop her own vision of foreign policy.

By 1983 the Soviet Union had reached a critical point in its history. After years of ossification under an elderly and unimaginative Politburo leadership, the communist system was in dire need of a radical overhaul. The Soviet economy was buckling under the weight of an excessive military budget, although it was difficult for outsiders to assess the seriousness of the problems that it faced. The country's ailing, inefficient bureaucracy was clearly in need of reform. At the same time the USSR continued to view the non-communist world with suspicion. This was highlighted early in

September 1983 by the shooting down of a South Korean airliner which had strayed into Soviet airspace, an act for which the regime refused to apologise. Two months later, the Soviet leadership genuinely believed that a NATO military exercise codenamed Able Archer 83 could be a cover for a surprise US nuclear strike on their territory. We should not underestimate the seriousness of this final acute phase of Cold War tensions.

Thatcher was conscious of the need to reassess relations with the Soviet Union, whilst commanding its respect by maintaining a position of strength in any future talks. Although aware of the weaknesses of the communist system, she and her inner circle did not predict the rapidity with which, in less than a decade, the USSR would collapse. For the foreseeable future, Thatcher believed, the West must live alongside the Soviet Union and it was in its interests to open up dialogue with the Kremlin. Reagan was willing and able to outbid the Soviets on defence, maintaining his country's superpower status by investing about 7 per cent of US national income in armaments, so that Moscow had to spend about 30 per cent of its budget in order to keep pace. This was not a viable strategy for a cash-starved Britain. The commitment, as a member of NATO, to an annual 3 per cent increase in the national contribution to the alliance budget imposed a significant strain on the economy. A more constructive approach to the Cold War enemy was required.

By 1983, Thatcher was actively seeking independent, informed advice on the nature of the Soviet regime and all aspects of its economy and society. She had less contact now with more ideologically committed, hard-line Cold War thinkers, such as intelligence expert Brian Crozier, who had been an important source of information during her years in opposition. Nor was she content to rely solely on the resources of the Foreign Office establishment. It was typical of her intellectual curiosity, and her thoroughness, that she organised a seminar on the Communist bloc at Chequers in September 1983, attended by a number of academic specialists as well as by the relevant ministers and officials. According to his own account it was one of the invited scholars, Oxford professor Archie Brown, who identified the member of the Soviet hierarchy who was most likely to promote change within the system. This was Mikhail Gorbachev, aged fifty-two at the time of the Chequers seminar and therefore the youngest of the Soviet governing elite. Brown described him as 'the best-educated member of the Politburo and probably the most open-minded' and as someone who 'might well be the most hopeful choice from the point of view both of Soviet citizens and the outside world'.[15] This recommendation reinforced Thatcher's growing belief, supported by the Foreign Office, that greater contact with the Eastern bloc was in Britain's best interests. She began to differentiate much more between the various communist satellite regimes, tentatively seeking to establish points of contact with those which seemed most amenable to Western influence. For example, early the following year, she paid a visit to Hungary, whose government had introduced some cautious market reforms within the context of continued one-party political control.

More important was the growth of a personal link between Thatcher and the coming man of the USSR. She first made contact with Gorbachev at Soviet leader, Yuri Andropov's funeral in February 1984, when the British Prime Minister impressed the younger man by waiting respectfully in the freezing cold as the cortege passed by. Her attendance at the funeral was itself significant: she had not travelled to Moscow for that of his long-serving predecessor, Leonid Brezhnev, who had died in November 1982. This was followed, in December 1984, by a meeting at Chequers which enabled Thatcher and Gorbachev to get to know each other better. Famously, she told a BBC interviewer after the talks that she liked Gorbachev and that 'we can do business together'.[16] It was a timely visit for, the following March, Gorbachev became General Secretary of the Soviet Communist Party when Andropov's successor, the equally infirm Konstantin Chernenko, died after little more than a year in office. This was, however, far from a meeting of minds. Thatcher and Gorbachev vigorously argued the respective merits of the free market and the centrally planned economy. She raised the issue of human rights for dissidents within the USSR, and accused the Soviets of providing financial support for miners in Britain, who were using force to prosecute their long-running strike: 'the Soviet Union's fellow-Communists who could not get their own way through the ballot box were opting for violence'.[17]

Through their arguments the two leaders evolved a mutual respect which provided the basis for further progress. In his memoirs Gorbachev paid tribute to her as 'a self-confident woman, the gentle charm and feminine façade disguising a rather tough and pragmatic politician. Her nickname the 'Iron Lady' is very apt.'[18] She was impressed by Gorbachev's willingness to discard his official brief, and to engage in debate about fundamental issues. Thatcher was aware, however, that notwithstanding his genuine human warmth, and his desire to reform the Soviet system, he remained a believer in communism. She also made it clear that he stood no chance of dividing her from the Americans; the Atlantic alliance would remain the essential foundation of British policy.

Arms and the woman: nuclear defence and the Cold War

Thatcher's ingrained adherence to the American camp meant that she never truly played the part of an intermediary between Reagan and Gorbachev. In any case, independently of the links she was forging with the Russian leader, by 1985 the US was moving away from the posture of unbending opposition to the Eastern bloc which it had adopted in the early Reagan years. Thatcher's advocacy did, however, help to persuade Reagan that Gorbachev was to be taken seriously, when some voices in the US administration were urging a more sceptical approach. In addition, Thatcher's high standing with conservative opinion in America helped Reagan to reassure his public that constructive engagement with the Soviets was now possible.

Even at this stage, however, when Thatcher's influence on the world stage was at its height, there were difficulties in the relationship with America. Although outwardly she and Reagan often seemed to speak with one voice, this apparent unity masked an important difference between them on the subject of nuclear weapons. In March 1983, the President had announced that the USA was working on a project known as the Strategic Defence Initiative, which was soon to be popularly dubbed 'Star Wars' after the well-known series of science fiction films. SDI involved plans for the construction of space-based laser systems, capable of destroying intercontinental nuclear missiles at the point on their trajectory when they temporarily left the earth's atmosphere. If such a scheme could be realised, it would make redundant any opposing state's most potent weaponry. Knowing that the USSR's ailing economy could not hope to compete on equal terms with such a technologically advanced development, Gorbachev became anxious to have SDI included in any negotiations on arms reduction. For Reagan, however, Star Wars was not merely a winning card in the struggle for a decisive advantage over the Soviet Union. In spite of his popular image as a one-dimensional Cold War crusader, the President in fact had a deep moral anxiety about the destructive power of nuclear weapons, and wanted to find some way of ensuring their ultimate abolition.

This presented Thatcher with an acute dilemma. Her academic background made SDI an intriguing technological concept, and she also sensed the opportunities in research and development which it might offer her own country's scientific industry. On the other hand, in common with other West European leaders, she feared that Reagan's enthusiasm might place in jeopardy the American nuclear umbrella, under which they had sheltered from the Soviet threat for forty years. The situation called on all her resources of diplomatic skill as she sought to find a way of guaranteeing European security without alienating her most powerful global partner. Thatcher was also able to exploit her inside knowledge of Washington, in order to secure allies within the Reagan administration who did not share the President's millenarian vision of a nuclear-free world. Meeting Reagan at the presidential country retreat, Camp David, in December 1984, she was able to secure a written understanding that research into SDI would continue, but that its deployment would be a matter for future negotiation. The meeting was a good illustration of Thatcher's business-like approach and of her effective use of her personal link with Reagan. She had in effect secured an undertaking from the Americans that they would not abandon the concept of nuclear deterrence. As Press Secretary Bernard Ingham, who accompanied the Prime Minister, put it, she did not go to Camp David 'to argue for the sake of argument. She went to clinch. And the only way in international diplomacy to clinch it is to set out your conclusions on paper.'[19]

The limits of Thatcher's ability to exercise influence in a world still dominated by the two superpowers were, however, underlined with painful clarity when Reagan and Gorbachev met at Reykjavik in Iceland in October 1986 to discuss arms control. In the event, no substantive agreement was reached, as a consequence of Reagan's refusal to accede to Gorbachev's demand for SDI to be put on the bargaining table. What alarmed Thatcher, however, was how close the two men had come to an agreement to eliminate all nuclear weapons. As an unqualified believer in nuclear deterrence she was horrified by the threat to the future of Trident, which was due to replace Britain's ageing Polaris system within the next decade. If the US abandoned its own nuclear programme, it was hardly likely to supply such a weapon to an ally. Without it, Britain would be left vulnerable to the Soviet Union's huge superiority in conventional weapons. Thatcher likened Reykjavik to an 'earthquake': 'there was no place where you could put your political feet, where you were certain you could stand'.[20] Unusually, she confided in President Mitterrand her belief that Reagan saw SDI as the way to win himself a place in the history books: 'it's harder to deal with someone who has a dream than someone who has a real objective'.[21] In a subsequent meeting with Reagan, Thatcher secured an undertaking that the Trident programme would be protected. Even in this instance, however, she was fortunate to find allies in Washington, in the form of the US Joint Chiefs of Staff, who had already used their own powers of persuasion with the President.

Thatcher had helped to prepare the ground for a deal on the elimination of intermediate range missiles from Europe, towards which the superpower leaders were moving by 1987. She had helped to persuade the Soviet leader that he could not win the arms race, and also that Reagan was sincere about seeking a balanced reduction of nuclear forces. But as final agreement drew nearer, her own importance to the process necessarily diminished. This was masked by two spectacular public relations coups in the course of the year. In March, she paid a highly publicised, and very successful, official visit to the Soviet Union. Dramatically attired in a fur hat and new Aquascutum outfit for a tour of the capital city, she impressed ordinary Muscovites with her panache. In the words of her speech writer and admirer, Ronald Millar, 'the embodiment of the free world, she came on like a modern Tsarina, hailed in triumph by a Communist people'.[22] The visit also saw the Prime Minister attend a Russian Orthodox ceremony at Zagorsk monastery, symbolising the reformist Soviet regime's new-found spirit of tolerance towards other belief systems. In another indication of the openness of debate which Gorbachev had encouraged, Thatcher took part in a television interview in which she openly challenged the Soviet arms build-up.

Nine months later, Gorbachev stopped off to meet her at Brize Norton air base in Oxfordshire, on his way to sign the Intermediate Nuclear Force (INF) treaty with Reagan. It was a fitting recognition of the part she had played in the unexpected evolution of this triangular relationship. At Brize Norton Gorbachev accepted an invitation to make an official visit to Britain, which took place in April 1989. Thatcher also took the opportunity, in interviews given after the air base meeting, to emphasise once again her commitment to deterrence – 'I want a war-free Europe, not a nuclear-free Europe' – and although she welcomed the forthcoming superpower arms control agreement, she stressed that Britain's small arsenal would remain unaffected.[23] Yet it was perhaps more accurately indicative of her junior partner status that, after Gorbachev had flown on to America, Thatcher was left to telephone Reagan to give her assessment of the Soviet leader's frame of mind. She was not to share a stage with the two superpower leaders as they appeared before the world's media in Washington.

From thaw to flood

Almost a year after the signing of the INF treaty, Reagan hosted Thatcher at the White House for the last time before his retirement in January 1989. It was, predictably, a celebratory occasion on which the two leaders paid fulsome tribute to each other, without a hint of their past differences. With his successor, George Bush Senior, whom Thatcher had known as Vice-President during the Reagan years, her relations were never as close. This was partly because the incoming President wanted to make his own mark on foreign policy, without being defined by what had gone before. But there were also important differences of personality and approach. Bush took an essentially pragmatic, managerial view of world affairs, encapsulated in his famous admission that he did not possess 'the vision thing'. In her memoirs Thatcher suggested that he 'had never had to think through his beliefs and fight for them when they were hopelessly unfashionable as Ronald Reagan and I had had to do'. This meant that he had to seek solutions to problems 'which to me came quite spontaneously, because they sprang from my basic convictions'.[24] In particular, Bush did not understand Thatcher's opposition to greater European unity, which she began to articulate from her September 1988 Bruges speech onwards. With a US administration in place which preferred to deal with a more closely integrated group of European countries, Thatcher feared the loss of her much prized influence in Washington.

Other, wider factors help to explain the differences between Thatcher and the USA's new leader. International relations moved rapidly in the first year of the Bush presidency, leaving Thatcher identified with policy positions which soon appeared outdated, and this was a source of frustration for the new US administration. The autumn of 1989 saw the collapse of communist regimes in the former Soviet satellite states of Eastern Europe. Remarkably, unlike his hard-line predecessors in the Kremlin, Gorbachev did not to attempt to prop up the USSR's client regimes in East Germany, Hungary, Czechoslovakia and Poland, instead leaving their leaders to make their own terms with the movements of popular protest which were poised to sweep away communist rule. Only in the Baltic states, which the Soviet leadership considered more fundamental to its own security, did the regime contemplate intervention. Conscious of the USSR's economic weakness, and anxious not to jeopardise the benefits of his newly established links with the West, he chose the path of restraint. What had been a tentative thaw in the Cold War had now become a flood.

The unravelling of the Eastern bloc took Thatcher, along with most of her contemporaries, by surprise. In theory this was the outcome for which she and other Western Cold Warriors had longed. On the other hand, the changes introduced a new and unsettling instability into international relations. There had always been an ambivalence in her attitude towards Gorbachev and his reform strategy within the Soviet Union. George Shultz approvingly recalled a remark she had once made, that 'Gorbachev thinks there are problems with the way the system works; he thinks he can make changes to make it work better. He doesn't understand that *the system is the problem*.'[25]

As the Soviet leader's hold on power weakened, however, Thatcher was slow to adapt. She was surprisingly reluctant to acknowledge the diminishing importance of the personal relationship on which she had placed such emphasis over the past five years. Viewing Gorbachev as a bulwark of stability, she was anxious about the effect of any changes on his position. Her foreign policy adviser, Percy Cradock, recalled discussing with Thatcher, late in 1988, how Britain should react to Soviet suppression of a possible revolt in the Baltic states. Her response was to say that she would speak out, but Britain's interest in the stability of the region would override the promotion of freedom in Eastern Europe. Her preferred policy was to encourage individual states to develop ties with the West and to undertake economic and political reforms. Events over the course of the following year would reveal Thatcher to be hopelessly out of step with the pace of change. As late as November 1989, the month that the Berlin Wall came down, she was insisting to Bush that 'the US must keep a "substantial presence" in Europe' and that 'the cold war would not be over until the end of the century'.[26] Her American host listened politely, but mentally he had moved on to a new European scenario which Thatcher was unwilling to accept.

Thatcher was particularly slow to come to terms with the dramatic sequence of events in Germany, which by early 1990 made reunification likely in the near future. Bush was relaxed about the prospect, provided that the new German state was anchored in both NATO and the European Community as a guarantee of its democratic credentials. In May 1989, he publicly referred to America and West Germany as 'partners in leadership',[27] raising the concern in Thatcher's mind that a strong, united Germany might replace Britain as the USA's closest European ally. In truth she was not the only Western leader to feel a sense of alarm at the speed with which reunification had appeared on the agenda. François Mitterrand shared her concerns, telling

her in a private meeting in January 1990 that the prospect of
unity had 'delivered a sort of mental shock to the Germans'. Its
effect, he said, was 'to turn them once again into the "bad"
Germans they used to be'. He differed from Thatcher, however,
in his recognition that other European states would have to
accommodate themselves to reality. For her part she insisted that
if the members of the European Community made their opposition clear to the Germans, they could delay reunification: 'German
policy was to test how far they could go with the rest of us, and
at the moment they were getting away with too much'.[28] In fact
this was not feasible. There was no real chance of mobilising the
US and the leaders of the European Community in a futile stand
against an outcome fervently desired by millions of ordinary
Germans.

Many commentators consider that Thatcher's extremely negative approach reflected an inability to move beyond a fear of
German domination, which dated back to her wartime childhood.
Although she did not envisage a revived German military threat,
in the words of Douglas Hurd, her last Foreign Secretary, 'she
argued that unification would unbalance Europe by adding fifteen
million disciplined Saxons and Prussians to what was already
Europe's leading economic power'.[29] She knew few Germans at
a personal level and was left untouched by the well-meaning
attempts of Chancellor Kohl to build a closer relationship with
her. After an informal visit to his home town, during which Kohl
tried hard to impress her with the culture and catering of his
native Rhineland, she confided to Charles Powell on the return
journey, 'My God, that man is so German'.[30] The Chancellor's
hospitality had failed to overcome Thatcher's fundamental prejudice against his country.

On German reunification, Thatcher's real position was that
she wanted to see it achieved gradually, rather than to block it
forever; but this was not how she came across. In Percy Cradock's
words, 'the fact that it was not all-out opposition, merely a plea
for care and delay mattered little; the press had the caricature
they needed'.[31] She gave the impression that Germany was not
to be trusted, and that she wanted to sustain the post-war division of the country, sponsored by the four victorious powers.
Particularly damaging were reports of a seminar convened at

Chequers in March 1990, to which Thatcher, accompanied by Douglas Hurd and Charles Powell, invited a number of scholarly experts on German history. The holding of such an event was typical of Thatcher's laudable desire to gain a fuller understanding of a particular issue. What was worrying, however, was that she ignored the subtleties of the academic arguments aired at the meeting to reach her own, over-simplified conclusions regarding German national characteristics. According to a memorandum prepared by Charles Powell, which later leaked to the press, these included 'angst, aggressiveness, assertiveness, bullying, egotism, inferiority complex, sentimentality'.[32] In the words of George Urban, a scholar who began as an admirer of Thatcher but became disillusioned by her embrace of national stereotypes,

> Germany is, deep down in her mind, still Britain's real foe. Russia, although not to be trusted either, is a distant factor . . . but also a balancing factor . . . in her subconscious thinking I nevertheless detected a hankering for the verities of the Second World War, if not the First.[33]

Thatcher's concerns were to some extent understandable. As Charles Powell has argued, at the time there was no guarantee that West Germany might not be pressured by the Soviet Union into leaving NATO as the price of absorbing the East. Having invested so much political capital in building up a good relationship with Gorbachev, she was also anxious to see the German situation resolved in a way that did not risk destabilising his position: 'his co-operation was essential to dismantling the Cold War, but it could only be secured by taking reasonable account of Soviet interests, rather than rubbing his nose in the collapse of the Communist system'.[34] She was not the only one to be taken by surprise by the rapid disintegration of the USSR; in fact Gorbachev and his state would be gone by Christmas 1991, little more than a year after her own departure from office. With hindsight, Thatcher would have been better advised to adapt to a process which she could not prevent, rather than taking a stand which could only alienate her European allies and reduce the influence she wielded in Washington.

Crisis in the Gulf

It was an event far from Europe and unconnected to the Cold War that enabled Thatcher, shortly before her ejection from office, to recover some of her old intimacy with the USA. This was the invasion of Kuwait by Saddam Hussein, dictator of Iraq, in August 1990. The threat to nearby Saudi Arabia, and to the oil resources of the Gulf region, alarmed Thatcher, who was clear from the beginning that a robust response was required. To her the situation was analogous to Argentina's violation of the Falklands, eight years earlier, and in her opinion appeasement was out of the question. She was in a position to make her views felt because by coincidence both she and Bush were scheduled to speak at a conference in Aspen, Colorado. There is some dispute over how far Thatcher needed to push the President into sharing her own views. In her memoirs she described his response to the crisis in a positive light, noting that although initially he was prepared to give an Arab solution time to work, he also insisted that this must include the withdrawal of Iraqi troops from Kuwait. Much was subsequently made of a phrase she used in conversation with the President, that 'this is no time to go wobbly',[35] although it is now acknowledged that this referred to a specific disagreement over the action to be taken after two Iraqi tankers violated the Western blockade of the Gulf. Bernard Ingham, who accompanied Thatcher to the US, stated that 'George Bush had a backbone before he arrived in Aspen and did not acquire it from Mrs Thatcher'.[36]

More importantly, as it became clear that only a concerted build-up of military strength in the Gulf would dislodge Saddam's grip on Kuwait, the crisis restored Britain's importance in America's eyes. With the partial exception of France, no other European state offered practical support. Germany, understandably distracted by the more pressing issue of reunification, did not live up to the role for which Bush had optimistically cast it when he took office. Thatcher was delighted to find herself part of a small Anglo-American group in Washington, shortly after the initial meeting at Aspen, at which joint strategy was worked out. Earlier suspicions that Bush may have resented her claims to influence, based upon her personal relationship with his predecessor and her long experience as a head of government, were banished. Thatcher's knowledge of running a war, acquired in the Falklands conflict, was now of practical value. In her remaining months as Prime Minister she busied herself in building unity among the Arab states and organising the transfer of British troops, aircraft and equipment to the region. Although the actual fighting did not take place until after John Major had succeeded her as Prime Minister, she had taken the initial decisions which had committed Britain to a military solution.

The liberation of Kuwait raises an interesting question about how Thatcher would have acted, had she still been in power early in 1991. Bush and Major were careful to keep within the parameters of the resolutions passed by the United Nations, which authorised intervention to expel Iraqi forces from the territory they had occupied, but did not permit further action to topple Saddam. In her memoirs Thatcher expressed regret that the allied success was not followed through so that Saddam was disarmed and had to face his own people as a clearly beaten leader, which might have triggered his overthrow. She complained that 'the opinion of the UN counted for too much and the military objective of defeat for too little'.[37] Nonetheless it seems unlikely, given her habitual respect for international law, and the Bush administration's strictly defined agenda in Kuwait, that she would have behaved very differently to her successor.

The global role: image and reality

Thatcher's importance in the international arena was underpinned by a fortuitous conjunction of personalities and events. She derived her influence from the fact that the Cold War entered a critical phase just as she was beginning to find her feet as Britain's leader. For much of her premiership she had to work with two individuals, Reagan and Gorbachev, who in their different ways responded positively to her. As their relationships developed she was able, through sheer tenacity and vigilance for British interests, to maximise her influence, taking care to assert her independence where she felt that this was necessary. By dint of continuous activity she enabled Britain to punch above its weight in international affairs even if, in the last analysis, this sustained the illusion rather than restored the reality of great power status. The fragility of her diplomatic achievement, and the dangers of too great a reliance on personal relationships in foreign affairs, was exposed in her last years in power, with Reagan's replacement by Bush and the weakening of Gorbachev's domestic position. Although the Gulf crisis enabled her to reassert her standing with the US leadership, this was a recovery based once again on a particular set of circumstances. Thatcher's personality equipped her best for action in emergencies, where the choices were, or appeared to be, clear-cut. It was an outlook which enabled her to play a prominent role in the divided world of the Cold War, and it was perhaps fitting that she left the stage just as it was giving way to a new, and in many ways more complex, set of international problems.

Notes

1 Quoted in *Time Magazine*, 3 December 1984, cited in Graham Stewart, *Bang! A History of Britain in the 1980s* (London, Atlantic Books, 2013), p. 212.
2 Sir Geoffrey Howe, *Conflict of Loyalty* (London, Macmillan, 1994), p. 393.
3 US: MT Letter to President Carter (Soviet Brigade in Cuba), 2 October 1979, www.margaretthatcher.org/document/112237 (accessed 23 August 2014).
4 Speech at 'Youth for Europe' Rally, 2 June 1979, www.margaret thatcher.org/document/104088 (accessed 23 August 2014).
5 Quoted in Hugo Young, *One of Us* (London, Pan, 1990), p. 255.
6 Quoted in John O'Sullivan, *The President, the Pope and the Prime Minister: Three Who Changed the World* (Washington, Regency Publishing, 2006), p. 179.
7 Quoted in George Urban, *Diplomacy and Disillusion at the Court of Margaret Thatcher* (London, I.B. Tauris, 1996), p. 95.
8 Quoted in O'Sullivan, *The President, the Pope and the Prime Minister*, pp. 140–1.
9 Quoted in Geoffrey Smith, *Reagan and Thatcher* (New York and London, W.W. Norton, 1991), p. 98.
10 Radio interview for BBC World Service (phone-in), 30 October 1983, *Margaret Thatcher: Complete Public Statements 1945–1990 on CD-ROM* (Oxford, Oxford University Press, 1999), 83_393.

11 House of Commons Debates, 26 October 1983, Grenada (invasion), vol. 47, cols 294–5, http://hansard.millbanksystems.com/commons/ 1983/oct/26/grenada-invasion (accessed 19 August 2014).

12 George Shultz, *Turmoil and Triumph: My Years as Secretary of State* (New York, Charles Scribner's Sons, 1993), p. 340.

13 Quoted in Mark Garnett and Ian Aitken, *Splendid! Splendid! The Authorized Biography of Willie Whitelaw* (London, Jonathan Cape, 2002), p. 314.

14 Percy Cradock, *In Pursuit of British Interests: Reflections on Foreign Policy under Margaret Thatcher and John Major* (London, John Murray, 1997), p. 14.

15 Archie Brown, 'Margaret Thatcher and the End of the Cold War' in W.R. Louis (ed.), *Resurgent Adventures with Britannia: Personalities, Politics and Culture in Britain* (London and New York, I.B. Tauris; Austin, Harry Ransom Center, 2011), p. 265.

16 TV interview for BBC, 17 December 1984, www.margaretthatcher. org/document/105592 (accessed 23 August 2014).

17 Soviet Union: No. 10 record of conversation (MT–Gorbachev), 16 December 1984, www.margaretthatcher.org/document/134729 (accessed 1 January 2015).

18 Mikhail Gorbachev, *Memoirs* (London, Doubleday, 1996), p. 160.

19 Bernard Ingham, *Kill the Messenger* (London, Fontana, 1991), p. 258.

20 Quoted in Smith, *Reagan and Thatcher*, p. 214.

21 Quoted in Philip Short, *Mitterrand: A Study in Ambiguity* (London, The Bodley Head, 2013), p. 440.

22 Ronald Millar, *A View from the Wings* (London, Weidenfeld & Nicolson 1993), p. 311.

23 Radio interview for IRN (talks with Gorbachev at Brize Norton), 7 December 1987, www.margaretthatcher.org/document/106984 (accessed 23 August 2014).

24 Margaret Thatcher, *The Downing Street Years* (London, Harper Collins, 1993), pp. 782–3.

25 Shultz, *Turmoil and Triumph*, p. 568.

26 Cold War 'will last until 2000', 25 November 1989, www.margaret thatcher.org/document/110782 (accessed 23 August 2014).

27 Quoted in John Campbell, *Margaret Thatcher: Volume Two: The Iron Lady* (London, Vintage, 2008), p. 631.

28 German unification: memorandum of conversation (MT and President Mitterrand), 20 January 1990, www.margaretthatcher.org/document/ 113883 (accessed 23 August 2014).

29 Douglas Hurd, *Memoirs* (London, Little, Brown, 2003), pp. 381–2.

30 Iain Dale (ed.) *Margaret Thatcher: A Tribute in Words and Pictures* (London, Weidenfeld & Nicolson, 2005), p. 233.

31 Cradock, *In Pursuit of British Interests*, p. 111.

32 Cold War: Chequers Seminar on Germany (Summary Record), 24 March 1990, www.margaretthatcher.org/document/111047 (accessed 23 August 2014).

33 Urban, *Diplomacy and Disillusion*, p. 132.
34 Charles Powell, 'We are still feeling the tremors from the Berlin Wall's collapse', *Daily Telegraph*, 22 August 2009.
35 George Bush and Brent Scowcroft, *A World Transformed* (New York, Alfred A Knopf, 1998), p. 352.
36 Ingham, *Kill the Messenger*, p. 262.
37 Thatcher, *Downing Street Years*, p. 828.

9 Building and resisting European union: 1979–1990

Always a Eurosceptic?

Margaret Thatcher's attachment to the United States as Prime Minister was balanced by a no less pronounced lack of enthusiasm for the European Community. It has become customary to trace Thatcher's scepticism – which verged on open hostility in the later stages of her premiership – back to negative memories of her upbringing in wartime Grantham, where Europe was seen as a source of conflict and fear. Many commentators have contrasted her attitudes with the more positive approach of her slightly older male contemporaries, such as Heath, Whitelaw and Carrington, whose military service in 1939–45 brought them into direct contact with the consequences of rampant nationalism on the battlefield. Their experience of combat, it is argued, encouraged them to regard European integration in an essentially positive light, giving them a broader perspective than that vouchsafed to the youthful Margaret Roberts. There may be something in this analysis but it cannot take account of the variety of attitudes towards Europe exhibited by other members of their generation. It does not explain, for example, the cautious, pragmatic response of James Callaghan to the Community, or the outright opposition of Enoch Powell, both of whom undoubtedly had a 'good war'. Nonetheless, those who knew Thatcher personally often referred to the way in which her childhood experiences influenced her later attitudes. Jonathan Aitken, for example, argues that as a mature politician 'she had moved on, but not nearly as far as most British people who had been teenagers in the dark days of

the 1940s when Britain stood alone'.[1] Sir Geoffrey Howe concluded that she must have long concealed her hostility to the Community, giving vent to it only in her final years as Prime Minister.
Recalling their membership of the government which had taken
Britain into Europe in 1973 in his memoirs, he wrote that in the
late 1980s she was, 'subconsciously at least', marking 'her escape
from the collective responsibility of her days in the Heath Cabinet –
when European policy had arrived, as it were, with the rations'.[2]

Howe was of course writing as a devoutly pro-European former
colleague, who resigned from Thatcher's government on the issue
of relations with Europe in November 1990. He had also witnessed her active encouragement, after her fall from office, of the
Eurosceptic faction in John Major's Conservative Party. In the
1990s, with the Tories deeply divided over further European
integration, she became the guiding light for a new generation
of right-wingers, some of whom were close to willing a British
exit, whilst on the other hand the party's diminishing band of
pro-Europeans excoriated her as a source of internal party strife.
The events of the decade after her downfall undoubtedly affected
retrospective judgements of her record in office. A dispassionate
assessment of Thatcher's involvement with Europe, however, must
take note of the way in which her attitudes evolved in response
to events across the whole of her eleven years in power. She was,
for the greater part of her premiership, more pragmatic and
perhaps less consistent than both her warmest admirers and bit-
terest critics may have been prepared to admit. Within the framework of certain basic attitudes and prejudices, she reacted to a
changing context in ways which do not always fit the familiar
stereotype.

Early encounters

It would be fair to say that, as Leader of the Opposition in
1975–9, Thatcher did not view Europe as a major priority. It
was noted that, although she gave loyal support to the idea of
staying in the Community, she played a rather low-key role in
the events of the 1975 referendum which confirmed British membership. She may have felt that it would go some way to healing
the wounds caused by her recent ousting of Heath from the party

leadership, if she stood aside to let him to play a more prominent part in the 'Yes' campaign – or perhaps she simply could not summon up enthusiasm for the cause. Douglas Hurd, who accompanied Thatcher on her first visit to the institutions of the Community in December 1977, remembered her saying that 'she would have no time to run the European policy of her Government, because for eighteen months she would have to concentrate entirely on the British economy'.[3] This was, of course, an impractical stance for a prospective head of government, and one which Thatcher did not attempt to put into practice on taking office in May 1979.

With the Labour Party now moving towards an increasingly Eurosceptic posture, it made sense for Thatcher – for party political reasons, if nothing else – to strike a moderately pro-Community note in public. This probably explains her decision to depict the Callaghan government as weak and divided when, in December 1978, it decided not to join the Exchange Rate Mechanism (ERM) of the European Monetary System – an attempt by the Community's founding members to link their currencies together, in order to promote greater monetary stability. Correspondence between Thatcher and her senior Shadow Cabinet advisers certainly does not suggest that there was anything approaching agreement, at the highest level of the party, on what was to prove a highly controversial issue for her government in the following decade. It was no doubt a source of relief for the Conservative leadership that it fell to a Labour government to make the initial response to a project which was so fraught with uncertainty.

At this stage few observers foresaw that Thatcher would prove to be so much more confrontational than any of her predecessors in her relations with the European Community. Roy Jenkins, until recently a senior Labour minister but now temporarily removed from the British party political scene as President of the European Commission, recalled that in 1979 'my rational thought (over-optimistic as the eleven and a half subsequent years turned out) was that a Conservative government would be better for Britain's relations with Europe'.[4] On the eve of the 1979 election, *The Times* anticipated that a Conservative government would 'put Europe higher on the country's scale of values and be less carping in its criticisms of European institutions'.[5] Her public statements at this stage, whilst certainly not indicating any sympathy with visionary schemes of supra-nationalism, suggested that she saw the Community as an important economic zone and also – less predictably – as a means of strengthening the defences of the West in the Cold War. Thus, addressing a 'Youth for Europe' rally a month after she became Prime Minister, she reminded her audience of the importance of removing barriers to trade and movement within the Community, and also declared that 'our European ideal insists on the capacity of the Community countries together with our other NATO allies to defend our way of life against any military threat from outside'.[6] This did not, however, translate into active support for anything resembling the pooling of defence forces at European level. She remained sceptical of the Western European Union, a Cold War era organisation created by the European Community's six founding nations and Britain, following the 1948 Brussels Treaty, with the objective of co-ordinating European security in association with NATO. As Foreign Secretary, Howe found it difficult to secure Thatcher's agreement to the reactivation of WEU in the mid-1980s. At heart she remained suspicious of a body promoted keenly by France – not then a member of NATO – and instead put her trust unambiguously in the Atlantic alliance.

In private, from the start of her premiership, Thatcher evinced a basic caution about the realities of Britain's relationship with the other member states. Lord Soames, a pro-European Cabinet colleague in the early years, who had once served as Britain's ambassador to Paris, characterised her position at this stage as that of 'an agnostic who continues to go to church. She won't become an atheist, but on the other hand she certainly won't become a true believer.'[7] Her annotations on a brief prepared for the incoming Prime Minister by Cabinet Secretary Robert Armstrong, which covered a range of European issues, are revealing. Where he had advised 'an open-minded approach to the concept of a zone of monetary stability in Europe', Thatcher wrote that 'I doubt whether this can be achieved by a currency system. Indeed it can't unless all the underlying policies of each country are right'. On the Common Fisheries Policy, Whitehall's senior mandarin had defined Britain's requirements as virtually exclusive access for its fishermen within twelve miles of the country's coastline, and preferential access in areas beyond this limit. Against this the premier noted, 'I want a 50 mile exclusive control zone. It is much simpler than having to monitor two zones.'[8]

On both issues, Thatcher was already highlighting her instinctive preference for the uncomplicated pursuit of British interests, and her sense that the Community was composed of individual states, each with its own distinctive needs and characteristics. There was little 'communitarian' sentiment here, rather an indication that she saw Europe as a forum within which states sought to gain advantage over their fellow members; in the words of foreign policy adviser Percy Cradock, as 'pre-eminently an area of struggle, an arena'.[9] No less significant was the exclamation mark she placed next to Armstrong's report on the Community's first, hesitant steps towards a social dimension, entailing proposals for 'concerted action to combat unemployment (such as an agreement on shorter working hours)'.[10] It is not too fanciful to see this robust response as foreshadowing Thatcher's opposition, in her third term, to the European Commission's Social Charter, which aimed to entrench working people's rights across the Community, and which she saw as an unwarranted interference with the working of the free market.

The budget question

The first important area in which Thatcher engaged with other European leaders, on becoming Prime Minister, was an issue which came to be known by its initial letters, 'BBQ' – the 'British Budgetary Question', sometimes rendered as the 'Bloody British Question'. Edward Heath's acceptance of unfavourable terms for Britain, as the price of admission, meant that Britain was now the second highest net contributor to the Community's finances after Germany. Funding was organised in a way which worked against a country like Britain, which depended heavily on food and manufactured imports from outside Europe. Moreover, with a relatively small and efficient agricultural sector, Britain derived little benefit from European subsidies under the Common Agricultural Policy. It was anticipated that, without reform, in 1980 Britain's net contribution would amount to some £1,000 million. The situation was exacerbated by the fact that at the time, in terms of Gross Domestic Product per head, Britain was only the seventh wealthiest Community member. Thatcher was determined to negotiate a fairer settlement for Britain – to recover what she repeatedly called 'our money'. At a time of economic stringency, the suggestion that the problem might be resolved by increasing the overall Community budget, so that more might be spent on Britain, was clearly unacceptable. The government was united on the principle of securing a rebate. She was also in step with public opinion. An ITN poll conducted in November 1979 showed that 55 per cent of respondents felt that the Prime Minister was 'handling the Common Market in the right way'. Tellingly, a similar proportion favoured a British exit from the Community. In addition, on this issue Thatcher enjoyed the broad support of the Labour opposition. It seems clear that, had the Callaghan government won the 1979 election, it would have taken on the task of negotiation. With the slightly patronising tone in which he so often addressed Thatcher across the floor of the Commons, Callaghan suggested that in bargaining for more equitable treatment from Britain's partners, she was continuing the work that his government had begun: 'It is fair to say that we took the shine off the ball and that it is now for her to hit the runs'.[11]

It is unlikely, however, that any alternative British Prime Minister would have exhibited quite the same combination of blunt speaking and sheer determination with which Thatcher approached the issue. Her two main opposite numbers – French President Giscard d'Estaing and West German Chancellor, Helmut Schmidt, who had both been in office since 1974 and enjoyed a close working relationship – did not make it easy to reach agreement. Giscard, in particular, scarcely troubled to conceal his lofty disdain for a premier whom he clearly viewed as a narrow-minded and decidedly inferior newcomer. Even at their first official meal he was not prepared to waive the protocol which dictated that, as head of state, he would be served before his guest, a mere head of government; in the words of Carrington's private secretary, George Walden, 'French inflexibility overcame French *galanterie*'.[12] His and Schmidt's lack of sympathy for Thatcher's arguments betrayed a deeper sense that she had violated the customary means of resolving disputes, through a lengthy process of diplomatic give and take.

The feeling that she was isolated served to stiffen Thatcher in her intransigent refusal to accept the compromise settlements offered at summits in Dublin in November 1979 and Luxembourg in April 1980. She was narrowly persuaded to accept an interim agreement negotiated the following month by Carrington and his deputy, Ian Gilmour, which offered a two-thirds refund over a three year period. In a bad-tempered exchange at Chequers, after the Foreign Office team had come to report on their progress at Brussels, Thatcher at first flatly refused to approve the deal they had secured. In the course of the meeting, both Prime Minister and Foreign Secretary threatened to resign. In the end, Gilmour effectively disarmed her opposition by briefing the press that the outcome was in fact a personal success for the Prime Minister. With headlines like 'It's a deal!' (*Daily Mail*) and 'Maggie wins a bit more loaf' (*Evening Standard*) in the following day's press, it became impossible for her to maintain her opposition.

It was not until the June 1984 Fontainebleau summit, however, that a final settlement was reached. Thatcher won few friends with her dogged pursuit of a permanent rebate but in truth the interim agreement reached in 1980 created the prospect of continuous year by year bargaining, and any British Prime Minister would have had to reopen the issue. Thatcher was aided by the fact that, from 1981 to 1982, Europe's two most important countries had new and less experienced leaders. Both men had long-term integrationist aspirations for Europe but they had not yet got into their stride when Thatcher renewed her demands. She had little rapport with the new West German Chancellor, Helmut Kohl, whose Christian Democrat ideology had little in common with his British counterpart's free market philosophy. Nor did the two ever become personally close, although Kohl tried harder than his British counterpart to lift the barriers between them. With François Mitterrand, however, who had succeeded Giscard as French President, Thatcher developed a surprisingly effective personal relationship. There was a certain chemistry between the two: 'He likes women, you know,'[13] remarked the Prime Minister to Robert Armstrong, as Mitterrand took his leave after their first meeting at Chequers. She was also grateful to the French leader for his support during the Falklands conflict. At a practical level, as the head of state whose turn it was to chair the European

Council in 1984, Mitterrand was anxious to deal with the rebate question, which he regarded as an obstruction to progress on other matters. The fact that the Community was anxious to secure unanimous agreement on an increase in its resources from higher VAT contributions gave her a lever in the last phase of the negotiations. In a final piece of hard bargaining, Thatcher was able to persuade her antagonists to raise their offer from 65 to 66 per cent, thus enabling her to claim that she had secured a more impressive-sounding two-thirds rebate.

Most of Thatcher's colleagues, and indeed Foreign Office officials, who might have been expected to have little sympathy for her hard-line stance, accepted the justice of her case, and were even prepared to admit that more emollient tactics were unlikely to have brought about the same results. At the same time, they noted the way in which the prolonged budget struggle made it harder to work with Britain's partners in later years. However strong her argument may have been, Thatcher's style had used up precious reserves of credit with her opposite numbers in the Community. Carrington's verdict on her performance was typically understated: 'I have little doubt,' he wrote, 'that Margaret's firmness and intransigence were the key factors in getting us a proper settlement: but I cannot pretend that the resultant atmosphere made all our foreign relations easier to conduct.'[14] Those who had to work with her after the budget wrangle knew what to expect. According to *Times* journalist John Ardagh, the French view of Thatcher was, 'that woman is an old-fashioned nationalist with no feeling for the European ideal'.[15] Roy Jenkins suggested somewhat condescendingly that 'by negotiating roughly – by grocer's economics if you like', she had sacrificed the possibility of Britain sharing the leadership of Europe alongside France and Germany; a 'loss of opportunity, far greater than any hundreds of millions which she's gained by saying "I want my money back"'.[16]

On her side, the experience of the budget dispute had made Thatcher much warier of the European Community. The second half of her premiership would see a growing tension, never fully resolved in her own mind, between two conflicting pressures. On the one hand she remained conscious of the need to gain what she could for Britain, by engaging with the leaders of other member states and the institutions of the Community. At the same time, she felt increasingly that the process itself entailed a progressive loss of national sovereignty and freedom of action, which at some point would have to be resisted.

The Single European Act

The middle years of Thatcher's premiership coincided with a new phase of advance for the Community. Although the idea of a single European currency had been first canvassed as early as 1970, the uncertain international economic climate of the following decade meant that little progress on this, or on other projects directed towards closer union, had been made. After the admission of Britain, Ireland and Denmark in 1973, the enlargement of the Community stalled until the entry of Greece in 1981. The final expansion of the Thatcher era took place in 1986, when the arrival of Spain and Portugal took the membership of the Community to twelve states. By this stage, with a more promising economic outlook and the appointment in January 1985 of a new Commission President, Jacques Delors, the Community was on the brink of rapid progress towards closer integration.

At first Thatcher supported the choice of Delors, a former French finance minister committed to the removal of the remaining internal barriers to trade within the Community. On the subject of completing the European single market she shared common ground with the dynamic, purposeful head of the Commission. Time would show, however, that their views on the further development of the Community, once restraints on the movement of labour, capital, goods and services had been lifted, would be markedly different. Where Thatcher embraced a minimalist vision for Europe, largely limited to the creation of a genuinely free market, Delors wanted to go beyond this to provide working people with stronger protection from the vagaries of capitalism. He also shared with the leaders of France, West Germany and other key players, a desire for eventual monetary union, and for closer political integration. Thatcher resented what she saw as the pretensions of an official who was seeking to enlarge his sphere of activity. There developed between the two a mutual sense of irritation, which sometimes became evident in public.

Sitting alongside Delors at a European Council press conference in London, for example, she dominated the proceedings, ignoring him until a question was asked about Community funding and the Common Agricultural Policy. When the Commission President declined to answer, she sarcastically commented, 'I had no idea you were the strong silent type.'[17] Such put-downs – increasingly typical of Thatcher in the second half of her premiership – did nothing for good relations with an influential figure in the Community.

There was a paradox at the heart of Thatcher's support for the Single European Act, passed in 1986, which paved the way for the completion of the single market. Many of the restrictions that she wanted to abolish were the result of national governments protecting their own interests, through protectionist rules which limited free competition within the Community. In order to extend the reach of market forces across Europe, however, it was necessary to strengthen the Community's central institutions at the expense of individual member states. As Delors later reflected, 'Mrs Thatcher did not realise the extent to which her acceptance of the Single Act brought her along the conveyor belt to closer union.'[18] An early indication of this was the clash between Thatcher and one of the two British Commissioners who served with Delors, Arthur Cockfield. The latter had been a member of her own Cabinet, earning a reputation as a committed free marketer as Trade Secretary in 1982–3. Once appointed to Brussels, however, Cockfield took up his new supra-national responsibilities with the thoroughness and dedication which the post required. He began his term of office by rapidly identifying 300 separate measures needed to achieve a full 'common market' by 1992.

Thatcher admired Cockfield's contribution to the single market programme but felt betrayed by his willingness to push the authority of the Community, as she saw it, into new areas. In her memoirs she described him as 'a natural technocrat of great ability and problem-solving outlook' but as 'the prisoner as well as the master of his subject', who found it all too easy to 'go native'.[19] According to Howe, Thatcher never accepted the understanding that, once appointed by a particular member state, a Commissioner was 'expected to abandon any national or party loyalty and to give his collegiate allegiance to the Commission itself'.[20]

She was mistaken in her assumption that a British appointee would be willing to act effectively as the agent of his own national government. The mismatch between the Prime Minister's nationalistic instincts and Cockfield's commitment to the Community agenda was highlighted by a frosty exchange between the two on the subject of indirect tax harmonisation. Thatcher was taken aback to be told by Cockfield that this was provided for by the Treaty of Rome, the founding document of the Community, to which she had subscribed as a member of the Heath government when Britain first joined the Common Market. When a Downing Street official was sent to find a copy of the treaty, so that Cockfield could prove his point, it was received by the Prime Minister in silence. The Commissioner later wryly noted, 'I was to learn over the years that the Prime Minister's hard knowledge of European matters was somewhat lacking. And that when at a loss, in Burke's words, she "depended on her imagination for her facts".'[21]

The clash over tax harmonisation was a foretaste of a more serious difference of perspective between Thatcher and her European partners. The central issue was that in order to bring about internal freedom of trade within the Community, it was necessary to allow the extension of qualified majority voting, whereby each member state was allocated a number of votes in proportion to its population. Unless this method of decision-taking was adopted, it would be possible for an individual state to derail progress towards the single market by the exercise of its national veto. At the June 1985 Milan summit Thatcher tried to block the calling of a full intergovernmental conference (IGC), which she feared might lead on to further constitutional developments, over which Britain would have little control. Her preference was for an informal agreement to set aside the requirement for unanimity on the single market issue; but she was outmanoeuvred by the summit chairman, Italian premier Bettino Craxi. An IGC, with a broader agenda than the completion of the single market, was duly convened at Luxembourg in December 1985.

The outcome was the Single European Act, which spoke of making 'concrete progress towards European unity' and monetary union. It represented a significant loss of national sovereignty, extended the power of the European Parliament and Commission, and paved the way for the single currency. These were all developments to which Thatcher would be sternly opposed. At the time, however, she was determined to push the measure through Parliament, which was achieved with dissent from only a handful of hard-liners. Even George Gardiner, a Conservative backbencher who would join the Eurosceptic Referendum Party a decade later, voiced support for what he called the 'pragmatic British way', and characterised qualified majority voting as the only way to overcome national protectionism.[22]

Thatcher and her supporters were later to claim that she had been deceived by her fellow heads of government, whilst her critics expressed astonishment that she had signed the Single European Act without apparently understanding its wider implications. Reflecting on the emphatic Euroscepticism of her later years, Thatcher's successor, John Major, wrote that he could not understand why she failed at Luxembourg to seek a UK opt-out from the process of economic and monetary union. He guessed that she may have accepted the phrase because it appeared in the preamble to the treaty and she viewed it as an unrealistic aspiration. 'That seems quite possible,' he argued, 'but if so it was a bad misjudgement.'[23] It seems totally out of character for Thatcher not to have had a full appreciation of what she was signing. David Williamson, a senior European policy adviser, stated that she explicitly told him, 'I have read every word of the Single European Act.'[24] It may be that she misinterpreted the text, reading into it what she chose to see, and that she underestimated her peers' commitment to making a reality of the longer-term aspirations that it contained. Perhaps she had convinced herself that, by force of will, she could successfully resist any unwelcome developments. Certainly she seems that to have had some reservations at the time, asking for more time to think through the implications before signing. The episode highlights a critical difference in the approach to negotiation taken by Thatcher and other European leaders. Whereas for her, each issue was a discrete problem to be solved, with a final outcome, they were accustomed to a continuous process of change and adjustment, in pursuit of a goal which took shape gradually over time. Thatcher had gained what she wanted and did not feel obliged to participate in the unfolding of a wider, less sharply defined European destiny.

The Bruges speech

The passing of the Single European Act marked the high point of Thatcher's positive engagement with the Community. With the passage of time she became convinced that it was moving in an increasingly federalist direction, which was fundamentally inimical to Britain's interests. She was particularly provoked by a statement made by Delors in July 1988, to the effect that within ten years, 80 per cent of the legislation affecting economic and social policy would be made at European level. Her response to this came in an interview on BBC Radio 2's Jimmy Young Show, a popular lunchtime programme on which she appeared from time to time. She was not wholly negative about European co-operation, accepting that there were some things that were better done by a group of countries, such as negotiating on trade matters with the USA, China and the USSR and – perhaps more surprisingly – making agricultural policy. She returned more than once, however, to the impossibility and undesirability of a 'United States of Europe', arguing that it was in all members' interests to 'trade more closely together and have fewer formalities across borders – but not to dissolve our own infinite variety, our own nationality, our own identity'.[25] Thatcher's assumption was that other states would be no more willing than Britain to transfer new powers to the supra-national institutions of the Community. In this she was to find herself increasingly out of step with her fellow heads of government, who did not share her anxiety that the Community was evolving in an unwelcome direction.

Thatcher's sense of alarm was heightened in September when Delors addressed the annual gathering of the Trades Union Congress, winning a warm reception for his vision of a growing social dimension for Europe. The speech was of decisive importance in persuading the Labour movement to abandon its suspicion of the Community as a capitalist club. Delors' insistence that the liberalising thrust of the single market could be counterbalanced by legally entrenched rights for workers, to be embodied in the Commission's Social Charter, drew an enthusiastic response from the conference. Ron Todd, leader of the powerful Transport and General Workers' Union, told the delegates that 'the only card game in town at the moment is in a town called Brussels, and it is a game of poker where we have got to learn the rules and learn them fast'.[26] By offering the unions the prospect of recovering the employment protection lost under her government, and restoring them to a position of political influence denied to them since 1979, Delors ensured Thatcher's implacable hostility to his concept of 'Social Europe'.

This was the background to Thatcher's next major intervention on the European stage, in the form of a speech at Bruges in September 1988. The drafting of the speech saw a prolonged tussle between Number 10 and the Foreign Office, with each side anxious to influence the tone that the Prime Minister would strike. In a private note on preparations for Bruges, senior mandarin Sir John Kerr wrote with typical diplomatic understatement that 'the Jimmy Young Show shows that the No 10 market for constructive language on the Community may still be poor'.[27] Typical of the more emollient line that the officials wanted her to take was the formula produced by Stephen Wall, private secretary to Sir Geoffrey Howe, on behalf of his political master:

> the Secretary of State agrees that a stronger Europe does not mean the creation of a new European super-state, but does, has and will require the sacrifice of political independence and the rights of national parliaments. That is inherent in the treaties.[28]

Such a sentiment was anathema to the Prime Minister. In the event the speech was substantially rewritten by her foreign affairs private secretary, Charles Powell, who instinctively shared and gave expression to Thatcher's growing Euroscepticism.

The Bruges speech was certainly not a 'little Englander' manifesto. It stated clearly that 'Britain does not dream of some cosy, isolated existence on the fringes of the European Community'. Thatcher amplified the point made in her Radio 2 interview two months earlier, that Europe needed to act in a united way in matters of trade, defence and external relations – though without attempting to subsume individual national identities in 'some sort of identikit European personality'. The speech also pointed the way towards a widening of the definition of Europe, to include those states still behind the iron curtain, at a time when few would have predicted the rapid collapse of communist rule: 'we shall always look on Warsaw, Prague and Budapest as great European cities'. The section of the speech which was to make the greatest impact, however, was the passage in which Thatcher warned against the growth of centralised power in economic and social matters: 'we have not successfully rolled back the frontiers of the state in Britain, only to see them re-imposed at a European level, with a European super-state exercising a new dominance from Brussels'. The speech was suffused with a sense of British exceptionalism. Whilst fully acknowledging the country's European cultural heritage, Thatcher went on to remind her audience of the sacrifices made by British troops to liberate the continent in two world wars. She also reminded her listeners of the strides that Britain had made in deregulating its economy: 'we wish we could say the same of many other Community members'. Declining to engage with the arguments around the establishment of a European central bank, she asserted her own priorities; member states should speed up the creation of a free market in financial services, and abolish exchange controls, just as Britain had done under her government.[29]

At one level, as in so many of her pronouncements as Prime Minister, Thatcher was expounding her belief in the need for Community members to take modest, incremental steps in order to procure practical benefits for all. Her hearers, however, took away a different and more negative message, which was amplified by the way in which an increasingly Eurosceptic press chose to present the speech. Writing in *The Daily Telegraph*, for example, right-wing journalist Simon Heffer described Thatcher as issuing 'her most uncompromising declaration yet of her intention to defend British parliamentary sovereignty against the EEC bureaucracy. In so doing she further inflamed her dispute with other European leaders over the nature of British participation in the EEC.'[30] The speech also inspired the founding in February 1989 of the Bruges Group, a think tank dedicated to combating the growth of a centralised Europe. Theoretically a cross-party group, in practice it was staffed and its meetings addressed mainly by Conservatives. Thatcher herself was not involved in its establishment, although she served as its president after leaving Number 10.

In the longer term it inspired a backlash against the power of Brussels among an important section of British intellectual opinion, buttressing the arguments of Conservative MPs who rebelled against the more pro-European stance of the Major government in the 1990s.

The Bruges speech and its aftermath highlighted a hardening of prime ministerial rhetoric, which worried the still broadly pro-European thinking of mainstream Conservatism. Officials in both London and Brussels were alarmed by the way in which Thatcher's increasingly outspoken statements contradicted the hitherto pragmatic thrust of British government policy. As an anonymous European official commented, 'it's her tone I can't stand. . . . Not all that she says is objectionable. It's the way she says it.'[31] It was almost as if Thatcher enjoyed goading those with whom she had to work in the Community. When asked to comment on the significance of the French Revolution, at the time of the bicentennial celebrations in the summer of 1989, she could not resist contrasting the violent extremism which had marred the course of events across the Channel with the orderly growth of liberty in Britain. A leading French newspaper, *Le Monde*, distilled her remarks into the headline, '"Les droits de l'homme n'ont pas commencé en France," nous déclare Mme Thatcher. ["The rights of man did not begin in France," Mrs Thatcher tells us.]'.[32]

A no less discordant note was struck in the June 1989 European Parliament elections – the only contest during Thatcher's premiership when Labour took more seats than the Conservatives. The party's campaign gave out mixed messages. In her final press conference before polling day Thatcher stressed that hers was 'the Party of Europe', whose role was to 'fight Britain's corner for a strong Britain in a strong Europe'.[33] At the same time a much more negative set of prejudices was on view, in the form of a prominently displayed Conservative poster which asked the electorate whether they wanted to exist on 'a diet of Brussels'. Tabloid-style language of this kind was out of step with the sentiments of most Conservative candidates in the election, whose preference for a constructive relationship with the representatives of other member states appeared to be undermined by their own leader's chosen emphasis.

Conflict over the Exchange Rate Mechanism

At the same time a more substantive divide over European policy was developing at the highest level of government. Nigel Lawson had been a strong supporter of British membership of the Exchange Rate Mechanism for many years. The Chancellor's most committed ally on the subject was Geoffrey Howe who, unlike him, saw ERM membership not merely as a means of controlling inflation, but as a step on the road to eventual monetary union. At a meeting of relevant ministers in November 1985, Lawson won the backing, on more pragmatic grounds, of a number of senior colleagues, including Deputy Prime Minister Willie Whitelaw, Trade and Industry Secretary Leon Brittan, and – more surprisingly, in view of his later Eurosceptic views – party chairman Norman Tebbit. Although she did not give her reasons at the time, Thatcher simply refused to contemplate joining. The truth was that, although she allowed it to be stated that Britain would join the ERM 'when the time was right' or, in some versions of the phrase, 'ripe', she was not prepared to take a step which she saw as a threat to the British government's control over economic policy. From March 1987, however, Lawson defied the prime ministerial veto by covertly 'shadowing the Deutschmark' – using the Chancellor's control over interest rates and intervening in the currency markets to prepare the ground for joining the ERM. Although he later insisted that Thatcher must have known that he was doing so, she claimed to have been kept in the dark until told what was happening by *Financial Times* journalists in an interview in November 1987. The truth seems to be that Lawson did not deliberately conceal his pursuit of an independent policy, but nor did he directly inform her of it.

Thatcher's hostility to the ERM was intensified by a further development in April 1989. This month saw the publication of the Delors report, which outlined a three stage advance towards full economic and monetary union. In the first phase all member states would join the ERM; in the second and third stages, a European central bank and a single currency would be created. The announcement of this planned progression confirmed Thatcher's fears regarding the direction in which the Community was travelling. By this stage policy arguments had intersected with the growing personal tensions at the top of the government. At a private meeting with Lawson in May, she ruled out further discussion of a date for joining the ERM with the menacing words, 'I must prevail' – a statement which indicated to the Chancellor that 'joining the ERM, as she saw it, had now become a battle of wills between her and me'.[34] The following month, shortly before she attended a European summit in Madrid, Lawson and Howe combined to demand a private meeting with her at which they both threatened resignation unless she agreed to set a timetable for entry. Thatcher regarded her two most senior colleagues' tactics as an 'ambush', motivated in part by Howe's personal frustration as he saw his chances of succeeding her as Prime Minister receding. When she wrote her memoirs she looked back with disdain on what she termed a 'nasty little meeting'.[35] In their defence, the Chancellor and Foreign Secretary argued that there had been no conspiracy, and that they believed that Britain would be in a stronger negotiating position on future proposals for monetary union if a timescale was announced. In fact at the council meeting Thatcher set no date, although she did announce clearer conditions for joining: Britain was prepared to do so once inflation had fallen to the European average, and progress had been made on the free movement of capital and abolition of foreign exchange controls.

For Thatcher, the conflict over ERM had by now become intensely political. She had given some ground at Madrid because she knew that she could not survive the threatened simultaneous departure of both her Chancellor and her Foreign Secretary. After both decided not to press their case to the point of resignation, she moved to weaken them. A reluctant Howe was removed from the Foreign Office in a reshuffle on 24 July, to be poorly compensated with the post of Leader of the Commons. As a consolation prize, at his request, Thatcher conferred on him the honorific title of Deputy Prime Minister, although a tactless press release from Bernard Ingham's office made clear that the role conferred no real authority. His replacement was the forty-six year old John Major, elevated unexpectedly from the junior Cabinet post of Chief Secretary to the Treasury, with no prior ministerial experience of foreign affairs. Thatcher treated Lawson, whose intellect she still respected, much more circumspectly, but he remained in place for only three more months. In spite of the more positive tone of her statement at Madrid, the Prime Minister further provoked Lawson by inviting her former economic adviser, the independent-minded Professor Alan Walters, back for a second stint in Downing Street after a period as a lecturer in the USA. Press publication of an earlier article he had written, describing the ERM as 'half-baked', brought matters to a head. Lawson resigned on 26 October 1989 on the grounds that he could not accept the presence at the heart of the government of a rival source of advice for the Prime Minister. Walters then relinquished his own post rather than continue to be an unwilling source of embarrassment for the Prime Minister. Lawson's departure forced Thatcher to carry out a further reshuffle, with Major replacing Lawson, and Douglas Hurd, a logical choice given his long diplomatic experience prior to entering Parliament, taking over as Foreign Secretary.

These frantic ministerial changes revealed the extent of Thatcher's isolation. Running through the personal antagonisms which were inflicting such damage on her government was an unresolved conflict over the part that Europe should play in the making of national economic policy. Considerations of political survival prevented Thatcher from giving the response towards which her instincts impelled her. In order to shore up her position she was obliged to promote individuals whose views on the ERM, and on Europe more generally, were significantly different from her own. A cartoon published in *The Independent* newspaper in June 1990 depicted Thatcher in the familiar guise of Britannia, a pound sign emblazoned on her shield, sitting on a raft which was being pushed by Hurd and Major towards an island marked 'European Monetary Union'. A possible compromise emerged that month in the form of Major's proposal for a 'hard ecu' as a common currency, to operate alongside national currencies – a concept which kept open the possibility of an eventual transition to a single currency but was more cautious than Delors' favoured timetable for monetary union. Thatcher finally agreed to join the ERM in early October, although by common consent the timing and the level at which the pound entered the system were serious mistakes. An exchange rate of 2.95 Deutschmarks to the pound was unrealistically high, and in just under two years, on 'Black

Wednesday' in September 1992, market pressure would force the Major government to suspend British membership.

Thatcher later admitted that she had taken Britain into the ERM because by the summer of 1990 she had come under over-whelming political pressure to do so – from her Cabinet colleagues and parliamentary party, the business community and the press. Domestic political considerations also led her to insist on a simultaneous cut in interest rates, designed to give some relief to the Conservative Party's core supporters. Within weeks it was made clear that entry had not moderated Thatcher's fundamental attitude towards further integration. At a summit held in Rome in October, Thatcher was angered to find that the other eleven member states had combined in an attempt to force the pace of progress towards stages two and three of the Delors plan. Facing the Commons on her return, she gave a measured defence of her position. In response to the questions which followed, however, she expressed her true feelings:

> the President of the Commission, M. Delors, said at a press conference the other day that he wanted the European Parliament to be the democratic body of the Community, he wanted the Commission to be the Executive and he wanted the Council of Ministers to be the Senate. No, no, no.[36]

This ringing challenge to the federalist camp horrified pro-Europeans. Two days later it led to Howe's resignation from the government, on the grounds that Thatcher's approach was dam-aging Britain's capacity to exercise influence within the Com-munity. His departure triggered the chain of events which, before the end of November, would bring about the Prime Minister's ejection from Downing Street. On the floor of the Commons, however, Thatcher's defiant stand drew widespread approval, as footage from the newly introduced TV cameras indicates. Sup-portive contributions came not only from a number of Conserva-tive MPs but also from the former SDP leader, David Owen, as well as Ulster Unionists and even some Eurosceptic Labour back-benchers. It was a question from one of the latter, Nigel Spearing, that led Thatcher into another admission which dismayed her more moderate colleagues. Her statement that the hard ecu was unlikely to be widely used, except for commercial transactions, undermined the argument that it could ever be more than a tactical device to head off the introduction of a single currency. Here again was the authentic Thatcher on display: the unscripted words from the heart at war with the pragmatic, measured official government line.

The balance sheet

Thatcher's conduct of relations with the European Community remains one of the most controversial aspects of her eleven years in Downing Street. She felt justified in the warnings she had sounded, as the process of European integration gathered pace from the 1990s. The experience of the June 1985 Milan summit, and still more of the meeting in Rome in October 1990, showed that Britain's partners would not hesitate to use the Community's procedural machinery to push forward their own agenda. It was easy to draw the lesson, as the ultra-Thatcherite Nicholas Ridley put it, that when the Prime Minister made concessions, for example in joining the ERM, she gained little in terms of goodwill:

> the evidence seems to be that the more she conceded to our partners, the more they believed she was weakening and the more they believed that Britain could be made to conform in the end. . . . Our partners in Europe are just as ruthless and determined to get what they want as she was.[37]

Committed Eurosceptics consider her to have reached the right conclusions, albeit belatedly, about an organisation which was moving inexorably towards the diminution of national sovereignty and the introduction of a single currency which, a decade after its adoption, would prove to be fraught with problems. Recalling her support for the completion of the single market in the mid-1980s, Bernard Ingham argued that 'this woman – who eventually was felled because of Europe – actually gave Europe the ambition to advance – and unfortunately it went in exactly the opposite direction that she wanted it to go'.[38]

To Thatcher's critics, on the other hand, her handling of Europe was one of her gravest misjudgements. Looking back on the year of his resignation, Lawson considered that 'ironically, by 1989 she had become the Community's great unifying force – and the unity she had forged was a unity against the UK'.[39] Even Jacques Chirac, Mitterrand's right-wing French premier, who had some common ideological ground with Thatcher, gave vent to his frustration with her at a meeting in February 1988: 'Whenever you start speaking, you get angry and lay down the law. How do you expect anyone to ask your opinion after that?'[40] By being consistently unyielding, it may be that Thatcher forfeited the chance of building alliances and exploiting differences among the other states, which might have enabled her to win some support on the issues that mattered to Britain. Certainly, in the short to medium term, she left a reputation for obstructiveness which her successors would struggle to overcome in their dealings with their European counterparts. And it is also the case that divisions over Europe, which reached to the very top of Thatcher's government, played a central part in bringing her long period of office to a close.

Notes

1 Jonathan Aitken, *Margaret Thatcher: Power and Personality* (London, Bloomsbury, 2013), p. 298.
2 Geoffrey Howe, *Conflict of Loyalty* (London, Macmillan, 1994), p. 538.
3 Douglas Hurd, *Memoirs* (London, Little, Brown, 2003), p. 244.
4 Roy Jenkins, *A Life at the Centre* (London, Macmillan, 1991), p. 493.
5 *The Times,* 30 April 1979, quoted in Paul Sharp, *Thatcher's Diplomacy: The Revival of British Foreign Policy* (London, Macmillan, 1999), p. 27.
6 Speech at 'Youth for Europe' Rally, 2 June 1979, www.margaret thatcher.org/document/104088 (accessed 4 October 2014).
7 Quoted in Hugo Young, *This Blessed Plot: Britain and Europe from Churchill to Blair* (London, Macmillan, 1998), p. 311.
8 Incoming brief: Cabinet Secretary's incoming brief for new PM ('European issues'), 4 May 1979, www.margaretthatcher.org/document/112779 (accessed 4 October 2014).
9 Percy Cradock, *In Defence of British Interests: Reflections on Foreign Policy Under Margaret Thatcher and John Major* (London, John Murray, 1997), p. 125.
10 Incoming brief: Cabinet Secretary's incoming brief for new PM ('European issues'), 4 May 1979, www.margaretthatcher.org/document/112779 (accessed 4 October 2014).

11 House of Commons, 26 June 1979 [Hansard, vol. 969, col. 289], quoted in John Campbell, *Margaret Thatcher: Volume Two: The Iron Lady* (London, Vintage, 2008), p. 60.

12 George Walden, *Lucky George: Memoirs of an Anti-Politician* (London, Allen Lane/Penguin, 1999), p. 194.

13 Quoted in Aitken, *Margaret Thatcher*, p. 299.

14 Lord Carrington, *Reflect on Things Past* (London, Collins, 1988), p. 319.

15 In *The Times*, 25 March 1984, quoted in Jim Buller, *National Statecraft and European Integration: The Conservative Government and the European Union 1979–1997* (London and New York, Pinter, 2000), p. 90.

16 Hugo Young and Anne Sloman, *The Thatcher Phenomenon* (London, BBC, 1986), p. 114.

17 Press Conference after London European Council, 6 December 1986, *Margaret Thatcher: Complete Public Statements 1945–1990 on CD-ROM* (Oxford, Oxford University Press, 1999), 86_367.

18 Quoted in Roy Denman, *Missed Chances: Britain and Europe in the Twentieth Century* (London, Cassell, 1996), p. 264.

19 Margaret Thatcher, *The Downing Street Years* (London, Harper Collins, 1993), p. 547.

20 Howe, *Conflict of Loyalty*, p. 404.

21 Lord Cockfield, *The European Union: Completing the Single Market* (Chichester, Chancery Law Publishing Ltd, 1994), p. 57. The quotation is from the noted eighteenth-century conservative thinker, Edmund Burke.

22 European Communities (Amendment) Bill, House of Commons Debates 23 April 1986, vol. 96, col. 358, http://hansard.millbank systems.com/commons/1986/apr/23/european-communities-amendment-bill (accessed 4 October 2014).

23 John Major, *The Autobiography* (London, Harper Collins, 1999), p. 150.

24 Quoted in Young, *This Blessed Plot*, p. 336.

25 Radio interview for BBC Radio 2 Jimmy Young Programme, 27 July 1988, *Margaret Thatcher CD-ROM*, 88_258.

26 Quoted in Kristine Mitchell, 'From Whitehall to Brussels: Thatcher, Delors and the Europeanization of the TUC', *Labour History*, vol. 53, issue 1 (2012), p. 5.

27 Europe: John Kerr to Patrick Wright, 28 July 1988, http://www.margaretthatcher.org/document/111779 (accessed 4 October 2014).

28 Europe: Stephen Wall minute (Geoffrey Howe's criticisms of No 10 draft of MT Bruges speech), 1 September 1988, www.margaretthatcher.org/document/111785 (accessed 24 September 2014).

29 Speech to the College of Europe ('Bruges Speech'), 20 September 1988, www.margaretthatcher.org/document/107332 (accessed 4 October 2014).

30 *The Daily Telegraph*, 21 September 1988, p. 1.

31 Quoted in *The Times*, 23 September 1988, cited in Sharp, *Thatcher's Diplomacy*, p. 169.
32 Thatcher, *Downing Street Years*, p. 753.
33 Press Conference concluding European Election campaign, 14 June 1989, www.margaretthatcher.org/document/107700 (accessed 4 October 2014).
34 Nigel Lawson, *The View from No. 11: Memoirs of a Tory Radical* (London, Bantam Press, 1992), p. 918.
35 Thatcher, *Downing Street Years*, p. 712.
36 House of Commons debates, 30 October 1990, European Council (Rome), http://www.publications.parliament.uk/pa/cm198990/cmhansrd/1990-10-30/Debate-1.html (accessed 4 October 2014).
37 Nicholas Ridley, *'My Style of Government': The Thatcher Years* (London, Hutchinson, 1991), pp. 160–1. Reproduced by permission of The Random House Group Ltd and Peters Fraser & Dunlop (www.petersfraserdunlop.com) on behalf of the Estate of Nicholas Ridley.
38 Quoted in 'Forging the Union', BBC Radio 4, Part 3: 'Breaking down the borders', broadcast 21 August 2006.
39 Lawson, *View from No. 11*, p. 899.
40 Quoted in Philip Short, *Mitterrand: A Study in Ambiguity* (London, The Bodley Head, 2013), p. 438.

10 Decline and fall: 1988–1990

A brutal exit

With hindsight it is clear that Thatcher's political position was weakening long before November 1990, when Michael Heseltine launched his bid for the Conservative Party leadership, setting in motion a series of events which led to her deposition within a matter of weeks. There were numerous worrying indicators during her final term of office. The decision to introduce an ill-considered reform of local government finance, in the form of the unpopular 'poll tax', was by common consent one of the greatest domestic policy blunders of the post-war era. The economic situation began to deteriorate within a year of the June 1987 general election victory, and by the time of Thatcher's resignation Britain had officially entered recession once again. Internal divisions over Europe brought in their train a series of high profile Cabinet resignations: Nigel Lawson in October 1989, Nicholas Ridley in July 1990 and, most seriously, Sir Geoffrey Howe at the beginning of November – the event which directly triggered Heseltine's challenge. Underlying all these issues was a growing perception that Thatcher's least attractive character traits – her desire to dominate, coupled with a growing sense of self-sufficiency and a disinclination to heed warning signs – were becoming more marked with the passage of time. In the words of a friendly observer, Tim Bell, after the 1987 election 'she was more autocratic and more opinionated, the hubris had increased and her judgment was slipping – all of which meant more enemies and a lot more trouble'.[1]

At the time, however, few expected Thatcher to be brought down until the event itself was almost upon them. Although Labour were consistently ahead in the polls in her final year in Number 10, and Thatcher's personal approval rating fell to an all-time low of 23 per cent in April 1990, she had weathered similar storms a decade earlier. It was hard to believe that a premier who had won three consecutive general elections could not rally in time for a fourth. Not since the toppling of Neville Chamberlain fifty years before, in the exceptional circumstances of a wartime crisis, had a premier been ousted without suffering either a breakdown in health or defeat by the electorate. In his memoirs, published a year after her downfall, Nicholas Ridley confessed that in spite of concerns about the direction of economic policy, he had not anticipated the dramatic turn of events: 'In retrospect, it is easy to see that in the vaults of Parliament there was by now a gunpowder barrel waiting to be ignited. But it was hard to see at the time.'[2] The recollections of Ridley, a Thatcher intimate, tally with those of senior BBC political correspondent, John Sergeant. He considered that Thatcher's hold on power did not look shaky until her last week in Downing Street. 'She had held office with such confidence and determination,' he later wrote, 'that even the more cynical journalists found it difficult to imagine that she might soon be gone. . . . She seemed invulnerable.'[3]

The person most affected by the suddenness and brutality of her removal was, of course, Thatcher herself. To a unique degree among holders of the premiership, she had lived almost completely for political life, with little time or inclination for extraneous interests. Although she denied that she had ever cared for the trappings of office, her desire to exercise power had not diminished by the time of her sixty-fifth birthday, which fell during the October 1990 Conservative Party conference. What hurt most of all was that she had not been given the opportunity to face the voters once more, but had been unseated by the withdrawal of support by her own parliamentary colleagues, followed by the desertion of her own Cabinet. It was a sequence of events which she described, in the TV film accompanying the publication of her memoirs three years later, as 'treachery with a smile on its face'.[4] Thatcher's characteristically personal interpretation does not, however, provide an adequate explanation of her downfall. In order to understand the reasons for her departure, we need to explore the range of policy issues, rivalries and anxieties which coalesced during her third term in Number 10.

The poll tax blunder

Without doubt the most damaging single decision of Thatcher's final years in office was her attempt to revolutionise the financing of local government. She had long been dissatisfied with the domestic rating system, which provided a proportion of the revenue gathered by councils. The rates were levied on the assessed value of individual properties and were easy to collect. They were, on the other hand, unpopular with householders who found that making a small improvement to their homes could result in an increased bill. Many users of local services, such as tenants of rented houses and flats, were exempt; and the system took no account of residents' income. What drove the government actively to seek an alternative to rates, however, was the high spending of many Labour councils in the 1980s. Thatcher became convinced that a new system was required which would enable electors to compel local authorities to exercise restraint. Her response was the adoption of the community charge, to be paid by all individuals at a flat rate. Although Thatcher disliked the term, thinking that it would be construed as a levy on voting, it became widely known as the 'poll tax', from the old English word for a head. The underlying principle was to ensure that all citizens made a contribution towards the cost of the services they received. In Thatcher's mind it would constitute a self-acting check on municipal extravagance, removing the need for further rate-capping by central government. If the electors knew the true cost of local authority services, the argument ran, they would ensure through their votes that they received value for money. In an aside to one of her confidants Thatcher returned to the values of her Grantham childhood, recalling that 'my father always said that everybody should pay something even if it's only sixpence'.[5] Unfortunately the implementation of the new charge would not prove quite so simple and straightforward.

Thatcher was not the sole author of the charge and, characteristically, was initially cautious about the idea of replacing the rates with a new system. It was devised by two bright, ambitious junior members of the Department of the Environment, William Waldegrave and Kenneth Baker. They sold it to the premier and her senior colleagues – with the notable exception of Nigel Lawson, who did not attend the gathering and was to be a consistent critic – at a presentation at Chequers in March 1985. It was introduced first of all in Scotland, at the express behest of the Conservative Party north of the border, after a revaluation of rated property there had caused widespread middle-class anger in 1984–5. It was implemented earlier than planned in England and Wales, without a transitional period of 'dual running' with the rating system, following pressure from the 1987 Conservative conference. The poll tax was the product of many hands. Nonetheless, more than any of her colleagues, Thatcher became the public face of the charge, always prepared to champion it vigorously and oblivious to its defects until too late in the day. Defending the policy on a visit to Bradford, shortly before the introduction of the charge in the spring of 1990, she insisted that the rating system had been inherently inequitable:

> For only half your local electorate to pay rates, and half those who vote don't pay rates, was desperately unfair. . . . I might tell you, I have had several widows living alone who have thanked me today, and said, 'Three cheers for the community charge! I was paying as much as next door, and they have four or five earners, and it wasn't fair.'[6]

Those who welcomed the new charge, however, were usually less vocal in their support, and they were greatly outnumbered by those who saw it as deeply unjust. Although people on lower incomes were granted rebates, there was no real attempt to link the charge to an individual's capacity to pay. Even Kenneth Baker, who had moved to be Education Secretary in May 1986, was dismayed by the requirement for students – most of whom had irregular earnings at best – to pay 20 per cent of the charge. In practice it proved hard to collect, with many non-payers evading detection simply by not registering to vote. In addition, government forecasts of the size of the bills proved to be a gross underestimate. The average charge per adult turned out to be £360, with some bills much higher than this, whereas a figure of £278 had been widely discussed not long before. The situation was exacerbated by Lawson's refusal to use Treasury funding to ease its introduction. Some councils increased their spending, knowing that the government would take the blame.

Public anger boiled over on 31 March 1990, the day before the charge was introduced in England and Wales, with riots in Trafalgar Square. More than 300 arrests were made and 460 people, most of them police, were injured. As running battles raged, and smoke billowed above shops almost within sight of Downing Street, it became clear that the charge lacked popular legitimacy. More significant than these violent scenes in London, however, were the numerous peaceful protests by law-abiding members of the public, many of them natural Conservative voters. Home-made banners with slogans such 'Thatcher's tax must be axed', held aloft by dismayed and angry pensioners, showed where the wider public placed the blame for the new charge. Ministers entrusted with defending the policy found themselves under pressure from hostile and despairing constituents. Chris Patten, Thatcher's last Environment Secretary, told journalist Hugo Young about a financially struggling couple in his Bath constituency, for whom the arrival of the first poll tax bill was the final straw. The charge was, he said, 'like a heat-seeking missile, homing in on low-rated housing which contained exactly the marginal votes the Tories needed to keep or get'.[7] The tax was widely blamed for the loss of the Mid-Staffordshire by-election to Labour, on a 22 per cent swing, in March 1990.

Conservative back-benchers' confidence in Thatcher's leadership was now seriously rattled as many, especially those with marginal seats in the north and the Midlands, began to fear for their own chances of re-election. Even Douglas Hurd, whose rural Oxfordshire constituency lay in the Conservative heartlands, had the gravity of the situation underlined for him when eighteen councillors resigned from the party to sit as independents. After a depressing day spent dealing with hostile correspondence, he realised too late that the charge was flawed, writing in his diary that 'we are in the deepest pit yet, the bitter letters pour in'.[8] By defending the tax so unequivocally, Thatcher had ensured that the full burden of public opprobrium would fall directly upon her. For the rest of her premiership, the poll tax remained the issue most often cited as the cause of her growing unpopularity. When Michael Heseltine challenged her for the party leadership, Cranley Onslow, the chairman of the backbench 1922 Committee, told Thatcher that voting would turn on whether or not it could be significantly modified. It was indicative of Thatcher's personal identification with the tax that she insisted that she 'could not suddenly pull a rabbit out of a hat' in order to win over her critics.[9] By this stage, in fact, only the withdrawal of the community charge would have succeeded in pacifying most of them.

The clash with Lawson and Howe

The difficulties surrounding the introduction of the poll tax were compounded by the effects of a worsening economic situation. The boom which had helped to win Thatcher her last general election was running out of steam barely a year later. As inflation returned, Lawson was obliged to raise interest rates from a low point of 7.5 per cent in May 1988 to 13 per cent by the end of the year and a staggering 15 per cent by October 1989. The ensuing hike in mortgage repayments threatened the interests of aspiring, home-owning new Tory voters and placed the once popular Chancellor's credibility in jeopardy. With the government's reputation for economic competence at risk, as adverse press coverage of the Treasury's policies grew, the relationship between Prime Minister and Chancellor deteriorated. Here was the making of a very serious rift between two strong personalities. Lawson stood out among Thatcher's ministers for his intellectual self-confidence; it is hard to imagine any other member of her Cabinet telling the Prime Minister to shut up so that another colleague could be heard, as he did on one occasion. By 1989, mutual respect and an ability to work productively together had turned to barely concealed mistrust.

As we have seen in Chapter 9, behind the growing personal antagonism between Prime Minister and Chancellor was a fundamental divergence of opinion on the merits of joining the European Exchange Rate Mechanism. In the early summer of 1989, Thatcher confronted an alliance between Lawson and Geoffrey Howe on the issue. These two senior ministers had not hitherto worked particularly closely together. In spite of his wide-ranging responsibilities as Foreign Secretary, Howe was an assiduous networker, who took the trouble to address a variety of Conservative audiences on a regular basis. The Chancellor, by contrast, was a solitary politician, who believed implicitly in his own technical expertise and had no real ambition to move higher than his current post. Indeed, as a comparatively poor man with a young family to support, it was logical that he would seek more remunerative employment in the private sector after leaving office at a time of his own choosing. Nor did Howe and Lawson share a complete identity of views. The Foreign Secretary was always a more committed European idealist, whereas for Lawson participation in the ERM was an anti-inflationary tool, which he did not see as a prelude to full economic and monetary union. Their joint attempt to compel Thatcher to commit herself to a date for joining, in the so-called 'Madrid ambush' of June 1989, was a pragmatic manoeuvre, born of a coincidence of objectives. Its sequel, Howe's removal from the Foreign Office in a reshuffle carried out on 24 July, caused further damage to relationships at the top of the government. Then, three months later, Lawson resigned in protest at Thatcher's appointment of Professor Alan Walters, an academic who was an outspoken critic of the ERM, as her economic policy adviser.[10]

The disruption of the government in the second half of 1989 shed an unflattering light on Thatcher's management of her colleagues. In later years she rationalised the events of the autumn by maintaining that the argument over Professor Walters was a pretext for Lawson to leave the government. He had resigned rather than stay to face the consequences of the inflationary pressures which had resurfaced in the latter part of his stewardship – a line of argument which Lawson vehemently rejected. Charles Powell stated that:

> Mrs Thatcher took the view that really Nigel Lawson was by then pretty pessimistic about his own policies and the fact that interest rates were rising pretty steeply, that he was increasingly bearing the brunt of unpopularity within the Conservative Party, within the country, for his policies and that Alan Walters' position was almost an excuse for him, not a serious issue.[11]

Walters added his own criticism of Lawson, characterising the episode as an illegitimate attempt by the Chancellor to dictate Thatcher's choice of staff: 'the substantive content was ERM and so on,' he argued, 'but the break point as far as the distribution of power is concerned, and that's what politics is about after all, is that she would not give him power to determine her advisers.'[12] Thatcher gave a somewhat incoherent justification of her own actions, in an uncomfortable TV interview two days after Lawson's resignation. Sounding flustered and defensive, she repeated endlessly that the former Chancellor's position had been 'unassailable' and that 'advisers are there to advise, ministers are there to decide'.[13] It was an explanation which failed to carry conviction and, for many observers, it raised questions about the stability of her government.

Lawson's abrupt exit obliged Thatcher to carry out a hasty reshuffle, only three months after she had installed the senior team with whom she had expected to enter the next general election campaign. Ironically the freshly promoted individuals were well suited to their new appointments. John Major was moved from the Foreign Office to replace Lawson, at last heading the department in which he had served his apprenticeship as Chief Secretary. In broadening his experience of high office, Thatcher was attempting to bring on a candidate whom she saw increasingly as her most promising successor, although of course she had no intention of creating a vacancy in the near future. Douglas Hurd, an experienced diplomat whose natural pro-Europeanism would take second place to his instinctive sense of public service and loyalty to the Prime Minister, replaced Major as Foreign Secretary. David Waddington, a traditional right-winger who saw eye to eye with Thatcher on most issues, was moved from the post of Chief Whip to take Hurd's place in the Home Office. Nonetheless the episode reeked of panic and many insiders began to question how Thatcher could have allowed relations with Lawson to deteriorate to such an extent. Norman Fowler, a middle-ranking minister who was to step down from government for family reasons two months later, noted in his diary that although he expected her to hang on for the time being, by showing preference for an adviser she had forfeited the friendship of her political colleagues, and 'the question is not whether she will go but when'.[14]

Bunker mentality

Under the Conservative Party's rules it was possible for a contender for the leadership to come forward at the start of the parliamentary year. In the years of Thatcher's supremacy no challenger had emerged. The resignation of Lawson, combined with growing unease about the poll tax, encouraged a little known backbencher, Sir Anthony Meyer, to offer himself in November 1989. Not even the candidate regarded himself as a credible alternative leader. In the ranks of the parliamentary party he was noted for his eccentric views – he was the only Conservative MP to have opposed the Falklands War – allied to an air of aristocratic disdain for Thatcherism. But that was not the point. He stood in order to register a protest against her style of government and, in particular, her increasing hostility to European integration. For such an obscure figure to win thirty-three votes, and for a further twenty-seven MPs to abstain, was worrying. To Thatcher's more perceptive colleagues, it raised the question of the impact that a more serious rival might have. Meeting after the declaration of the result, early in December 1989, the members of her campaign team discussed the lessons of the contest. All of them were aware that a number of MPs had voted for Thatcher reluctantly. If the economic situation deteriorated further, in eleven months' time some of those with marginal seats might think that they stood a better chance of success under a different leader. Not all went as far as the most critical member of the group, Deputy Chief Whip Tristan Garel-Jones, who talked about 'the beginning of the end of the Thatcher Era' and felt that there was no certainty of her winning the next general election. They did, however, agree that the Prime Minister should make herself more accessible to backbenchers. There was also concern at her dependence on Charles Powell and Bernard Ingham, the 'sentries in the bunker', whose influence tended to distance Thatcher from her parliamentary colleagues. Europe was also acknowledged as a problem. Thatcher needed, they felt, to strike a different tone and to recognise that many younger Conservatives were concerned at the danger of Britain becoming isolated within the Community.[15]

None of these were warnings to which Thatcher cared to pay attention. Several observers considered that by the late 1980s she was beginning to lose her acute political sensitivity. The length of her period in office and a growing self-confidence, reinforced by the flattery of her closest advisers, were often cited in explanation. Social Democrat leader David Owen, for example, felt that 'since 1987 her political antennae were no longer receiving, only broadcasting'.[16] There were also signs that her famously inexhaustible energy was beginning to flag. West German Chancellor Helmut Kohl later recalled that 'she would doze off during summits and would then nearly fall off her chair, clutching her handbag'.[17] On the other hand she continued to be hyperactive, interfering in the affairs of government departments and promoting legislation on a range of issues, from the introduction of identity cards for football supporters to the prosecution of former Nazi war criminals living in Britain. She also developed a habit of visiting the scene of major disasters, including several rail crashes and the April 1989 Hillsborough football stadium tragedy, on the principle that as the person in charge of the country she had to be seen to show concern. The relentlessness of her compassion for the victims was in danger of becoming a source of ridicule by the end of the decade. One journalist claimed to carry a card saying: 'In the event of an accident, I do not wish to be visited by the Prime Minister'.[18] She also maintained a punishing schedule of foreign travel, enjoying her status as the Western world's longest serving national leader, and running the risk of becoming out of touch with domestic political developments. Kenneth Baker, who became party chairman in the July 1989 reshuffle, recalled warning her frequently that 'the plaudits are abroad but the votes are back home'.[19]

A more surprising political weakness was her failure to promote a cadre of like-minded MPs. Some ideologically sympathetic and long-serving members of the parliamentary party received only minor office or were not asked to join the government at all. An example was the Eurosceptic Teddy Taylor, her Shadow Scottish Secretary who lost his seat at the 1979 election. Although he returned to the Commons at a by-election less than a year later, he was never one of Thatcher's ministers. Even after 1981, when she had purged most of the 'wets' from the Cabinet, the core of Thatcherite members remained remarkably small. Some, of course, fell by the wayside for personal reasons. Cecil Parkinson returned to the Cabinet after the 1987 election but was never the candidate for high office that he had briefly been before his fall from grace four years earlier. Nicholas Ridley was the closest of her ministerial colleagues in the final years, but he never rose above the middle-ranking posts of Environment and Trade and Industry. Thatcher would have liked to have appointed him Chancellor after Lawson's resignation, but she recognised that her outspoken friend's 'scorn for presentational niceties' ruled him out.[20] The circumstances of his abrupt resignation in July 1990 demonstrated that she was right to be cautious. *The Spectator* published some indiscreet remarks about the threat of German domination of Europe, which he made in the course of lunch with the magazine's editor, the son of the former Chancellor, Dominic Lawson. Ridley's departure was sealed by a front cover cartoon depicting him as a naughty schoolboy, running away after daubing a Hitler moustache on a poster of West German Chancellor Helmut Kohl.

The truth was that there was a marked shortage of potential governmental talent on the party's right wing. By 1989–90 the Prime Minister had become dependent on the goodwill of Tories who, although they owed their promotion to her, were not at heart card-carrying loyalists. She persuaded herself that John Major was of her way of thinking, largely because of his work as Chief Secretary of the Treasury, overlooking the evidence of his instinctive moderation on social and European issues as she steadily promoted him. Fellow MP Edwina Currie, with whom Major had an affair in the mid-1980s, judged that it was easy to misinterpret his real attitudes by concentrating unduly on his classic rise from humble origins: 'the newspapers think Major is Thatcherite, just because he grew up in Brixton and went to grammar school; but he's much more complex than that, more pragmatist than anything else'.[21] In spite of their different backgrounds, Major and Douglas Hurd found considerable common ground in their approach to politics as they moved up the Cabinet ladder. 'I like and trust him more and more,' wrote the latter in his diary,[22] as the two men got to know each other through informal social contact. Thatcher's inability to establish easy relations with her senior colleagues prevented her from developing a fuller understanding of her new Chancellor's personality. Another problem – a characteristic she shared with other long-serving leaders – was the growing list of disappointed office-seekers in the parliamentary party. *Times* journalist Robin Oakley calculated that, by the time of the Meyer challenge, fifty-eight Conservative MPs had lost their positions in government, and a further ninety-seven had never been invited to serve.[23] The result was that, when Thatcher came under pressure, she found herself dangerously isolated. Reviewing backbench opinion in March 1990, junior minister Alan Clark noted that 'her "constituency" in this place depends solely on her proven ability to win General Elections. But now this is in jeopardy she has no real Praetorian Guard to fall back on'.[24] She was soon keenly to feel the absence of a dependable core of support.

Howe's resignation

At the heart of the government, Thatcher's difficult relationship with Sir Geoffrey Howe worsened still further after his reluctant transfer from the Foreign Office. He soon discovered the empti-ness of the title of Deputy Prime Minister. His exclusion from the centre of power was such that he found out from the Queen in October 1990 that Thatcher had finally decided to join the ERM. Howe's side-lining was a fresh blow in a process which had seen him frequently belittled by the Prime Minister in front of others. It was not merely that his pro-European views were increasingly out of harmony with those of his boss; she also seemed to dislike him on frankly personal grounds. As Tim Bell recalled, Howe was a regular target for bullying: 'he was grey and mumbled and shuffled and she despised all those things'.[25] Lawson remembered the embarrassment felt by other ministers as she treated her longest serving colleague as 'something halfway between a punchbag and a doormat'.[26] The quiet, gentlemanly Howe chose to ignore the premier's provocations rather than retaliating. As others testified, however, the resentment went deep. Lord Carrington, for example, related to Woodrow Wyatt late in 1989 that 'what he is saying to me every time I see him . . . is that he hates her and that she has been horrible and he wishes she would go'.[27] Rather than confront her face to face, he resorted to coded messages in public speeches, subtly distancing himself from the Prime Minister.

The issue which finally brought about Howe's resignation was Thatcher's general conduct of relations with Britain's European partners. This had long been a source of differences between the two. At the time of the 1984 Fontainebleau summit, at which the question of Britain's budget rebate was finally settled, he had outlined their different negotiating styles for the benefit of British journalists. He compared his own approach to a police line, which was flexible enough to adjust itself to crowd pressure without giving way, whereas 'the Prime Minister builds a brick wall. It resists. The disadvantage is that if her position becomes untenable, she ends up having to knock it down.'[28] Thatcher's Bruges speech and the dispute over the ERM were signposts on the road to separation. The breaking point finally came with Thatcher's celebrated 'No! No! No!' response to the prospect of further European integration, delivered in the Commons with Howe sitting alongside her, after her return from the European leaders' summit in Rome at the end of October 1990.

Thatcher's supporters subsequently argued that Howe had not resigned over a substantive issue of policy. His departure came shortly after Britain had finally joined the ERM, and in his resignation letter he stated that he did not want to see the imposition of a single currency. What concerned him, he told the Prime Minister, was that 'the mood you have struck . . . will make it more difficult for Britain to hold and retain a position of influence' in the debate on the future of economic and monetary union. He also indicated unease at her management style, with the statement that 'Cabinet government is all about trying to persuade one another from within' – a principle which, he argued, also applied within the European Community.[29] He made no mention of her treatment of him as a colleague, and later denied that personal factors had influenced his decision. In her memoirs Thatcher professed not to understand the exact reasons for his decision, whilst recognising that growing personal differences between them had made his resignation unavoidable at some point. Her main concern was that the loss of the last surviving member of her original Cabinet would leave her in an exposed position – a fact of which commentators at the time were not slow to take note. Author and television personality Gyles Brandreth, who had just decided to seek selection as a Conservative candidate, wrote in his diary, the day after Howe's resignation: 'There's a wonderful picture in *The Times* of the Thatcher Cabinet in 1979. Eleven years later and there's not one of them left. She's eaten every single one'.[30] The sense of decline was heightened by the fact that only two weeks before the Liberal Democrats had won the Eastbourne by-election, which had been triggered by the IRA's murder of the sitting Conservative MP, Thatcher's former parliamentary private secretary, Ian Gow.

Thatcher did her best to move on from Howe's resignation with a reshuffle in which John MacGregor, the quietly loyal Education Secretary, was appointed Leader of the House, with Kenneth Clarke taking his place. The real damage, however, was yet to come. On 13 November Howe delivered a speech in the Commons in which he explained his resignation. It was delivered in the deadpan tones of a politician whose manner had once been likened to the spectacle of 'a much-loved family tortoise, creeping over the lawn in search of a distant tomato'.[31] The content of the speech, however, was unexpectedly harsh. The core of his argument was that Thatcher's increasingly vocal and impulsive initiatives on European policy were making it virtually impossible for her colleagues to maintain a constructive relationship with Britain's partners. The language he used ensured that MPs listened with surprise, amusement and growing appreciation, whilst his victim writhed uncomfortably on the front bench. He accused Thatcher of presenting a 'nightmare image' of ill-intentioned foreigners, scheming to 'extinguish democracy', to 'dissolve our national identities' and to lead Britain 'through the backdoor into a federal Europe'. Employing a rather odd metaphor, he compared her to a cricket captain who breaks the team's bats before they go out to face the bowling. Calling in aid quotations from Winston Churchill and Harold Macmillan, he depicted Thatcher as out of step with the established policy of the Conservative Party. He maintained that under her leadership, Britain was in danger of losing the benefits offered by participation in the European mainstream. Her perceived attitude, he said, 'risks minimising our influence and maximising our chances of being once again shut out'. He concluded by presenting his reluctant resignation as the only way to resolve a 'tragic conflict of loyalties with which I have myself wrestled for perhaps too long'.[32]

Howe delivered his speech to a Conservative parliamentary party which was by no means as Eurosceptic as it would be a decade later. Most MPs were probably not overly concerned at this stage by the threat of a continental 'super-state'; but nor did they share the great enthusiasm for Europe manifested by the former Deputy Prime Minister. In his memoirs Howe himself placed 'Europe' behind the poll tax, Thatcher's unpopularity with voters and dismay at her style of government, in his explanation of growing disenchantment with her.[33] Tory MPs' main concern, in the opinion of Nigel Lawson, was not with the substance of policy: 'it was rather that they sensed that she was handling Europe badly, and feared that she would split the party over it'.[34] Howe's speech had crystallised a mounting sense of unease, even of alarm, regarding the nature of Thatcher's leadership and her chances of securing a fourth general election victory for the Conservatives. Self-preservation, rather than ideological conviction, would determine the course of events at Westminster over the next week.

Heseltine's challenge

Howe did not intend the speech as a preliminary to launching a party leadership bid of his own. Although he was outwardly unambitious, Thatcher considered that he had nurtured hopes of succeeding her in Number 10, which were by now slipping away. He must have realised that it was too late for him to seek the premiership. But nor is there any evidence that he had concerted his actions with the most plausible contender to the throne, Michael Heseltine. Indeed, although the latter had been courting the goodwill of Tory MPs ever since his resignation almost five years earlier, he had little contact with his former Cabinet colleagues. He had been assiduous in visiting backbenchers' constituencies and speaking for them, whilst being careful never to appear to be posing an overt threat to Thatcher. His oft-repeated formula, to which he adhered right up to November 1990, was that he could not envisage the circumstances in which he would stand against her, and that he expected her to lead the party into the next election, and to win. Suddenly, with the awed reaction to Howe's speech, the circumstances *had* changed. The expectation on the part of the press, that a contest was now imminent, had been recklessly encouraged by Bernard Ingham's taunts that it was time for Heseltine to 'put up or shut up'. Now he chose the former, realising that his credibility depended on not delaying longer.

Michael Heseltine offered a potent appeal to Tory MPs who feared for their political futures if Thatcher remained Prime Minister. Opinion polls in the week before the leadership contest indicated that the former Defence Secretary was a definite electoral asset. The research carried out by seven different polling organisations suggested that if Thatcher continued as leader, the Conservatives were likely to lose to Labour by an average of 10 per cent, whereas Heseltine would give them a lead of 5 per cent. Unlike Sir Anthony Meyer, he was a plausible alternative leader, with a track record in government as well as a charismatic public image. He struck a more positive note on Europe than Thatcher and extended the prospect of a review of the hated poll tax. He was adept at flattering those who had been excluded from office over the previous eleven years, shamelessly suggesting to them that their talents had been overlooked. By no means all MPs, of course, were seduced. Many of those who had entered the Commons in 1983 or 1987 were still fervent admirers of Thatcher. Heseltine's resignation over the obscure issue of Westland had left doubts about his judgement and his restless ambition. It was not a foregone conclusion that Thatcher would be driven from office. For that to happen, it was necessary for her and her supporters to make a number of critical mistakes in the week between Heseltine's announcement of his candidacy and the first ballot on 20 November.

The most obvious error was in the lack-lustre nature of Thatcher's re-election team. Former Cabinet minister Sir George Younger, who had managed the campaign against Meyer, was unable to devote himself fully a second time because he was committed to a new post as chairman of the Royal Bank of Scotland. Peter Morrison, Thatcher's parliamentary private secretary, was worryingly complacent about the Prime Minister's chances of success. The Conservative parliamentary party constituted a small, devious and panicky electorate, many of whom clearly did not tell the truth when canvassed. Morrison was naïve in believing the assurances of support he was given, and insufficiently pro-active in seeking votes. With only slight exaggeration George Gardiner, a loyalist backbencher, later related that 'people speak of a Margaret Thatcher campaign. In truth there was only one person who was running a campaign, and that was Michael Heseltine. . . . I had friends who were rung up in their bath by Michael Heseltine.'[35] Another problem was that, in contrast with the situation in 1989, the whips' office, now headed by Tim Renton, adopted a stance of strict neutrality in the contest. Renton testified to his own lack of commitment to his boss in his memoirs, recalling her complaining at the time of Howe's resignation that 'she needed a friend in Cabinet and that I was always suggesting people who were opposed to her philosophy'.[36] He was a curious choice for the post he occupied, admitting that he disagreed with her views on Europe and that he abstained in the leadership election. Renton's predecessor, David Waddington, later regretted that he had accepted promotion to the Home Office a year earlier, musing in his memoirs whether, had he still been running the whips' office, he might have succeeded in mobilising vital additional votes for her.[37]

Thatcher herself was partly to blame for her failure to secure re-election. Her only direct contribution to the campaign was to attack Heseltine, most vehemently in a *Times* interview published the day before voting took place, as an instinctive left-winger whose succession would place in jeopardy her own achievements. His published statements, she claimed, were 'more akin to some of the Labour party policies: intervention, corporatism, everything that pulled us down'.[37] Such claims made a poor impression on MPs, suggesting a desperate attempt to shore up her position at the expense of the truth. If they had any substance, how had it been possible for her to tolerate Heseltine in her Cabinet for almost seven years? Another tactical error was the decision, at Thatcher's personal insistence, to shorten the length of the campaigning period to just a week. This reduced the opportunities for local Conservative associations, a majority of whose members were probably supportive of Thatcher, to put pressure on their members to remain loyal. The timing also meant that she would actually be in Paris, at an international conference marking the end of the Cold War, when the first round of voting was held.

Some of her advisers considered it unwise for her to be out of the country, when she should have been at Westminster, consolidating support. She was too ready to assume that her own record spoke for itself, and mistakenly believed that it would work in her favour to be seen on the world stage at such a time.

The exit

Thatcher received the result of the first round by telephone at the British embassy in Paris, where she was preparing to attend an official entertainment for the assembled heads of government. Some of her entourage later stated that this was when they realised she was finished. She had received 204 votes to Heseltine's 152, with sixteen MPs abstaining. Under the rules laid down for leadership contests, in order to secure an unequivocal victory, an incumbent had to win an overall majority plus 15 per cent of those entitled to vote. She was just four votes short of the required total. Without hesitation she addressed journalists outside, telling them that she intended to let her name go forward to a second ballot. Some of her followers, such as party chairman Kenneth Baker, were uneasy that she made the announcement so precipitately, although in truth it is hard to see what else she could have done if she wanted to stay in the race. Any delay would have signalled an acceptance of defeat. The very prospect of a second round, however, spelt trouble.

For a serving Prime Minister of Thatcher's experience to be unable to win outright was a shock. It was likely that a number of MPs who had reluctantly voted for her in the first round would now see her cause as irretrievably damaged, and would withdraw their support if she stood again. The warning signs were clear on her return to London. Her two sponsors in the first round, Douglas Hurd and John Major, agreed to support her nomination once again but the latter, who was recovering from a wisdom tooth operation, appeared momentarily to hesitate when asked for his endorsement by telephone. There is no evidence that a campaign had been started on Major's behalf before Thatcher had left the field, and he positively discouraged friends who wanted to promote his cause. Nonetheless, a number of influential Conservatives had already started to think about who was best placed to run against Heseltine. Soon after the result of the first ballot had been announced, about a dozen members of the government met at Tristan Garel-Jones' house in Catherine Place to consider this question. Most felt that Hurd, who was still in Paris with the Prime Minister, was the most credible candidate. Almost without exception the attendees had psychologically moved on from the Thatcher era.

Initially Thatcher tried to tough it out, telling reporters in Downing Street on 21 November: 'I fight on, I fight to win'. That evening, however, following the advice of Peter Morrison and the Energy Secretary, John Wakeham, who had found himself cast as her final campaign manager, she decided to seek the advice of her Cabinet colleagues. Thatcherites such as Cecil Parkinson and Tim Bell would later argue that she should have seen the Cabinet as a group, since it would have been harder for them to oppose her openly. Instead she saw them individually in her room at the Commons. The line that most of them took was so similar that it seems clear that they must have conferred together whilst waiting for their audience. Hardly any of them unequivocally urged her to fight on. Most stated that they would support her if she chose to stand again, but they expected her to lose. Few were quite as brutal as Kenneth Clarke, who told her that her inevitable defeat would leave the party split, and advised her to stand aside so that Hurd or Major could take on Heseltine. Some, such as David Waddington, were genuinely distressed as they gave their assessment. Only a handful of junior ministers and backbenchers, who arrived belatedly in an attempt to bolster Thatcher's spirits, urged her to fight on regardless of the cost. It was her inability to mobilise her most senior colleagues which led her, on the morning of 22 November, to announce her resignation.

In her memoirs Thatcher revealed her true bitterness at what she regarded as betrayal by those whom she had elevated to high office. The chapter in which she chronicled her downfall is headed 'Men in Lifeboats'. She found her final Cabinet meeting, at which she told her colleagues of her decision, a traumatic experience. By the afternoon Thatcher had recovered sufficiently to deliver a defiant final performance in a no-confidence debate initiated by the opposition. In a wide-ranging defence of her eleven years at the top, she insisted that her government had 'rescued Britain from the parlous state to which socialism had brought it', had extended ordinary people's freedom of choice and power over their own lives, and ensured that 'we are no longer the sick man of Europe'. Responding ebulliently to interruptions from across the floor, at one point she exclaimed, 'I am enjoying this.' She closed on a positively Churchillian note, reminding her listeners of the Falklands conflict, and of the preparations which were then in progress to expel Iraq's forces from Kuwait. She spoke of 'a sense of this country's destiny: the centuries of history and experience which ensure that, when principles have to be defended, when good has to be upheld and when evil has to be overcome, Britain will take up arms'.[39] It was an extraordinary performance from a Prime Minister who had been toppled only a few hours earlier. The popular press the following day reflected the sense of shock at Thatcher's abrupt departure, with the *Daily Express* asking, 'What have they done?' and the *Daily Mail* excoriating Tory faint-hearts with the headline, 'Too damn good for the lot of them'.

Thatcher remained Prime Minister until after her successor had been chosen on 27 November. In the second round Major emerged as the winner, taking 185 votes to Heseltine's 131 and Hurd's 57. The Chancellor owed his success to the fact that he was more widely trusted in the parliamentary party than the flamboyant Heseltine and, as a self-made, meritocratic figure, he was judged to have greater electoral appeal than the Old Etonian Foreign Secretary. He also benefited from Thatcher's open support for his candidacy and the fact that he was considered most likely to cement her legacy. No doubt MPs who felt some guilt at Thatcher's despatch were able to assuage their consciences by voting for her favoured successor. On 28 November she left Downing Street for the last time, containing her emotions as she delivered a brief final statement to the waiting media, in which she spoke of leaving the United Kingdom 'in a very, very much better state than when we came here eleven and a half years ago', and stated that Major had 'the makings of a great Prime Minister, which I'm sure he'll be in a very short time'.[40] Only as she was driven away did the cameras capture the glimpse of a tearful fallen leader, through the window of the car, which would become the defining image of Thatcher's final hour in office.

Notes

1 Tim Bell, *Right or Wrong? The Memoirs of Lord Bell* (London, Bloomsbury, 2014), p. 130.

2 Nicholas Ridley, *'My Style of Government': The Thatcher Years* (London, Hutchinson, 1991), p. 232. Reproduced by permission of The Random House Group Ltd and Peters Fraser Dunlop (www.petersfraserdunlop.com) on behalf of the Estate of Nicholas Ridley.

3 John Sergeant, *Give Me Ten Seconds* (London, Macmillan, 2001), p. 3.

4 Quoted in *Thatcher: The Downing Street Years: Part 4: Wielding the Knife* (BBC2, 1993).

5 Sarah Curtis (ed.), *The Journals of Woodrow Wyatt*, Volume 1 (London, Macmillan, 1998), p. 467, entry for 20 December 1987.

6 TV Interview for Yorkshire TV (visiting Bradford), 28 February 1990, *Margaret Thatcher: Complete Public Statements on CD-ROM, 1945–1990* (Oxford, Oxford University Press, 1999), 90_062.

7 Chris Patten, 25 June 1990, quoted in Ion Trewin (ed.), *The Hugo Young Papers: Thirty Years of British Politics – Off the Record* (London, Allen Lane, 2008), p. 299.

8 Douglas Hurd, *Memoirs* (London, Little, Brown, 2003), p. 399.

9 Jonathan Aitken, *Margaret Thatcher: Power and Personality* (London, Bloomsbury, 2013), p. 634.

10 For further details on the events covered in this paragraph, see pp. 209–11.

11 Quoted in 'Not while I'm alive, he ain't – Part 4', presented by Brian Walden on The Westminster Hour, BBC Radio 4, 21 April 2002, http://news.bbc.co.uk/1/hi/programmes/the_westminster_hour/1940421.stm (accessed 14 December 2014).

12 Quoted in 'Not while I'm alive, he ain't – Part 4', http://news.bbc.co.uk/1/hi/programmes/the_westminster_hour/1940421.stm (accessed 14 December 2014).

13 TV Interview for The Walden Interview (Lawson's resignation), 28 October 1989, *Margaret Thatcher: Complete Public Statements on CD-ROM, 1945–1990* (Oxford, Oxford University Press, 1999), 89_408.

14 Norman Fowler, *A Political Suicide: The Conservatives' Voyage into the Wilderness* (London, Politico's, 2008), p. 51.

15 Leadership election: George Younger's 'post-mortem meeting notes' (MT campaign team's secret discussion), 6 December 1989, http://www.margaretthatcher.org/document/111437 (accessed 14 December 2014).

16 David Owen, *Time to Declare* (London, Michael Joseph, 1991), p. 784.

17 Quoted in 'The lady's not for waking', *The Sunday Times*, 12 October 2014.

18 Quoted in Richard Vinen, *Thatcher's Britain: The Politics and Social Upheaval of the Thatcher Era* (London, Simon & Schuster, 2009), p. 262.

19 Kenneth Baker, *The Turbulent Years: My Life in Politics* (London, Faber and Faber, 1993), p. 363.
20 Margaret Thatcher, *The Downing Street Years* (London, Harper Collins, 1993), p. 717.
21 Edwina Currie, *Diaries 1987–1992* (London, Time Warner, 2002), p. 62, entry for 8 May 1988.
22 Douglas Hurd, *Memoirs* (London, Little, Brown, 2003), p. 396.
23 John Campbell, *Margaret Thatcher Volume Two: The Iron Lady* (London, Jonathan Cape, 2003), p. 695.
24 Alan Clark, *Diaries: In Power 1983–1992* (London, Weidenfeld & Nicolson, 1993), p. 289, entry for 28 March 1990.
25 Bell, *Right or Wrong?,* p. 137.
26 Nigel Lawson, *The View from No. 11: Memoirs of a Tory Radical* (London, Bantam Press, 1992), p. 653.
27 Sarah Curtis (ed.), *The Journals of Woodrow Wyatt*, Volume 2 (London, Pan, 2000), p. 207, entry for 11 December 1989.
28 Quoted in Philip Short, *Mitterrand: A Study in Ambiguity* (London, The Bodley Head, 2013), p. 381.
29 Geoffrey Howe, *Conflict of Loyalty* (London, Macmillan, 1994), p. 650.
30 Gyles Brandreth, *Breaking the Code: Westminster Diaries May 1990–May 1997* (London, Weidenfeld & Nicolson, 1999), p. 17, entry for 2 November 1990.
31 David McKie, *Guardian* journalist, 17 July 1986, quoted in Gyles Brandreth (ed.), *The Oxford Dictionary of Humorous Quotations* (Oxford, Oxford University Press, 2013), p. 290.
32 Personal Statement, House of Commons Debates, 13 November 1990, vol. 180, cc. 463–5, http://hansard.millbanksystems.com/commons/1990/nov/13/personal-statement (accessed 14 December 2014).
33 Howe, *Conflict of Loyalty*, p. 670.
34 Lawson, *View from No. 11*, p. 1001.
35 Quoted in *Thatcher: The Downing Street Years: Part 4: Wielding the Knife* (BBC2, 1993).
36 Tim Renton, *Chief Whip: People, Power and Patronage in Westminster* (London, Politico's, 2004), pp. 79–80.
37 David Waddington, *Memoirs: Dispatches from Margaret Thatcher's Last Home Secretary* (London, Biteback, 2012), p. 222.
38 Interview for *The Times*, 17 November 1990, www.margaretthatcher.org/document/107869 (accessed 14 December 2014).
39 Confidence in Her Majesty's Government, House of Commons Debates, 22 November 1990, vol. 181, cc. 446–453, http://hansard.millbanksystems.com/commons/1990/nov/22/confidence-in-her-majestys-government (accessed 14 December 2014).
40 Remarks departing Downing Street, 28 November 1990, www.margaretthatcher.org/document/108258 (accessed 14 December 2014).

11 Life after political death: 1990–2013

A painful adjustment

Thatcher adapted with great difficulty to her downfall. It was particularly hard for her to be removed from office in the midst of allied preparations for the ejection of Saddam Hussein's forces from Kuwait, which led in January 1991 to the short, successful campaign known as the first Gulf War. In the longer run Thatcher never truly reconciled herself to her abrupt departure from Downing Street, and found it difficult to carve out a new role for herself. She was clearly too dominating a figure to accept a post in her successor's Cabinet, and John Major was realist enough not to offer one. Her controversial reputation also ruled out taking a post as chair of an international organisation; there had been loud laughter, during her exuberant performance in the no confidence debate on 22 November 1990, when Labour MP Denis Skinner had jokingly proposed her as head of the soon to be created European Central Bank. Instead, for more than a decade, Thatcher projected herself as a global figure, occupying her time and supplementing her income with the publication of her memoirs and an intensive programme of lecture tours in the United States, the Far East and elsewhere. In 1991, she founded the Thatcher Foundation, whose original purpose was to promote the spread of ideas of freedom and enterprise, especially in the former iron curtain countries of Central and Eastern Europe. It evolved into an educational trust and the repository, through the creation of a CD-ROM and a comprehensive website, of Thatcher's written and spoken words. Yet hers was not a dignified retirement in which she assumed the Olympian role of international states-woman, detached from national politics. Her interventions in the affairs of the Conservative Party, which were halted only by the deterioration of her physical and mental health in her late seventies, did her reputation little good and arguably harmed the prospects of her successors.

Thatcher and Major

The practicalities of everyday life, after the loss of the Downing Street support system, proved a considerable challenge for the former Prime Minister. She and her husband had purchased a suburban house in Dulwich in anticipation of their retirement, without considering its suitability for someone who wanted to continue playing as active a role as possible in public life. The couple eventually settled in a more central location in London's upmarket Chester Square, where a small circle of friends and supporters from the worlds of politics, journalism and academia paid court. She became a focus for right-wing Conservatives, organised in a number of bodies such as the Bruges Group and the No Turning Back Group, whose purpose was to keep alive the ideas for which their heroine stood. Influence and admiration were, however, poor substitutes for the reality of power. Tim Bell recalled that, in the first years after the loss of office, 'she would talk about how she still could not stop expecting her car to turn into Downing Street, and of course, it always carried on'.[1]

Thatcher's disillusion with her successor set in remarkably early. She resented his abandonment of the poll tax in favour of a banded property-based charge, the council tax, even though this was no more than a recognition of political reality. Just as unreasonably, she objected to Major's appointment of Michael Heseltine to his Cabinet as Environment Secretary, even though she had given senior posts to those she had defeated for the party leadership fifteen years earlier. To have kept such a powerful figure on the backbenches, out of deference to Thatcher's sensitivities, would have been unthinkable for an incoming Prime Minister seeking to establish himself in office. More seriously, she began to grumble, mainly in private but occasionally in public, that Major was not committed to preserving her legacy. This was hard to square with the fact that, at least until after his general election success in April 1992, he retained most of the Cabinet whom she had originally appointed. She and her followers gave out the message that he was a grey man without definite ideas, who was by implication unworthy to fill her shoes. Asked by her daughter to explain her earlier promotion of a man she now found so unsatisfactory, Thatcher replied that 'he was very good at doing what I asked him to do. I assumed that he believed in what he was doing.'[2] Some years later a puzzled Douglas Hurd asked her why, if she thought so little of Major, she had given him her unequivocal support in the second round of the November 1990 leadership contest. Tactlessly forgetting that Hurd had himself been a contender, she confided in him that 'he was the best of a *very* poor bunch'.[3]

Thatcher's attitude towards her successor unavoidably led parallels to be drawn with the way in which Edward Heath had harassed her as Prime Minister. Thatcher was, however, in a stronger position than he had been to inflict damage on the government of the day. Heath had attacked Thatcher on such a wide range of policy issues – condemning her refusal to contemplate an incomes policy, calling for a negotiated settlement of the Falklands crisis and opposing privatisation, tax cuts and the abolition of the GLC– that it was all too easy to dismiss his criticisms as proceeding from nothing more than bad temper at his own supersession. Unlike Heath, she commanded significant support on the backbenches and among opinion formers in the media. Thatcher also enjoyed the continuing regard of the Conservative rank and file, who greeted her enthusiastically at successive party conferences. Party activists' warmth did, however, diminish a little as evidence grew of her disloyalty to the current leadership. She also posed a less serious challenge to Major after she decided to take up a seat in the House of Lords following the 1992 general election.

Nonetheless, the main issue on which Thatcher chose to attack her successor's policy was one with toxic potential for Conservative unity. It was the question of closer European integration that drew her ire above all. The flashpoint was Major's signing of the Maastricht Treaty in December 1991, which transformed the Community into the European Union. Hard-line Eurosceptics were not reassured by the fact that he had won opt-outs for

Britain from the process of economic and monetary union, and from the Social Chapter, which introduced new regulations of working conditions. The drawn-out process of securing parliamentary ratification of the treaty was particularly tense since, following the April 1992 general election, Major had a much smaller majority of twenty-one to work with, and so every vote in the House of Commons counted. The government's position was further weakened by the onset of massive speculation in the money markets, leading on 16 September 1992 to the suspension of sterling's membership of the Exchange Rate Mechanism. Thatcher openly welcomed the events of 'Black Wednesday', arguing that the ERM had turned out to be much more rigid than was believed to be the case when Britain had joined, barely two years before. By staying in the system after its lack of flexibility had become apparent, the government had been obliged to keep interest rates high, with dire consequences for home owners and businesses. She treated the crisis as a vindication of her own instincts. Now that the pound had been allowed to float, she stated, it was possible to devise 'an economic strategy which works with markets, not against them . . . we must return to the policy of domestic monetary control that worked throughout most of the 1980s'.[4] This was not entirely fair since although the inflation rate – her chosen measure of successful economic management – initially fell, it had returned to double digits by the time she left office.

Thatcher's barely disguised glee at the collapse of an exchange rate policy in which she had never believed was accompanied by the open demonstration of her hostility to Maastricht. She tested her relationship with Major almost to destruction by encouraging a small band of right-wing MPs to rebel against the government. Defenders of the Prime Minister countered that it was entirely possible to envisage Thatcher herself negotiating on Britain's behalf as he had done, if she had still been in office. After all, she had surrendered a greater measure of national sovereignty when she signed the Single European Act. By now, however, liberated from the constraints of office, she had come to regret the way in which the 1986 Act had paved the way for what she saw as creeping European federalism. Addressing the House of Lords in June 1993, she maintained that 'we got our fingers burned under the Single European Act', as majority voting – originally intended only to enable the completion of the single market – had been extended into a range of additional policy areas. Maastricht, she argued, would represent an unacceptable further enlargement of this process, amounting to 'an overwhelming centralisation of decisions by bureaucracy at the expense of democracy and at the expense of accountability to the electorate'.[5] Although the treaty was eventually ratified, the episode left lasting scars on the party. For his part, Major was deeply bruised by an exhibition of disloyalty which Thatcher would not have tolerated in others during her own term of office. In his memoirs he directly blamed his defeat in the 1997 general election on the internal party disunity which began at this time. He also expressed his anger that she chose to speak out in public rather than expressing her concerns privately.[6]

Less predictable than her clash with the government over Europe was the stand that Thatcher took over another foreign policy development of the 1990s, the gradual disintegration of Yugoslavia and the attempts of Serbia to prevent the other constituent parts from winning their independence. From the start, Thatcher insisted on the right of Croatia, Slovenia and Bosnia-Hercegovina to self-determination, and criticised the Major government for its steadfast refusal to support intervention, even the supply of arms to assist those struggling against Serb aggression. Her position was based partly on ideological hostility to the communist-led regime of Slobodan Milosevic in Belgrade, but also on humanitarian grounds, as evidence accumulated of Serbian atrocities, particularly against Bosnian Muslims. It was a stance which aligned her with a much wider range of opinion than her campaign against Maastricht had done, including a number of voices on the left – Michael Foot, for example, emerged from retirement to make a documentary film about the unfolding tragedy. For Thatcher, the Major government's insistence that Western intervention could only cause the crisis to escalate was further proof of its weakness. She felt a degree of vindication when NATO air strikes in August 1995 eventually brought the Serbs to the negotiating table, leading in November to guarantees for Bosnian independence in the Dayton agreement. Thatcher drew support for her traditionalist view of foreign policy from the prolonged blood-letting in the Balkans. Speaking to an American audience before the crisis ended, she contrasted the successful conduct of the Gulf War with the West's slowness to take action against Serbia. Strong military action, directed for a specific purpose, would prevail against an aggressor where well-meaning internationalism had failed. Idealistic talk of a new world order in the aftermath of the Cold War had proved premature: 'only nations are capable of acting with the necessary decisiveness and purpose, provided always that they have strong leadership'.[7]

Writing and fighting her corner

The publication of her memoirs was another way in which Thatcher contrived to project her views to a wider audience. For commercial reasons the volume dealing with the most important phase of her career, *The Downing Street Years*, appeared first, in the autumn of 1993. It was accompanied by a four part BBC TV series in which Thatcher and a number of her leading contemporaries gave extensive interviews. Whilst making due allowance for the former premier's desire to make her case and to stress her own role in events, together they constitute an indispensable source for the historian. A second volume, on her life before the 1979 election victory, was published two years later. Entitled *The Path to Power*, it is an oddly structured work, with the book's autobiographical core followed by four chapters in which she gave her own commentary on events since she had left office. Thatcher was not a natural author. The project was tackled in much the same way as her speeches had been produced, with a team of research assistants offering ideas and drafts, and the whole work being revised until it met with her satisfaction. In a rare example of modesty, Thatcher confided in journalist Hugo Young that 'it was much harder work than a general election. . . . She wrote and wrote, and dictated as well, and then others laid hands on it'. She aimed to write as she spoke, and found it hard to get the right inflections into print: 'she expressed herself envious of people like me who knew how to write and had done it for a long time'.[8]

As was only to be expected in the febrile political atmosphere of the mid-1990s, the media focused largely on the clues supplied by both books regarding Thatcher's thoughts on her successor. The month after the appearance of *The Path to Power*, with the Tory civil war over Europe continuing, Major sought desperately to lance the boil by challenging a representative of the Eurosceptic camp to fight him for the party leadership. When a member of his own Cabinet, Welsh Secretary John Redwood, stepped forward, Thatcher indiscreetly stated that the candidates were both 'good Conservatives'.[9] In the event, however, despite pressure from some of her advisers to the contrary, she did not abandon Major. Residual loyalty to the party's official leadership, possibly combined with the fact that she did not regard any of the potential challengers on the right as wholly suitable, stayed her hand for the remainder of Major's premiership. Indeed, at the May 1997 election she gave the Prime Minister her public support and somewhat uneasily campaigned alongside him. Although she was known to admire the efforts of Tony Blair, who had become Labour leader in July 1994, to move the party away from its socialist roots, she asserted that its public embrace of free market economics represented a surface change rather than a sincere conversion: 'imitations are still fakes'. At the eleventh hour she endorsed Major as the leader who had carried forward her own approach, based upon 'the basic truths about human nature, about markets, about limited government and about national pride'. She also condemned as 'radically subversive' New Labour's programme of constitutional change, comprising House of Lords reform, Scottish devolution, the possibility of proportional representation at Westminster and further European integration.[10] This did not, however, prevent her from accepting a well-publicised invitation from a triumphant Tony Blair to revisit Number Ten shortly after his landslide victory.

Thatcher played a role in the election of the next two Conservative leaders, William Hague in June 1997 and Iain Duncan Smith in September 2001, both of whom came from the right. She supported them largely to prevent the party's leading pro-European candidate, Kenneth Clarke, from being elected. Both leaders had an ambivalent relationship with her, unable wholly to distance themselves from her on account of her continued standing with party activists, but unwilling to be too closely identified with an individual whose interventions in politics were increasingly erratic. She won few admirers for her campaign on behalf of the retired Chilean dictator, General Augusto Pinochet. He was arrested whilst on a visit to Britain in October 1998 at the behest of a Spanish judge, who sought to have him extradited for trial on charges of torture dating back to the 1980s. Thatcher's regard for the general stemmed from gratitude for the support given to Britain by Chile – uniquely among Latin American countries – during the Falklands conflict. She argued that he should be allowed to return to his homeland rather than forced to answer charges in Spain. Although the plea for extradition was eventually turned down on legal grounds, and it was also true that Pinochet had voluntarily made way for a democratic system of government in Chile, Thatcher's involvement was embarrassing for the Conservative leadership. Pinochet's record of human rights abuse was exactly the kind of association that modernising Tories, seeking to develop a more tolerant and inclusive image for their party, did not want.

Thatcher's last extended political statement came in March 2002 with the publication of a third book, *Statecraft: Strategies for a Changing World*. It took the form of a series of commentaries on the international scene and contained a number of by now familiar warnings and prescriptions. The role models for future action were clearly identified. Ronald Reagan's pursuit of American military superiority and defiance of Soviet ambitions was credited with successfully ending the Cold War. Over the past decade the West had mistakenly assumed that the world was a less dangerous place and had allowed its guard to slip. She was characteristically firm in her support for American action against the Islamic terrorist groups responsible for the 9/11 bombings in New York and Washington, which had occurred the previous autumn, and was prepared to support the removal from power of Saddam Hussein in Iraq, which she regarded as the world's most significant 'rogue state'. The most noteworthy passages in the book, however, concerned the growth of the European Union, which she saw both as doomed to eventual failure and as fundamentally inimical to British interests. She lamented the failure of successive governments, including her own, to secure more favourable terms for British membership, and concluded that if this could not be achieved, the United Kingdom should contemplate leaving. Membership of the North American Free Trade Area, she suggested, might be the best alternative. Her overall message was pessimistic in the extreme:

> that such an unnecessary and irrational project as building a European super-state was ever embarked upon will seem in future years to be perhaps the greatest folly of the modern era. And that Britain, with her traditional strengths and global destiny, should ever have been part of it will appear a political error of historic magnitude.[11]

The final years

By the turn of the century, as she reached her mid-seventies, Thatcher's physical health was deteriorating. Trouble with her teeth affected her speech, and it was rumoured that, after a self-disciplined approach to alcohol in office, she was now drinking too much. Her short-term memory was beginning to fail. Former MP George Walden depicted Thatcher in decline, her eyes with 'a far-away look, like an actress endlessly on the point of delivering her curtain speech', conversing distractedly in a series of quotations, whilst 'her over-immaculate hair set off the ravages of her face'.[12] After a series of minor strokes, in March 2002 she finally bowed to medical advice and stopped giving speeches. From now on she issued only occasional brief public statements and when she appeared in public, the media inevitably commented on her increasingly visible frailty. The death of Denis in June 2003 was a major blow. She did not see as much of her family as she would have liked. Mark had married an American and contact with her two grandchildren, who were brought up in Texas, was infrequent; Carol lived largely in Switzerland. In October 2005 she marked her eightieth birthday with a large party at which, in a partial gesture of reconciliation, Geoffrey Howe and Nigel Lawson – though not Michael Heseltine – were present. It was also noteworthy that, with yet another Conservative Party leadership election about to take place, among the guests were the two candidates of the right, David Davis and Liam Fox. There was no invitation for the champion of the party's centre-left, Kenneth Clarke, nor for the eventual winner of the contest, David Cameron, who belonged to a younger generation whom she scarcely knew.

Portrayals of Thatcher in the work of writers and performers continued through her declining years. Criticism of her record became less overt with the passage of time. She made a cameo appearance, dancing with the central character at a party in Alan Hollinghurst's prize-winning 2004 novel *The Line of Beauty*, which vividly depicted the materialism of mid-1980s Britain. Different episodes of Thatcher's career were portrayed on film in *The Long Walk to Finchley* (2008), about her search for a parliamentary seat in the 1950s, and in *Margaret* (2009), which centred on her fall from power. The former even managed to evoke some sympathy for her as a career woman, struggling against the entrenched male chauvinism of the age. Most controversial was *The Iron Lady* (2011), in which American actress Meryl Streep played an elderly Thatcher, with episodes from her career recalled in a series of flashbacks. Although Streep successfully captured Thatcher's physical appearance, speech and mannerisms, some critics felt that the film's focus on its subject's mental deterioration was insensitive and in questionable taste.

The public events in which Thatcher took part in her last decade tended to underline the fact that she was increasingly a figure of the past. In June 2004, she attended Ronald Reagan's funeral in Washington, accompanying the former President's family to the interment which followed at his California home. Since it was judged unwise for her to attempt to deliver it in person, she had pre-recorded a tribute to her old transatlantic ally, which was played at the service. In February 2007, she was guest of honour at the opening of the UK's Cold War Museum at RAF Cosford, and that spring she attended a series of events marking the twenty-fifth anniversary of the Falklands conflict. In the same year, Thatcher was accorded an unprecedented honour for a still living ex-premier when a statue of her was erected in the Houses of Parliament. As her years in office receded into the past, she also began to enjoy a degree of cross-party regard, with two invitations to Downing Street and one to Chequers from Labour Prime Minister, Gordon Brown. On one of these occasions she was present at the unveiling of her portrait in Number 10. Her final visit to her old home was in June 2010, as the guest of the first Conservative Prime Minister in thirteen years, David Cameron. From time to time the public were afforded more informal glimpses of her relaxing in London parks. There were signs of an unsuspected, gentler side to her character as she enjoyed the company of animals and showed appreciation of gardens.

As Thatcher's health continued to decline, it was announced in December 2011 that her office in the House of Lords was closing. A year later, after a minor operation, it was judged that she could no longer manage the stairs in her London house and she spent her final months in the comfort of a private suite at the Ritz Hotel. It was there, following a further stroke on the morning of 8 April 2013, that she died aged eighty-seven. In death Thatcher continued to divide opinion as she had done in life. Respectful tributes were paid by representatives of Britain's political establishment, former Cabinet colleagues and current and retired world leaders. Parliament was recalled from the Easter recess to allow members of both houses to mark her passing, and there were appreciative remarks on her patriotism and global impact by David Cameron, Tony Blair and others. A more hostile response came from deprived areas where the impact of her policies on manufacturing industry and the trade unions had not been forgiven. Opponents used social media in an attempt to send the song 'Ding Dong! The Witch is Dead' to the top of the music charts – it reached number two – and there were street parties in Brixton, Liverpool and Glasgow. In a sarcastic allusion to her privatisation policies, left-wing film-maker Ken Loach called for her funeral to be put out to tender and the cheapest bid accepted: 'it's what she would have wanted'.[13]

Nine days after her death Thatcher was given a ceremonial funeral, with military honours, at St Paul's. She had been closely involved in the planning and had ruled out additional features associated with a full state funeral, such as a lying in state and a RAF fly-past, which she felt would have entailed unjustifiable added expense. Nonetheless, with the exception of Winston Churchill almost half a century earlier, it was the most elaborate farewell to a former premier in modern times. The coffin travelled on a gun carriage with military escort on the final phase of the journey to the cathedral, where the funeral was conducted in the presence of the Queen and the address was given by the Bishop of London. Crowds lining the route were in general respectful, with occasional bursts of applause, and fears of significant protests in central London were not borne out. The ceremony was followed by a private cremation, attended only by a handful of family members and close friends, and the ashes were later interred at the Royal Hospital, Chelsea. The debate on Thatcher's legacy, which had begun long before her death, would now intensify.

Notes

1 Tim Bell, *Right or Wrong? The Memoirs of Lord Bell* (London, Bloomsbury, 2014), p. 144.
2 Quoted in Alistair McAlpine, *Once A Jolly Bagman: Memoirs* (London, Weidenfeld & Nicolson, 1997), p. 271.
3 Douglas Hurd, *Memoirs* (London, Little, Brown, 2003), p. 404.
4 Article for *The European* (Maastricht), 8 October 1992, www.margaretthatcher.org/document/108305 (accessed 28 December 2014).
5 House of Lords Speeches, European Communities (Amendment) Bill, 7 June 1993, www.margaretthatcher.org/document/108314 (accessed 28 December 2014).
6 John Major, *The Autobiography* (London, Harper Collins, 1999), p. 362, pp. 613–14.
7 Speech to the Aspen Institute ('Managing conflict – the role of international intervention'), 4 August 1995, www.margaretthatcher.org/document/108346 (accessed 28 December 2014).
8 Ion Trewin (ed.), *The Hugo Young Papers: Thirty Years of British Politics – Off the Record* (London, Allen Lane, 2008), p. 400.
9 Quoted in Anthony Seldon, *Major: A Political Life* (London, Phoenix, 1998), p. 579.
10 Article for *Daily Telegraph* ('The boneless wonder of New Labour'), 1 April 1997, www.margaretthatcher.org/document/108369 (accessed 28 December 2014).
11 Margaret Thatcher, *Statecraft: Strategies for a Changing World* (London, Harper Collins, 2002), p. 410.
12 George Walden, *Lucky George: Memories of an Anti-Politician* (London, Allen Lane, 1999), pp. 379–80.
13 Quoted in *The Independent*, 9 April 2013, p. 7.

12 The Thatcher legacy

Thatcher and Thatcherism

This study began with an insistence that historians should look behind the image of a dominant leader, so often distorted by the adulation of her admirers and the vituperation of her detractors, to assess the real significance of Margaret Thatcher's career. The strength of her personality, and the length of her period of office, make it all too easy to exaggerate the part she played, and to see her almost as the embodiment of 1980s Britain. This book has drawn attention to the constraints within which Thatcher acted in her years of power. It has highlighted her caution as well as her radicalism, and her capacity for change alongside her adherence to certain core values. We have seen how, as Prime Minister, to a great extent she acted in response to events rather than implementing a preconceived master plan.

Earlier chapters have provided numerous examples of Thatcher's inconsistency. She espoused and then abandoned the pursuit of strict targets for the control of the money supply; she staunchly opposed and eventually joined the European Exchange Rate Mechanism. Initially slow to adopt privatisation and the poll tax, she later became a passionate advocate of both. She concluded settlements in Rhodesia, Hong Kong and Northern Ireland which went against her innermost convictions. Before leaving office she had turned decisively against the process of European integration which, in the Single European Act, she had done so much to promote. Any discussion of Thatcher's legacy needs to be informed by the recognition that she was a practical politician who evolved over time, rather than the incarnation of a static ideology. It is also important to highlight how her governments formed part of the continuity of post-war British politics and government, as well as the ways in which they marked a break with the recent past.

It suited some of Thatcher's opponents – and, from a different perspective, some of her followers – to depict her as an aberration from the mainstream of British Conservatism, as the bearer of a doctrine alien to the traditions of the party she led. It is true that she attracted support from many who never identified themselves explicitly with the Conservative Party. Alan Walters, Bernard Ingham and John Hoskyns had all supported Labour at various points in their earlier careers. Thatcher enjoyed the confirmation of her attitudes and policies provided by intellectual converts from socialism such as Paul Johnson, a past editor of the left-wing *New Statesman*, whilst former Labour MP Woodrow Wyatt was a confidant. Some commentators suggested that, with her desire to shrink the state, to lower direct taxation and promote competition, she was at heart a classical liberal in the mould of Gladstone, a hundred years earlier. The claim was made disparagingly by some of her critics, in a bid to establish that she was not a true Conservative. Mark Garnett and Ian Gilmour, for example, insisted that

> Thatcherite ideology was largely inspired by nineteenth-century liberalism, as expounded (though hardly updated) by American and continental writers, further distilled by the odd assortment of rationalists and communist converts [an allusion to Alfred Sherman, who had served on the republican side in the Spanish civil war] who staffed her favourite think-tanks.[1]

This is to exaggerate the extent to which Thatcher departed from mainstream Conservatism. In the early 1950s Churchill had reacted against the statism of the Attlee governments, whilst, at the end of the decade, Macmillan had presided over a culture of consumerism no less shameless than that of the Thatcher era. John Nott, recalling his time as Trade Secretary in her first government, wrote that 'it is a complete misreading of her beliefs to depict her as a nineteenth-century Liberal' and insisted that her nationalist instincts took precedence over her theoretical commitment to free trade: 'emotionally she was an authoritarian and a protectionist'.[2] Thatcher openly admired what she recognised as 'Victorian values' of self-help, industry and sobriety, but these were never the sole preserve of one party. In her robust emphasis on the pursuit of British interests and hostility to constitutional change, she stood much closer to the ideas of Disraelian Conservatism than she did to the internationalist and reform-minded outlook of his Liberal opponents. Indeed she consistently refused to allow her wet Tory critics a monopoly of the concept of 'one nation'. The difference was that, whereas for Gilmour and his like it stood for a tradition of benevolent paternalism, for her it carried a connotation of assertive patriotism.

Although as party leader Thatcher adopted a more overtly populist tone than her recent predecessors, most Conservative governments over the previous century had combined defence of the free market and private property with an emphasis on law and order and national defence. When asked to define the concept of 'Thatcherism', she usually characterised it as an endeavour to restore widely accepted common sense values, from which Britain had temporarily departed in the 1960s and 1970s. Interviewed in 1988, she insisted that what she stood for was 'not Thatcherism. It is much older than that'. She portrayed herself as being in step with mainstream public opinion in seeking to reverse the 'ratchet of socialism', which had advanced since 1945, and thus to make it possible for individuals to take more control over their lives.[3] It was an interpretation to which Thatcher continued to adhere, telling an overseas audience after her departure from Number 10 that she had not 'invented' Thatcherism but had 'rediscovered' it. 'The values, ideas and beliefs which I was privileged to be able to put into effect . . . were rooted in the experience of the past and reinforced by events in my lifetime.'[4]

Thatcher's repeated emphasis on the importance of economic freedom and individual choice and responsibility made her sound more doctrinaire than she really was. A prominent example was her May 1988 speech to the General Assembly of the Church of Scotland – commonly known as the 'Sermon on the Mound' after the Edinburgh venue where it was delivered – in which she linked her political philosophy to her religious and spiritual values. She drew attention to the words of the patriotic hymn, 'I vow to thee my country', in which the writer envisages the progress of each individual soul to salvation: 'not group by group or party by party or even church by church – but soul by soul – and each one counts'. The address antagonised left-leaning theologians such as Professor Duncan Forrester, who condemned what he termed Thatcher's notion of an 'individualist's paradise' as a distortion of the Christian gospel.[5] Even more controversial was the September 1987 interview in which she declared that 'there is no such thing as society'. It was a perhaps unwise phrase, destined to be quoted out of context. Elsewhere in the interview, she criticised those who were dependent on state welfare provision for 'casting their problems on society', and stressed the importance of people helping each other at local level. Evidently she felt the need to clarify her thoughts because, in an article published in *The Sunday Times* some months later, it was stated that she believed in society as a collection of people rather than an abstraction: 'she prefers to think in terms of the acts of individuals and their families as the real sinews of society rather than of society as an abstract concept'.[6]

Thatcher did have an understanding of society, but it differed from the vision of her collectivist opponents, who emphasised the role of government action in ensuring social justice. In her memoirs she outlined a model of social responsibility in which 'a living structure of individuals, families, neighbours and voluntary groups' would play a greater role. What she objected to was 'the confusion of society with the state as the helper of first resort'.[7] It was not, in fact, far removed from the notion of the 'big society' championed by David Cameron as Conservative leader two decades later, even though at the time he was usually viewed as a moderniser, ideologically distant from his predecessor. 'There is such a thing as society, it's just not the same thing as the state',[8] he declared in a perhaps unconscious echo of Thatcher's own message.

The difference was that Thatcher so often adopted a harsh, antagonistic tone which suggested a lack of sympathy with the less fortunate. On one occasion, for example, she spoke of those who 'just drool and drivel they care',[9] words which she clumsily withdrew when challenged by the interviewer. She made no secret of her own use of private health care, stating that it enabled her to have an operation at a time that suited her convenience[10] – a public relations blunder which later Tory leaders, determined to present themselves as champions of services used by the majority of voters, were careful to avoid. Yet she rejected as politically too difficult the more ambitious proposals put forward by right-wing think tanks, such as education vouchers to give parents a choice of schools, university tuition fees and, above all, anything which threatened the privatisation of the NHS. Spending on health increased by almost one third across the decade, even if the pressures imposed by an ageing population and more expensive medical procedures meant that the government still faced charges of underfunding. Nor did Thatcher undertake root and branch reform of the benefits system, in spite of her keen awareness of the problem of welfare dependency. Rising unemployment at the beginning and the end of her premiership made it difficult to cut spending on social security. Social changes which had first become evident in the 1960s, notably family breakdown, continued in the Thatcher years, so that the number of people reliant on income support and single parent benefits increased by more than 2 million over the decade. Total spending on social services fell by an insignificant amount, from 22.9 to 22.2 per cent of GDP.

Yet what endured in the popular imagination was the image of an uncaring leader, who neglected and even despised the poor and the services on which they depended. It was all too easy to parody Thatcher as the promoter of an enterprise culture whose other side was an unappealing, selfish materialism. The 'Henry Root letters' – the work of a satirist who wrote to a variety of public figures, using the imaginary persona of a retired Surrey fishmonger – provide a number of examples. Offering a bribe to the tutor of a Cambridge college if he will award a place to his intellectually undistinguished nephew, Root assures him that he is

> prepared to pay 'over the top' to achieve equality of opportunity. That's the Tory way. We voted for Mrs Thatcher so that those of us who had indulged in prudent house-keeping down the years could give their youngsters a flying start.[11]

Changing everything?

At least from 1975, Thatcher saw herself as a kind of Conservative revolutionary, whose mission it was to restore a set of values that had been temporarily side-lined in the years of muddle and compromise. Both in office and when reflecting on her achievements in retirement, she consistently projected herself as the author of a decisive breach with a failed post-war consensus. As early as 1977, when asked by an adviser what she had changed, she replied simply, 'Everything'.[12] This arresting statement was typical of Thatcher's penchant for self-dramatisation. After barely two years as opposition leader, she could hardly claim to have transformed even the culture of her own party, let alone that of the country. There were in fact important limits to her radicalism. Unlike Enoch Powell, for example, who had blazed the trail for monetarist economics in the 1960s, and whose championship of national sovereignty prefigured Thatcher's own later opposition to European integration, she did not question the centrality of the Atlantic alliance or the validity of nuclear deterrence. In this area, at least, she was a defender of the settlement established by the Attlee governments, whilst the unilateralist Labour Party of Foot and Kinnock represented a break with the direction of British foreign and defence policy over the previous three and a half decades. On Europe, too, it should be remembered that Thatcher broadly followed the precedent, set by recent Conservative and Labour governments, of seeking to maximise Britain's advantage within the Community. She did not contemplate the possibility of a British exit until long after her departure from office.

In other aspects of national life, the post-war consensus was already being eroded before Thatcher had established herself as premier. Although they did so in response to the onset of financial pressures, rather than through conviction, it was James Callaghan and his Chancellor, Denis Healey, who made the decisive breach with Keynesian economic management. Labour's premier told his shocked party conference, in the autumn of 1976, that it was no longer possible to 'spend your way out of recession and increase employment by cutting taxes and boosting Government spending', and publicly made a causative link between inflation and rising unemployment.[13] In many ways Thatcher accelerated the pace of developments which were already under way. The 1980s saw a marked shift from traditional industry towards a service-based economy, but this was part of a process which had begun decades earlier. The number of people working in the manufacturing sector had peaked in 1966 and had been in steady decline thereafter. Employment in coal mining fell from 230,000 to 57,000 in the course of the 1980s, but 300,000 mining jobs had been lost in the two previous decades. Thatcher's withdrawal of subsidies from inefficient enterprises undoubtedly played a part in reshaping the economy. More fundamental explanations, however, are to be found in the growth of global competition, combined with the impact of new technology. Over these forces the government had little control.

One of the most noted features of the Thatcher years was the widening gulf between the deprived areas of the industrial north and the increasingly prosperous south. High unemployment disproportionately affected those regions which had been dependent on ageing staple industries, leaving an abiding sense of grievance in the communities affected. One measure of this decline was the deteriorating position of the Conservative Party in these areas. By 1987 there were only three Conservative MPs in the largest cities of northern England. A closer examination, however, suggests a more complex picture. In several of these old urban centres, the turning point for the party's fortunes came much earlier. The Conservatives had held six of Liverpool's nine seats in the 1959 general election, a figure which fell to two in the 1964 contest. On Merseyside the key factors were the declining significance of the historic religious divide, which had delivered a Protestant working-class Tory vote for generations, reinforced from the 1970s by the decline of the docks. 1964 also saw Conservative representation halved in Manchester, Newcastle and Bradford, whilst it disappeared completely in Hull. On the other hand Conservative representation in Leeds and Sheffield did not completely vanish until the New Labour landslide victory of 1997. These results indicate the need for caution in ascribing too much significance to the 'Thatcher effect'. The intense hatred of her in large areas of the north tended to obscure the fact that her governments accelerated, rather than initiated, a long-term process of deindustrialisation. In their failure to provide those who had lost their jobs with alternative sources of employment, they recalled the attitudes of the National Governments of the 1930s, rather than the compassionate interventionism which had typified the post-1945 era. By creating the impression that people's livelihoods could be left to the unimpeded working of the market, Thatcher contributed to a lasting sense of disadvantage and inequality in areas of social deprivation.

Nowhere in the United Kingdom did this negative perception of Thatcher prevail with greater intensity than in Scotland. Yet the Conservative Party had been experiencing long-term decline there ever since attaining a high point in 1955, the last general election when it won a majority of Scottish seats. In Glasgow, as in so much of northern England, it was the 1964 election which saw the steepest fall, with the party reduced from five to two seats. Across Scotland as a whole the early years of Thatcher's leadership witnessed a modest revival for the party, from sixteen seats in October 1974 to twenty-two in 1979 and twenty-one in 1983. This figure fell to ten in 1987, though it was not until 1997 that the Conservatives disappeared entirely from the Scottish electoral map. Thatcher was clearly a contributory factor rather than the root cause of Conservative woes in Scotland. It is not entirely clear why she gained so little purchase on Scottish affections. As in northern England, her apparent indifference towards a part of the country which was heavily dependent on old staple industries must have played a part, although the steel-making plant at Ravenscraig, whose fate was the subject of anguished debate in the Thatcher era, did not actually close until 1992. It was a victim of foreign competition, far more than a casualty of policies determined in London. Some observers have suggested that there was a more fundamental cultural divide between Thatcher and the Scots. Ian Lang, a junior Scottish Office minister under Thatcher, who became Secretary of State in Major's government, controversially claimed that whilst she shared many of the values which had made it a great country, such as self-reliance and thrift, 'she didn't quite understand the extent to which Scotland was in thrall to socialism and the dependency culture', which 'was more deep-rooted than she realised'.[14]

Certainly Thatcher displayed more than her usual insensitivity in her approach to Scotland. The 'Sermon on the Mound' demonstrated a lack of sympathy for Scottish notions of egalitarianism and community. Once again it was the tone rather than the substance of Thatcher's policies that was so often at fault. She did not, for example, attempt to reform the central government public spending formula introduced under Callaghan, which gave Scotland a disproportionate share of funding. As we have seen in Chapter 10,[15] in introducing the poll tax in Scotland a year earlier than in England, Thatcher was responding to pressure from Scottish Conservative MPs, after an unpopular revaluation of the rates, rather than treating the country as a 'guinea pig' for the new charge. Nevertheless, it was an insensitive decision, after a general election which had seen her mandate to govern Scotland significantly weakened. Thatcher's failure to address her party's perceived lack of legitimacy north of the border helps to explain the growing demand for devolution, signalled by the creation of a Scottish constitutional convention in March 1989. This body united Labour, the Liberal Democrats and representatives of the churches and trade unions in support of a Scottish parliament, with only the Conservatives and the pro-independence Scottish Nationalists choosing not to be involved. It was a paradox of Thatcher's rule that she unintentionally paved the way for Scotland's reappraisal of its position within the Union in the next decade.

Although antipathy to Thatcher was more muted in Wales, her relationship with the principality in some respects mirrors the Scottish experience. The confrontation with the miners and the continued erosion of the old industrial base won her few friends in a part of the United Kingdom where coal and steel still possessed great symbolic significance. Yet in other respects the Thatcher government helped to preserve the special character of Wales, acceding to nationalist pressure for the protection of the Welsh language in broadcasting and schools. Some of the government's policies, such as the sale of council houses, were undoubtedly popular. Particularly after the arch-wet Peter Walker's appointment in June 1987, the Welsh Office was allowed considerable latitude in setting public spending priorities, working through regional agencies whose mainspring was far removed from 'Thatcherite' ideas. The Conservatives did not perform badly in Wales, increasing their modest total of MPs from eleven in 1979 to fourteen in 1983, falling to eight in 1987. As with Scotland, the party did not lose all its seats there until 1997. Yet Thatcher and Wales never warmed to each other. Her first Welsh Secretary, Nicholas Edwards, recalled her response to an unfavourable reception in Cardiff during the 1987 election campaign: 'Oh what dreadful people, we are really wasting our time – what is the point of all your efforts if they appreciate them so little'. Edwards considered that for her 'this was alien territory, far from the England that she knew and understood'.[16] There was some truth in Chris Patten's observation on Thatcher's 'achievement in making the Conservative Party an English national party'.[17] This was not her intention, but rather the consequence of a failure of imagination on her part, a lack of empathy with parts of the United Kingdom where her writ did not truly run.

An economic and social revolution?

In the short term Thatcher achieved, at best, only qualified success in her much-vaunted crusade to turn the British economy around. Taxation continued to take around 40 per cent of GDP, although the balance between direct and indirect taxes shifted decisively in favour of the latter, providing an incentive to the better off entrepreneurial 'wealth-creators' whilst disproportionately penalising those on low incomes. After initially bringing inflation down, she left office with it returning to double figures and Britain entering recession, from which it did not emerge for another three years. This was in large part the consequence of her and Lawson's willingness to set aside 'monetarism' in favour of the credit-fuelled, personal consumption-oriented boom which delivered electoral victory in 1987. Thatcher's Conservatives owed their electoral success to an ability to appeal to the self-interest of a disparate collection of groups – from prosperous merchant bankers and 'yuppies' to the traditional middle classes of the suburbs and shires, through to the upwardly mobile, aspiring workers who had bought their council houses and wanted to trade up to larger properties in more affluent areas. It was a fragile coalition, cemented mid-decade by the impact of the

'Falklands factor' and the splitting of the anti-Conservative vote which, under Britain's first past the post electoral system, enabled Thatcher to win elections with no more than 43 per cent of the popular vote. By the end of the decade the base of her support was being eroded by anger over the poll tax and anxiety over the economic downturn.

There is little evidence that Thatcher had succeeded in bringing about an ideological conversion of the electorate. Opinion polls consistently showed that public attitudes to the welfare state were closer to the values of the post-1945 consensus than to Thatcher's free market philosophy. Data presented in the 1988 edition of *British Social Attitudes*, for example, suggested that only 3 per cent of respondents supported the idea that taxes should be reduced and less spent on the NHS, education and benefits. In a MORI opinion poll in March 1989, after almost a decade of Thatcherism, 55 per cent wanted a society 'which emphasises the social and collective provision of welfare', compared to 40 per cent who preferred one in which 'the individual is encouraged to look after himself'.[18] Although there is no suggestion that a significant proportion of people were anti-business – still less that they were attracted by old-style socialist prescriptions for state control of the economy – it seems that the 'caring', collectivist ethos of the post-war era continued to exert a powerful emotional pull. This did not of course affect the outcome of the general elections fought by Thatcher as Conservative leader. Polling evidence also suggests that in the critical areas of leadership and managerial competence, she enjoyed a decisive lead over her Labour opponents. In a Gallup poll conducted as late as April 1990, 78 per cent of those questioned felt that she had greater determination than Kinnock and 60 per cent believed that she was better placed to win the respect of foreign leaders, whilst 58 per cent rated her more highly in terms of overall leadership ability.[19] Voters reacted more to the images projected by the parties and their leaders than to their policies on specific issues.

Where Thatcher undoubtedly made a difference was in the way in which she reasserted the authority of government, after a decade in which it had been widely called in question. Early in her premiership she stated that her government would continue to talk to the trade unions and listen to them, 'so long as it is understood that national policy is the responsibility of Government and Parliament'.[20] Thatcher not only pushed through far-reaching changes to employment law but also buried the corporatist approach to economic management, which had proved wanting in the industrial disputes of the 1970s. She was helped in this task, of course, by the impact of unemployment, which contributed to a fall in union membership from 13.2 million in 1979 to 9.8 million in 1990, significantly reducing their leaders' bargaining power.

Beyond this, Thatcher effectively redefined the role of the state, removing it from areas where she considered it to have acquired an illegitimate influence, such as the ownership of public utilities, and strengthening it in those areas for which it had traditionally been responsible, notably law and order, defence and currency stability. This was a formula to which she returned repeatedly: 'I believe you need very strong Government to be strong on those things which only Governments can do. And strong enough after that to leave the rest to the people because that is the essence of a free society.'[21] It is true that she embraced privatisation hesitantly at first, and her governments never extended it to coal, railways and the Royal Mail. She left the BBC licence fee untouched, even though she would have liked to see the corporation forced to compete in the market place alongside independent television channels. Cabinet papers released in 2014 show her asking whether a receiver could be invented which would not show BBC programmes, thus allowing purchasers to be exempt from paying the fee. From the 1980s, however, across a range of industries, privatisation was established as a standard means of delivering public services, and the British model became a template for other countries, especially in Eastern Europe and Latin America. From now on the debate would not be about state or private ownership, but about the accountability of privatised services to the consumer, the prices paid by the public and the sometimes excessive levels of remuneration enjoyed by the new companies' chief executives.

There were other consequences of Thatcher's encouragement of market economics and consumer choice. The number of owner-occupiers in England and Wales increased from 10.2 million in 1981 to 13.4 million a decade later, a development which was helped by the introduction of the right to buy scheme for council tenants. By restricting local authorities' ability to reinvest the proceeds in the construction of new properties, however, the policy contributed to a shortage of low-cost housing in London and the South-East by the turn of the century. Thatcher's promotion of property ownership, and the deregulation of the financial sector, must also take some responsibility for the unsustainable house price bubble and the bust which followed in the early 1990s. It is much harder to argue, as some critics have done, that her policies were to blame for the financial crash of 2007–8, which had its origins in the irresponsible lending practices of many banks and the collapse of the sub-prime mortgage market in the USA. It is true that in the long run, the 'big bang' reforms of the stock market encouraged a less cautious approach on the part of investment banks, leading to ill-advised mergers with high street banks. To lay responsibility at Thatcher's door, however, is to ignore the global nature of the crisis. It also overlooks the flawed model for bank regulation put in place by the incoming Labour government in 1997, which took little account of the growing interdependence of the financial services industry.

Thatcher had less success in changing the moral climate of British society and there is little evidence, in spite of her socially conservative rhetoric, that this was ever a key priority for her. Campaigners against the advance of 'permissiveness' saw her as a kindred spirit, even though in the 1960s she had supported the legalisation of abortion and homosexuality. On issues such as the family, crime and immigration control, she did little to promote a hard-line agenda. On the last of these the fate of Enoch Powell underlined the dangers, for a practical politician, of doing or saying anything which could be construed as racist. Thatcher explicitly ruled out the repatriation of immigrants and, in April 1990, provoked a parliamentary rebellion on the right, led by former minister Norman Tebbit, against a bill to grant approximately 250,000 Hong Kong residents British citizenship. Like many of her generation and class, Thatcher held strong views on the importance of harsh punishments to deter crime. She was the last Prime Minister to favour the return of the death penalty but rejected calls for a referendum on the issue, bowing instead to successive majority votes against restoration in the Commons.

Only one of her Home Secretaries, David Waddington, supported capital punishment, and the others did not come under prime ministerial pressure to change their minds.

Nor did Thatcher do much in practice to support campaigners for the defence of the traditional family. When a Catholic mother of ten, Victoria Gillick, challenged a 1980 Department of Health and Social Security ruling, allowing doctors to give contraceptive advice to girls under the age of sixteen without parental knowledge or consent, Thatcher was one of 200 Conservative MPs to register a protest. Five years later, however, when the Law Lords endorsed the DHSS's original position, the government declined to introduce legislation to overturn the verdict. Thatcher offered greater hope to Conservative moralists on the issue of homosexuality, which assumed political significance in the late 1980s following the emergence of the gay rights movement and public anxiety at the spread of AIDS. At the 1987 conference, for example, she condemned the socially liberal agenda of some left-wing local education authorities. She was in step with many Conservative activists in declaring that 'children who need to be taught to respect traditional moral values are being taught that they have an inalienable right to be gay'.[22] A rare example of legislation which took an explicitly moralistic standpoint was Section 28 of the 1988 Local Government Act, which made it illegal to promote homosexuality in schools. This was of greater symbolic than practical importance, as no prosecutions took place, and the relevant part of the bill was the result of an amendment by a Conservative backbencher, Jill Knight, rather than a government initiative.

Perhaps more surprising was the failure of the first female Prime Minister to do anything of significance to advance the cause of women's rights. Contemporaries noted that, although several women served in junior ministerial posts under Thatcher, only one was ever promoted to the Cabinet. This was Baroness Young, who served briefly as Leader of the Lords in 1981–3. In her personal life Thatcher maintained a traditional view of female domestic roles. During the 1983 election campaign she mocked Labour for focusing on women's issues, joking to her male colleagues that 'if they have their way, you'll soon be having the babies'.[23] Addressing the 300 Group, which had been formed to promote increased female representation in public life, she praised businesses which had begun to help women balance their work and family responsibilities, but offered no prospect of legislation to further the process. True to her individualist creed, she made clear that, just as she had risen by her own efforts – ignoring, of course, the financial support of a wealthy husband - other women should not be granted 'special favours'.[24] Cherie Blair, wife of Tony Blair and a prominent supporter of gender equality, considered that 'you can't underestimate the impact of the image of her outside Number 10' as a symbol of female achievement, but that Thatcher broke the glass ceiling for herself, 'and that was enough for her'.[25]

As in so many areas, Thatcher was a product of her time and background. She had reached maturity long before the appearance of the radical women's movement in the 1960s. There were, perhaps, practical reasons for her lack of interest in feminism. Not only was she justifiably proud of her own success, she was wary of being viewed as a one-dimensional political figure. When granted honorary membership of the Carlton Club, the exclusive preserve of male Conservative MPs, she accepted the honour without insisting on the doors being opened to all female members of the parliamentary party. Too close an association with women's issues might well have hampered her rise in a male-dominated political culture. She had to beat the men at their own game without claiming special privileges for her sex.

New Conservatives, New Labour

In spite of her three general election victories as its leader, Thatcher's medium-term impact on the Conservative Party was almost wholly negative. Her successor had to contend with the divisions over Europe which had started to emerge in her last two years as Prime Minister, and whose growth she did nothing to control in the mid-1990s. She left a parliamentary party which admired her without ever having been fully converted to her personal philosophy. Its leading figures, by the end of her time in office, were long-serving pragmatists such as Major, Hurd and Clarke, who had little real empathy with her. In the words of political scientist Andrew Gamble, writing four years after her downfall, 'the Conservative Party never became a Thatcherite party. It remained the Conservative Party led by Margaret Thatcher.'[26] Her influence over the party on the European issue reached its peak after her departure from Downing Street, with the retirement or marginalisation from 1997 of leading pro-Europeans such as Heseltine and Clarke, and the election of younger MPs who were deeply suspicious of the Brussels 'super-state'. One consequence of this shift, early in the twenty-first century, was that the party leadership took up a position of outright hostility to British participation in the European single currency.

In spite of her well-known rapport with grassroots Tory activists, Thatcher made remarkably little difference to the organisation of the Conservative Party. Except in the build-up to general elections, she tended to neglect the party machine. Nor did the composition of the parliamentary party change dramatically after 1975. She took little interest in candidate selection. The 1980s are best seen as continuing a trend which had been in progress for four decades: the supersession of the old Tory elites of the land, army and the bar by a new meritocracy dominated by business executives, solicitors, accountants and professional politicians. The number of Old Etonian Conservative MPs declined from one in four to one in ten between 1945 and 1992 – a shift, in one historian's words, from 'estate owners to estate agents'.[27]

The new generation of Conservative leaders viewed Thatcher with some unease. She could not be ignored whilst rank and file party supporters continued to venerate her memory. At the same time her pragmatic successors, operating in a political environment shaped by New Labour's successive triumphs in 1997, 2001 and 2005, were keen to distance themselves from aspects of her legacy which might jeopardise their electoral prospects. This was particularly true of David Cameron. Thatcher's popular association with economic materialism and moral authoritarianism made her a dubious icon for a Conservative Party moving cautiously in the direction of modernisation. Although the onset of the financial crisis of 2007–8 shifted the party in a more explicitly neo-liberal direction, with an 'austerity' agenda which recalled Thatcher's first years in Downing Street, in other respects Cameron sought to differentiate himself from his predecessor. In his first year as Prime Minister he pointedly observed that 'the

Conservative government of the Eighties made some good steps forward on choice and competition, but didn't understand enough about the public service ethos'.[28] In his talk of positive action to mend what he called a 'broken society', and his embrace of tolerant policies such as gay marriage, Cameron struck a distinctively 'unThatcherite' note.

More controversial is the nature of Thatcher's influence on the Labour Party. As Conservative leader she alternated between a tribal desire to crush her opponents and a more detached appreciation of the long-term need for a party of the centre-left, anchored in reality and purged of extremism. Interviewed on the eve of the 1987 election, for example, she expressed the view that Labour should 'drop the socialist side and then become much more like the kind of Labour party on the continent'.[29] This, of course, was the essence of the 'New Labour' project which came to fruition a decade later under the leadership of Tony Blair. In some ways Thatcher was a role model for Blair, who admired her commanding style of leadership. It was even more surprising to see her publicly praised and welcomed to Downing Street by Gordon Brown, whose 1989 book, *Where There is Greed,* had been dedicated to the Dunfermline East Labour Party and to his constituents, 'who have more reason than most to look forward to the end of the Thatcher era'.[30]

By establishing a new domestic settlement based around affording greater freedom for market forces, Thatcher compelled Labour to move towards the centre ground in order to make itself electable. This was a process which began hesitantly with Kinnock's 1989 policy review and was symbolised in Blair's rejection of old-style public ownership five years later. The cumulative shock of four successive electoral defeats made the party much more willing to shift its ground. One of the architects of New Labour, Peter Mandelson, went so far as to declare in June 2002 that 'we are all Thatcherites now' – a provocative phrase which drew criticism from Labour traditionalists. On closer examination, it appears that he was doing little more than celebrating the party's new-found realism in accepting the facts of economic life. 'Globalisation,' he wrote, 'punishes hard any country that tries to run its economy by ignoring the realities of the market or prudent public finances.'[31] As Mandelson acknowledged after her death,

Thatcher performed an indispensable service for Labour by reforming trade union law and privatising utilities. These were policies which would have split any Labour government which tried to implement them; but once they were in place, the party was able to make it clear that it was impractical to reverse them.

In other policy areas, however, it is hard to discern any clear connection. New Labour stood for British participation in the process of European integration and promoted a range of constitutional reforms, including Scottish and Welsh devolution and House of Lords reform, against which Thatcher had set her face. Her moralistic approach in retirement to the break-up of Yugoslavia has some common ground with the doctrine of international engagement, articulated by Blair in his April 1999 Chicago speech, and exemplified by his support for military action to drive Serbian forces out of Kosovo in the same year. As Prime Minister, however, Thatcher had espoused a much more limited and defensive conception of the national interest. She did not see it as Britain's role to promote democracy across the globe in the way that Blair seemed to envisage. In domestic policy, the New Labour governments showed themselves to be firmly in the British social democratic tradition in their efforts to eliminate child poverty, tackle social exclusion and improve the life chances of the disadvantaged. Blair signalled his party's embrace of social diversity by repealing Section 28, against which gay rights activists had campaigned for over a decade, and by legislating for civil partnerships. New Labour ministers sharply differentiated themselves from the Thatcher era in their emphasis on investment in the public services. Looking back after five years in office, Blair stated that 'the country has a different feel to the harshness of the Thatcher years', and celebrated Britain's emergence from the dominance of Tory values: 'elitism, selfish individualism; the belief that there is no such thing as society and its international equivalent – insularity and isolationism'.[32] New Labour's relationship with Thatcher would remain an ambivalent one. In his memoirs, Blair commended Thatcher for her awareness of the importance of choice and aspiration, whilst criticising her failure to grasp the role of government in securing for people the opportunities they needed: 'though she "got" one side of human nature, she appeared to ignore another'.[33] From Thatcherism to New Labour the line of descent did not run straight.

The triumph of personality?

For a long-serving premier, Thatcher showed a surprising lack of interest in changing the machinery of government. Perhaps it was easier, amid the press of events, to seek results by changing the personnel with whom she worked rather than the institutional structures. She mistrusted the civil service for its passive acceptance of 'managed decline', but valued individuals, such as Charles Powell, who were not stereotypical mandarins. She made use of the Policy Unit, inherited from the Wilson government, and the much older Downing Street Private Office as sources of advice. In 1983 she abolished the Central Policy Review Staff, which had been set up by the Heath government to assist the Cabinet in thinking strategically, but which had in fact contributed little of significance since the downfall of its creator. There was no National Security Adviser on the American model although Brent Scowcroft, who held the post under President Bush, informally regarded Charles Powell as his British equivalent. Nor did Thatcher create a permanent White House-style 'Chief of Staff' to run her Number 10 office, as Blair was to do after 1997. The only person to hold the post, David Wolfson, returned part-time to his business career before the end of the first term, after failing to get a grip on the operation of Downing Street. Sir Derek Rayner of Marks and Spencer was hired in the early years to run an Efficiency Unit, located within the Cabinet Office with a brief to root out bureaucratic waste, but he left in 1982, after it failed to acquire the authority of a full-blown ministry.

One of the few institutional innovations with long-term significance was the creation of the 'Next Steps' agencies from 1988. The purpose of these bodies was to carry out some of the functions of government departments at arm's length from Whitehall, under the management of chief executives rather than the direct control of ministers. Within ten years, 75 per cent of civil servants were employed by more than 100 executive agencies, such as the Driver and Vehicle Licensing Authority and Companies House, or by government departments run on the same lines. It entailed a radical rethinking of the way in which civil servants worked, with most officials now focused on service delivery, whilst a small core continued to give policy advice to ministers and ran Whitehall departments. It was typical of Thatcher that, fearful of antagonising the Treasury, she took some time to be persuaded before becoming an enthusiastic supporter of the initiative.

Above all, Thatcher left the memory of a leader who reached the top and imposed her vision through the force of her personality. Matthew Parris, who worked in her office when she was Leader of the Opposition, recalled the 'manic quality' with which she worked her bemused audience on a walkabout in a London street: 'she was happening. She had an unerring sense of how to happen.'[34] She was uninhibited by any sense of self-doubt or irony, giving herself to the task in hand with full attention. In office she grew immeasurably in confidence. A visitor, whom she was showing around Number 10 shortly after the 1979 election, remarked that there was no room for her own picture in the gallery of portraits of former premiers on the main staircase. '"Don't worry," she said with the trace of a smile, "I'll push all the others down."'[35] After 1990, some of those Conservatives who initially welcomed John Major's low-key, non-confrontational style experienced pangs of nostalgia for her more assertive approach. Sir Peter Tapsell, a veteran backbencher who was by no means a card-carrying Thatcherite, confided to a fellow MP that Major was 'an attractive man, intelligent and well-intentioned, but he doesn't frighten anybody does he? When Margaret came into the tea room the teacups rattled.'[36]

There is no doubt that Thatcher was a dominant, even a domineering personality, who used the considerable powers of the premiership to their fullest extent. This was especially true of the power to appoint, dismiss and move colleagues around; during the 1980s, Cabinet reshuffles became a regular feature of the political landscape, with the media anticipating the next round of ministerial musical chairs. Coached by Gordon Reece, Ronald Millar and others, she learned to project herself through television and the press, and she assumed some of the attributes of a 'presidential' leader, cutting a striking figure on the world stage. In the second half of her premiership, critics increasingly accused her of bypassing Cabinet and circulating fewer papers to aid its deliberations; of intervening arbitrarily in government departments and bullying their ministerial heads; and of working much more through small groups and private advisers. Her downfall in some ways reflected the Cabinet's long overdue reassertion of its constitutional role, against a premier who had become dangerously autocratic and isolated.

It would be wrong, however, to caricature Thatcher as a dictator. Even after the second election victory, which strengthened her control over the Cabinet, she rarely had a large enough cadre of like-minded ministers on whom she could rely. Hers was often a reactive government, whose fortunes were shaped by its response to a series of dramatic crises: the 1981 inner city riots, the Falklands, the miners' strike, Westland. As premier in the final decade of the Cold War, she played a more active and prominent international part than any of her predecessors since Macmillan, even if Britain's limited resources meant that hers was always a supporting role to Ronald Reagan and George Bush. The unexpectedly rapid collapse of East European communism in 1989–90 left her largely on the side-lines, uneasy at the pace of events as a united Germany re-emerged. In domestic policy there were many sporadic and not always fully thought out initiatives, especially in the late 1980s, when she belatedly turned her attention to the overhaul of health, education and local government finance. Terrifying though she could be, it was possible for a strong-minded Cabinet colleague to defy her: she shrank from sacking Heseltine at the height of the Westland affair; and Lawson shadowed the Deutschmark without her authorisation, signalling his opposition to the poll tax with a refusal to make funds available to blunt its impact.

A proper sense of historical perspective is vital in assessing Thatcher's impact. Sir Douglas Wass, who served as head of the Treasury during her first term, was correct to argue that some premiers, like Churchill in wartime, have exhibited 'presidential' characteristics, whilst others, such as Attlee and Wilson, have behaved like 'chairmen of committees'. The office of Prime Minister is shaped to a large extent by changing contexts and by the personality of the occupant. 'It's gone up and down over the course of history and I think it's quite possible we could revert to a chairman-type prime minister again.'[37] The point was well made by the contrasting styles of Thatcher's two immediate successors, Major and Blair. She did not irreversibly transform the premiership, and it would be premature to claim that she permanently changed the direction of society and the economy. By the time of her downfall, however, it was impossible to imagine a return to the less dynamic and efficient, but also more equal and united, society of the three post-war decades. Thatcher left the memory of an unusually driven leader, whose remarkable sense of direction and determination both inspired and antagonised her fellow citizens. British history between 1979 and 1990 would have been very different without her. She made an enduring mark, and her legacy will continue to fascinate and divide those who come after.

Notes

1 Mark Garnett and Lord Gilmour, 'Thatcherism and the Conservative tradition' in Martin Francis and Ina Zweiniger-Bargielowska (eds), *The Conservatives and British Society, 1880–1990* (Cardiff, University of Wales Press, 1996), p. 89.

2 John Nott, *Here Today, Gone Tomorrow: Recollections of an Errant Politician* (London, Politico's, 2002), p. 183.

3 Radio Interview for BBC Radio 2 Jimmy Young Programme, 27 July 1988, www.margaretthatcher.org/document/107075 (accessed 17 January 2015).

4 Speech in Korea ('The Principles of Thatcherism'), 3 September 1992, *Margaret Thatcher: Complete Statements on CD-ROM 1945–1990* (Oxford, Oxford University Press, 1999), 92_009.

5 Both extracts quoted in Jonathan Raban, *God, Man and Mrs Thatcher: A Critique of Mrs Thatcher's Address to the General Assembly of the Church of Scotland* (London, Chatto & Windus, 1989), p. 67.

6 Interview for *Woman's Own* ('No such thing as society'), 23 September 1987, *Margaret Thatcher CD-ROM*, 87_384. The *Sunday Times* statement, dated 10 July 1988, is in an appendix on the CD-ROM.

7 Margaret Thatcher, *The Downing Street Years* (London, Harper Collins, 1993), p. 626.

8 Simon Lee and Matt Beech (ed.), *The Conservatives Under David Cameron* (London, Palgrave Macmillan, 2009), p. 8.

9 TV Interview for BBC (eve of poll; 'drool and drivel they care'), 10 June 1987, www.margaretthatcher.org/document/106649 (accessed 17 January 2015).

10 Radio interview for BBC Radio 1, Election '87 (phone-in), 3 June 1987, *Margaret Thatcher CD-ROM*, 87_249.

11 Letter to the Senior Tutor, Magdalene College, Cambridge, 29 July 1979, in *The Complete Henry Root Letters* (London, Mandarin, 1992), n.p. The collection was originally published in 1980.

12 Patrick Cosgrave, *Thatcher: The First Term* (London, Bodley Head, 1985), pp. 26–7.

13 Kenneth Morgan, *Callaghan: A Life* (Oxford, Oxford University Press, 1997), p. 535.

14 *Thatcher and the Scots*, BBC Scotland TV programme shown in 2008.
15 See p. 220.
16 Iain Dale (ed.), *Margaret Thatcher: A Tribute in Words and Pictures* (London, Weidenfeld & Nicolson, 2005), p. 166.
17 Interview, 28 January 1992, in Ion Trewin (ed.), *The Hugo Young Papers: Thirty Years of British Politics: Off the Record* (London, Allen Lane, 2008), p. 335.
18 Ivor Crewe, '1979–96' in Anthony Seldon (ed.), *How Tory Governments Fall: The Tory Party in Power Since 1783* (London, Fontana, 1996), p. 406.
19 Ivor Crewe, 'Margaret Thatcher: As the British Saw Her', *The Public Perspective*, January/February 1991, p. 17.
20 Conservative Party: text of MT's speech to the Conservative Party Conference, 12 October 1979, www.margaretthatcher.org/document/119164 (accessed 17 January 2015).
21 TV Interview for LWT *Weekend World* ('The Second Term'), 15 January 1984, www.margaretthatcher.org/document/105503 (accessed 17 January 2015).
22 Speech to Conservative Party Conference, 9 October 1987, www.margaretthatcher.org/document/106941 (accessed 17 January 2015).
23 Thatcher, *Downing Street Years*, p. 296.
24 Pankhurst Lecture to the 300 Group, 18 July 1990, www.margaretthatcher.org/document/108156 (accessed 17 January 2015).
25 *The Independent*, 9 April 2013.
26 Andrew Gamble, *The Free Economy and the Strong State: The Politics of Thatcherism* (London, Macmillan, 1994), p. 213.
27 Byron Criddle in Anthony Seldon and Stuart Ball (eds) *Conservative Century: The Conservative Party since 1900* (Oxford, Oxford University Press, 1994), p. 161.
28 *The Daily Telegraph*, 18 January 2011.
29 Interview for *Daily Mail*, 11 May 1987, *Margaret Thatcher CD-ROM*, 87_163.
30 Gordon Brown, *Where There is Greed . . . Margaret Thatcher and the Betrayal of Britain's Future* (Edinburgh, Mainstream Publishing, 1989), ix.
31 *The Times*, 10 June 2002.
32 *The Daily Telegraph*, 13 March 2002.
33 Tony Blair, *A Journey* (London, Hutchinson, 2010), p. 318.
34 Matthew Parris, *Chance Witness: An Outsider's Life in Politics* (London, Penguin, 2013), p. 203.
35 'Thatcher Triumphant', *Time*, 20 June 1983.
36 Gyles Brandreth, *Breaking the Code: Westminster Diaries, May 1990–May 1997* (London, Weidenfeld & Nicolson, 1999), p. 107, entry for 29 June 1992.
37 Hugo Young and Anne Sloman, *The Thatcher Phenomenon* (London, BBC, 1986), p. 47.

Further reading

The website of the Thatcher Foundation (www.margaretthatcher.org) provides a wealth of constantly updated documentation for Iron Lady studies. This should be supplemented with *Margaret Thatcher: Complete Public Statements 1945–1990 on CD-ROM* (Oxford University Press, 1999), a resource which is available from the Curator of the Thatcher archives at Churchill College, Cambridge. Thatcher herself published three volumes of autobiography and reflection on the issues which concerned her after leaving Number 10. *The Downing Street Years* (Harper Collins, 1993) is the most important for students. As the title suggests, *The Path to Power* (Harper Collins, 1995) covers Thatcher's life and career up to the 1979 general election. Slightly awkwardly tacked on to this is a further section in which she gives her views on the European Union, foreign policy and other themes. In her final book, *Statecraft: Strategies for a Changing World* (Harper Collins, 2002) she returned to these and other concerns, including her response to global terrorism in the wake of the 9/11 attacks in the USA.

Brief introductions are provided by the relevant chapters in Vernon Bogdanor (ed.), *From New Jerusalem to New Labour: British Prime Ministers from Attlee to Blair* (Palgrave Macmillan, 2010) and in Robert Pearce and Graham Goodlad, *British Prime Ministers from Balfour to Brown* (Routledge, 2013). The first two volumes of Charles Moore's *Margaret Thatcher: The Authorized Biography* are entitled *Not for Turning* (Allen Lane, 2013) and *Everything She Wants* (Allen Lane, 2015). The third and final volume is expected in 2017. Moore's access to previously unavailable primary material, and the large number of interviews that he conducted, both with his subject and with people who knew her, places his work in a category of its own. Students should, however, still turn to John Campbell, *Margaret Thatcher: The Grocer's Daughter* (Jonathan Cape, 2000) and *Margaret Thatcher: The Iron Lady* (Jonathan Cape, 2003), or to the condensed version which appeared in 2009, for further insights. Although largely superseded by these later studies, Hugo Young's *One of Us* (Macmillan, 1990) contains some sharp judgements on Thatcher's career. Also worth noting are two broadly sympathetic biographies by writers who knew Thatcher well at different stages of her life. Robin Harris, who worked for her as a speech writer and helped her with her own books, wrote *Not for Turning: The Life of Margaret Thatcher* (Bantam Press, 2013). Jonathan Aitken, a Conservative MP throughout Thatcher's premiership, and the boyfriend of her daughter in the late 1970s, published a vivid portrait in *Margaret Thatcher: Power and Personality* (Bloomsbury, 2013). The book combines admiration for its subject, whose overthrow he clearly regards as a national tragedy, with a frank awareness of her domineering personality.

A remarkable number of Thatcher's former Cabinet colleagues have left memoirs of their time in office. The two most important are the accounts of Geoffrey Howe, *Conflict of Loyalty* (Macmillan, 1994) and Nigel Lawson, *The View from No. 11: Memoirs of a Tory Radical* (Bantam Press, 1992). *The Whitelaw Memoirs* (Aurum Press, 1989) contain less of value for students of Thatcher than does Mark Garnett and Ian Aitken, *Splendid! Splendid! The Authorized Biography of Willie Whitelaw* (Jonathan Cape, 2002). The Thatcher loyalist perspective is represented by Norman Tebbit, *Upwardly Mobile* (Futura, 1989), Nicholas Ridley, *'My Style of Government': The Thatcher Years* (Hutchinson, 1991) and Cecil Parkinson, *Right at the Centre: An Autobiography* (Weidenfeld & Nicolson, 1992). The last of these contains a particularly vivid account of the events which led to the toppling of Thatcher. Predictably more critical are Ian Gilmour, *Dancing with Dogma: Britain under Thatcherism* (Simon & Schuster, 1992), a manifesto for 'wet' Conservatism, and the autobiography of James Prior, *A Balance of Power* (Hamish Hamilton, 1986). Heathites who made the transition to office under Thatcher were

Kenneth Baker, author of *The Turbulent Years: My Life in Politics* (Faber and Faber, 1993), and Douglas Hurd, whose *Memoirs* were published by Little, Brown in 2003. John Nott, *Here Today, Gone Tomorrow: Recollections of an Errant Politician* (Politico's, 2002) is useful for the Falklands conflict. John Major's views on his predecessor can be found in the pages of *The Autobiography* (Harper Collins, 1999). The man who brought her down, Michael Heseltine, covered their uneasy relationship in *Life in the Jungle: My Autobiography* (Hodder and Stoughton, 2000). Thatcher's intellectual guru, Sir Keith Joseph, did not write memoirs but there is a good biography by Andrew Denham and Mark Garnett, *Keith Joseph* (Acumen, 2001). Among the testimonies of less central figures, mention should be made of John Biffen, *Semi-Detached* (Biteback, 2013), Norman Fowler, *Ministers Decide: A Personal Memoir of the Thatcher Years* (Chapmans, 1991) and David Waddington, *Memoirs: Dispatches from Margaret Thatcher's Last Home Secretary* (Biteback, 2012). Although no 1980s Cabinet minister has left diaries to compete with those of Barbara Castle and Richard Crossman for the two previous decades, the first two volumes of junior minister Alan Clark's *Diaries* (Weidenfeld & Nicolson, 1993 and 2000) contain numerous illuminating references to Thatcher.

Insights into what it was like to work for Thatcher are provided by Bernard Ingham, *Kill the Messenger* (Fontana, 1991), John Ranelagh, *Thatcher's People: An Insider's Account of the Politics, the Power and the Personalities* (Harper Collins, 1991), Alistair McAlpine, *Once A Jolly Bagman: Memoirs* (Weidenfeld & Nicolson, 1997) and Tim Bell, *Right or Wrong: The Memoirs of Lord Bell* (Bloomsbury, 2014). Two directors of the Number 10 Policy Unit wrote memoirs which reveal the frustrations of working for the Prime Minister: John Hoskyns, *Just in Time: Inside the Thatcher Revolution* (Aurum, 2000) and Ferdinand Mount, *Cold Cream: My Early Life and Other Mistakes* (Bloomsbury, 2008). Revealing asides are to be found in the three volumes of diaries kept by a Thatcher confidant, *The Journals of Woodrow Wyatt* (Macmillan, 1998–2000), edited by Sarah Curtis, and in the memoirs of speech writer Ronald Millar, *A View from the Wings* (Weidenfeld & Nicolson, 1993). A unique personal insight is supplied by Thatcher's daughter, Carol Thatcher, in *Below the*

Parapet: The Biography of Denis Thatcher (Harper Collins, 1997) and *My Story: A Swim-On Part in the Goldfish Bowl* (Headline Review, 2009). Two good sources of anecdotes and comment are Iain Dale (ed.), *Margaret Thatcher: A Tribute in Words and Pictures* (Weidenfeld & Nicolson, 2005) and Gillian Shephard, *The Real Iron Lady: Working with Margaret Thatcher* (Biteback, 2013).

There is a huge, and still growing, literature on the policies of the Thatcher government. Her ascendancy is placed in wider context by Brian Harrison, *Finding a Role? The United Kingdom 1980–1990* (Oxford University Press, 2010) and by Paul Addison, *No Turning Back: The Peacetime Revolutions of Post-War Britain* (Oxford University Press, 2010). Less conventional in its approach is Graham Stewart, *Bang! A History of Britain in the 1980s* (Atlantic Books, 2013), a good example of a recent vogue for studies which link popular culture with social and political history. A comprehensive and balanced overview is provided by Geoffrey Fry, *The Politics of the Thatcher Revolution: An Interpretation of British Politics 1979–1990* (Palgrave, 2008). Richard Vinen, *Thatcher's Britain: The Politics and Social Upheaval of the 1980s* (Simon & Schuster, 2009) is essentially a series of essays on different aspects of the period. E.H.H. Green, *Thatcher* (Hodder Arnold, 2006) also adopts a thematic approach. More overtly hostile is Eric Evans, *Thatcher and Thatcherism* (Routledge, third edition, 2013). Ben Jackson and Robert Saunders (eds), *Making Thatcher's Britain* (Cambridge University Press, 2012) is a wide-ranging collection of essays.

Thatcher's Labour opposite numbers have been well served by biographers. Kenneth O. Morgan has given us full portraits of *Callaghan: A Life* (Oxford University Press, 1997) and *Michael Foot: A Life* (Harper Press, 2007). Martin Westlake and Ian St John, *Kinnock: The Biography* (Little, Brown, 2001) is also to be recommended. A good account of the miners' strike is Francis Beckett and David Hencke, *Marching to the Fault Line* (Constable, 2009).

Thatcher's Northern Ireland policies are covered in Eamonn Mallie and David McKittrick, *Endgame in Ireland* (Hodder and Stoughton, 2001), which accompanied a major BBC TV series, and Michael Cunningham, *British Government Policy in Northern*

Ireland 1969–2000 (Manchester University Press, 2001). On Scotland we have David Torrance, *'We in Scotland': Thatcherism in a Cold Climate* (Birlinn, 2009). There is, as yet, no corresponding study of Thatcher's impact on Wales.

The fullest exploration of foreign policy is Paul Sharp, *Thatcher's Diplomacy: The Revival of British Foreign Policy* (Macmillan, 1999). On the defining episode of the first term we have Lawrence Freedman's two volume *The Official History of the Falklands Campaign* (Routledge, 2005). Richard Aldous, *Reagan and Thatcher: The Difficult Relationship* (Arrow, 2013) is a balanced assessment of the Iron Lady's most important overseas connection. It complements an excellent piece of 'instant history', Geoffrey Smith, *Reagan and Thatcher* (W.W. Norton, 1991). On the troubled relationship with the European Community see Hugo Young, *This Blessed Plot: Britain and Europe from Churchill to Blair* (Macmillan, 1998). Much can be gleaned from the memoirs of three of Thatcher's foreign policy advisers: Percy Cradock, *In Defence of British Interests* (John Murray, 1997), George R. Urban, *Diplomacy and Disillusion at the Court of Margaret Thatcher* (I.B. Tauris, 1996) and Robin Renwick, *A Journey With Margaret Thatcher: Foreign Policy under the Iron Lady* (Biteback, 2013).

The overthrow of Thatcher was chronicled in lively fashion by journalist Alan Watkins in *A Conservative Coup* (Duckworth, 1991). Further detail on the events of 1990 is provided in the first half of Tim Renton, *Chief Whip: People, Power and Patronage in Westminster* (Politico's, 2004). One can learn all one needs about a key issue in Thatcher's decline and fall in David Butler, Andrew Adonis and Tony Travers, *Failure in British Government: The Politics of the Poll Tax* (Oxford University Press, 1994). A more succinct account is to be found in Anthony King and Ivor Crewe, *The Blunders of Our Governments* (One World, second edition, 2014).

The literature on the significance of Thatcher's premiership is legion. Still important is Dennis Kavanagh, *Thatcherism and British Politics: The End of Consensus?* (Oxford University Press, second edition, 1990). Andrew Gamble, *The Free Economy and the Strong State* (Macmillan, second edition, 1994) focuses on the strengthening of the central state, which occurred alongside the liberation of the market in the 1980s. A similar thesis is offered in Simon Jenkins, *Thatcher and Sons* (Penguin, 2007), which extends its coverage to the Major and Blair eras. Shirley Letwin, *The Anatomy of Thatcherism* (Fontana, 1992) is an analysis by a leading Conservative intellectual. Richard Heffernan, *New Labour and Thatcherism: Political Change in Britain* (Palgrave Macmillan, 2001) examines Thatcher's impact on the Labour Party of Tony Blair. Tim Bale, *The Conservative Party from Thatcher to Cameron* (Polity Press, 2010) looks at her legacy for her own party. Peter Hennessy, *The Prime Minister: The Office and its Holders since 1945* (Allen Lane/Penguin, 2000) contains an important chapter discussing Thatcher's impact on the premiership. Louisa Hadley, *Responding to Margaret Thatcher's Death* (Palgrave, 2014) analyses the range of popular reactions to her passing.

Index